I Think, Therefore Who Am I?

Memoir of a Psychedelic Year

I Think, Therefore Who Am I?

Memoir of a Psychedelic Year

Peter Weissman

To order additional copies of this book, contact:
Xlibris Corporation
1-888-795-4274
www.Xlibris.com
Orders@Xlibris.com
32142

The one true vocation for man is to find out what is real.

—J. Krishnamurti

Before Almost Everything Changed

People hung out on the corner, smoking cigarettes, cars and trucks clattering by on the cobblestone avenue as Mark and I shuffled past, looking at Wechsler's column in the *Post*. There were other columnists as contemptible; Lerner, for instance, with his ossified anticommunism. But though Wechsler was against the war, as we were, he seemed more offended by the unmannerly protests than the killing, which galled us, and so we focused our anger on him.

"The cretin."

"The shithead."

I smacked my forehead in affected exasperation, to add emphasis, and Mark rattled the paper as if to shake some sense into it.

"The prick."

Then we'd plunge back in, briefly looking up to check the traffic light as we shuffled through the fecund cityscape of tenement buildings and bustling people, consigning them to the periphery, submerging ourselves in a world of commentary, which fell so maddeningly short of our expectations.

At Tompkins Park, the street we'd absently trod abruptly ended. Pausing, looking up, we would assess our circumstance, called upon to make an earthbound decision. What to do now? In what direction would we go? It was not a dispassionate question, for we were bound together in daily habit and preferred not to go our separate ways. But in fact we were by then tired of each other's predictable company, worn thin, and we'd say our good-byes and take separate paths: Mark to his cell, me to mine.

Not for long, though. A certain gradation of light filtering through a window would stir me, propel me back downstairs a few hours later and through the gray streets. Or maybe they weren't gray but only seemed so as I walked in my own fog past storefronts and stoops, brick facades and cars lining the curbs, garbage cans and fire escapes and opaque windows—

And stop, looking up, my feet, with a mind of their own, having measured the distance while I thought about other things. Wechsler, maybe. Or the price of eggs in China. And now I'd arrived at my destination.

There was no door to that building. I would enter, traverse the broken tile floor, take the worn marble steps two at a time to the sixth floor and rap on the door. After several seconds, while I stood reading the messages written on the painted surface, Mark would jerk it open, interrupting my absorption. He seemed to know so many people, a dozen friends and casual acquaintances, some of whom I'd actually met, bumping into them while traipsing the streets, or barging in on them when there was something we wanted to see on television.

Mark looked tired. He always looked tired, in his rumpled clothes, his light stubble beard seemingly unable to draw enough energy to cover his face. He'd rake a hand through his unkempt mane of dirty blond hair, a wake-up gesture, and with world-weary fatigue invite me in by moving aside.

In fact I was tired too, yawning so wide it hurt as he plunged right in with his latest thoughts, variations on themes we'd explored earlier, groping to express them in all their munificence, negotiating a mine field of torturous sentences, retreating to edit and emend what he'd already managed to articulate before moving on and veering in a somewhat different direction. It could be torture listening to him, impatient as I was. But then, I knew Mark would listen to me when I had the floor, for as long as it took. And when it was my turn, to ensure that I got my fair share of time, I'd veer back and forth as well, having developed a stutter of sorts myself, an artifice of indecisiveness. Or maybe, spending so much time together, I'd been influenced by him, the two of us similarly jittery and verbose.

Our apartments were similar too, with unwashed dishes and furry growths in the sink, dirty clothes heaped in corners. Though where I'd used the cracks on the walls as an outline for cartoon figures done in black marker, he'd taped or tacked over his crumbling plaster with magazine reproductions from *Life* or *National Geographic*. They were nondescript photos, did nothing to ameliorate the bleakness of the room as we sat on the unmade bed—a mattress on the floor—in the tiny railroad flat, examining the afternoon edition of the paper in the cloudy light that filtered in above the roofline of the adjacent building.

There were no new editorials or columns to lambaste, but the sports pages were now up-to-date, and we were big basketball fans. Occasionally we actually watched a game the night before, but it didn't matter—the box scores were enough for us to work up a plangent critique: whether the game was won or lost on foul shots, field goals, rebounds, or assists; or because so-and-so didn't play or had fouled out.

Eventually exhausting the possibilities, we'd come to our next customary activity, though we didn't think of it as that. We liked to think we were without a plan or a schedule, while subliminally mindful of the shifting light of day and impending night that moved us, or a sense of hunger, which would announce itself when we were putting on coats, ushering us along, leaving the dissected paper scattered on the floor of that dreary room.

Almost always we'd shuffle into the B&H, our restaurant, where I ordered tuna fish on thick pieces of challah and Mark studied the menu awhile before inevitably ordering mushroom-barley soup. And then, with the first bite, realizing how hungry we were—for this was usually our only real meal of the day—we'd shut up and eat like starving animals.

Meanwhile, it got darker, which was hard not to notice, no matter how much attention we paid to each other's circumlocutions. The twilight was intriguing, mysterious, contained the possibility of something different, yet fraught too with irrational uncertainty. Pausing outside the vapored window of the B&H after we'd eaten one day as dusk came on, I was taken by the street scene, its extraordinary dimension, the buildings compact, the sky a backdrop, rendering them shapes occupying space, which of course they were, but for some reason, I'd never noticed it before. And around me, in the life-size diorama, the motley cast of people were also more solidly real, moving this way or that, or sitting on cars parked at the curb, drinking from bottles in paper bags, as the law allowed. Now *there* was a conception—what the law allowed—on a planet in the universe; a grotesque regulation mocking the natural state of things.

Farther up the avenue—we were walking now, obeying the impulse that moved us whenever we found ourselves with nothing to read or talk about— the bars had begun to thrum with music, raucous laughter bursting from open doors, the dishabille atmosphere producing a cast of disreputable characters lounging in doorways and lingering on corners. On Tenth Street an old lady picked garbage out of a trash can, threw it back and rummaged deeper. On the next block, a beggar on crutches tottered out of nowhere and thrust out his hand, demanding payment, and as we veered away, his aggressive gesture seemed a cue, a signal conveyed to the hokhmuth of humanity of which we were a part, the already untethered world becoming a greater welter of sound and movement. Cars idling at the light roared forward, fumes billowing over the sidewalk; dogs snarled, straining at their leashes to get at each other; a distinct but unseen someone laughed; a bottle shattered in the street.

Mark and I bolted, racing to beat the tempo, and of course incidentally dancing to it, hurrying up one street and down another, flitting past our own plateglass reflections, plowing through smells and sounds, sensations the universe threw haphazardly in our path, heading for our next destination as to a haven.

On this evening, Mark, who knew more people than I did and usually led the way, chose a locked door building with a directory and buzzers, to keep the riffraff out, and we were buzzed into a small lobby, and took an elevator upstairs.

Gerry Gornish had a studio apartment. A table, chairs, kitchen appliances, and cupboards were at one end, and the rest of the pad was filled with stacks of newspapers and magazines, a wing chair, an unmade brass bed, and, most of all—for I was there for the first time and had not known what to expect—walls nearly covered with black and white photos of naked, buxom women. They posed astride chairs or reclining on the brass bed, inspecting their nipples, leering at the camera . . . In one, a slim woman with impressive breasts was on her knees, sucking Gerry's cock, his potbelly in profile, like those of the happy Buddhas in tourist shops in Chinatown.

He was undressing when we entered, and he and Mark talked while he sat in his bath—in the kitchen, tenement style—water slopping on the floor as Gerry soaped up and rinsed. I sat in the wing chair and threw a few words in their direction, but the gallery of naked women distracted me, though I tried to ignore it. The world of pornography, as it was and probably always will be, is rooted in casual disregard, and making money, of course. Not for the first time, I wondered about Mark's wide array of friends, which could include a Gerry Gornish along with the impassioned political types we often ran into at protest demonstrations.

Gerry got out of the tub, looking bloated and fishbelly white, patted himself dry with a towel and doused with talcum powder while explaining that he'd been preparing to leave when we showed up, had somewhere to go, was in somewhat of a hurry: an appointment uptown with a perfume diva and her entourage. Had we heard of her? No? Well, unlike us, these people worked by timetables and he couldn't keep them waiting . . .

We walked him downstairs and up to First Avenue, where he hailed a cab and we stood there as it drove away. It was full dark now, and it demanded our attention.

"There's a game on tonight," Mark said.

"Who's playing?" I asked.

Not that it mattered; some team or another. And he'd add, or I would: "It should be a good one."

We were neither of us enthusiastic now. We'd done this too many times.

So we set off for Alfie's, because he had a television set, though on a typical game night Alfie was as likely to be out as not, and then we'd move on to someone else Mark knew less well. That was our routine. We'd traipse, knock, and receiving no response, move on, quickly putting dark and questionable streets behind us, shifting nervously from foot to foot in hallways that conjured danger because they were ill-lit or so brightly lit that we might be seen by anyone watching through a peephole. It was a downward spiral from Mark's friends to his acquaintances to someone he might have met on a basketball court who had a set . . . like the near total stranger who questioned us through a door as we stood in a hallway, Mark recounting a schoolyard encounter as a dog threw itself against the barrier separating us, smelling strangers. Eventually, locks were undone and a grim-faced character appeared in the doorway, gesturing us inside with a sawed-off shotgun, the snarling dog chained to a wall now, baring its teeth as we tried to get comfortable in a room illuminated by the glowing screen.

"I'm glad you guys showed up," our host said. "I didn't know there was a game on tonight."

But he only paid passing attention to it, his glance skittering from the set to the window, where someone might leap into the room at any moment with a knife between his teeth. And with the growling dog in the kitchen and the sawed-off shotgun propped in a corner, within his reach, Mark and I had a hard time concentrating on the flickering figures on the screen. Afterward, on the street, we discussed the game, recalling snippets, perhaps to bring it into focus now that we were able to breathe without fear.

It was true: we loved basketball. But the point, when it got dark, was to lose ourselves. And so, we talked about the game on this night in the same way we'd talked about politics earlier and other unseen games in the afternoon, replaying it, reiterating the high points, imagining other possibilities, wrapping our thoughts around the real and the imaginary, speculating upon what would or would not have happened if this or that had occurred instead of that or this.

But we couldn't hold back the night forever, and eventually, falling silent, we headed with doomed resignation toward the night spots, the final chapter in our communal day.

Mark and I saw ourselves as rebels. We opposed the war and demonstrated against it. We were prepared to convince the draft board we were insane, homosexual, whatever it took, and to go to Canada, if it came to that. We excoriated the government, and authority in general. Yet as male adults taken with the notion of women and what it meant to be men, we lacked that rebellious bravado, wriggled under a microscope of our own scrutiny, pinioned by certain beliefs and their accompanying expectations. We never said so aloud, but shared the mind-set of cowards, and our protective companionship was constant reminder of our embarrassing failures with the other sex.

Appearing anxious to ourselves, much less those women we meant to impress and win over, we made the rounds of restaurants, coffeehouses, and bars, beginning with the Paradox, whose macrobiotic clientele appeared to pair off with unspoken signals as we sat sipping tea, pretending we enjoyed it. We moved on to the Annex, with its blaring jukebox, long bar, and women with glistening lips and polished fingernails, as brazen in their way as the objects on Gerry's walls, whom we couldn't imagine speaking to, much less winning over. And from there to the Forum, which was more amenable, with its woolly bohemians, but whose self-assured women in leotards appeared equally unapproachable.

What did it mean to be shy? Was there such a thing as shyness independent of fear? Or was the concept just an excuse? Like erudite professors, we discussed such things, and thus managed for a while to obscure the masculine safari in which we were so fumblingly engaged.

When the Forum closed—it was getting late now—we moved up the block to the Cave, a jazzy den throbbing with libidinous energy, men and women whispering huskily, eyeing each other with clear intent, for by then it seemed that all the world but Mark and I had made its nighttime assignations.

Usually it was our last stop, after which we would convince ourselves that we'd at least tried. On this night, however, in a fit of uncharacteristic optimism, we followed two women from the Cave to a no-name bar on Avenue A with red and white checkered tablecloths, and sat at the next table, talking about this and that while screwing up the courage to approach. They eyed us, appeared both interested and shy, like us, and as we continued to procrastinate, two other, less fainthearted lovers walked into the place, introduced themselves and sat down, showing us how it was done.

"I've gotta go," Mark said when we stood outside. "See you tomorrow."

"Yeah, tomorrow . . ."

And when he went his way, I went mine, slowly walking the now deserted streets to my building, oppressed by my own ineffectuality.

My Czechoslovak Awakening

Day after day I smoked one joint after another, inflating the ordinary into the poetic. My cramped handwriting on yellow scrap paper seemed a precious script, a relic in its time, as I recorded the details of my historical twentieth-century solitude: the zigzag pattern of fire escapes on buildings across the way, the orange-hued light of a setting sun casting long shadows across tenement facades, the landscape of tarpaper rooftops, the city beyond . . .

The red brick walls of Stuyvesant Town beyond Fourteenth Street stirred something more personal and definitive, the middle-class housing a doppelganger for my upbringing in a similar project, a comment upon my presence in an apartment whose cracked walls my immigrant grandparents would have recognized, its stark simplicity more real to me than the attitude of acquisitive prosperity. I was turning the clock back beyond my parents, eschewing electricity when the natural light of an overcast day faded in late afternoon and I lit a candle and wrote by the glow of its flame.

Always, I began with grand thoughts. And then, as the cannabis lost its influence, I'd revisit my overblown prose, cross out lines, whittle the whole thing down, strain toward a notion of perfection. By the time I was through, a dozen pages would have been reduced to a short poem, four to eight lines, maybe less, and I'd put down the pen, the indentations on cheap paper a braille, yellow pages curling at the edges like aged parchment.

I was twenty-three, and curiously hopeful, my life just beginning. And at the same time, I lacked confidence. Out on my own, finally, the tenement streets that intrigued me also held dread possibilities. Which might have been why I spent so much time in the apartment, and why, when I left, I'd move quickly, grabbing my coat and rushing out, pulling it on as I hurried down the six flights and into the encroaching darkness of twilight. In my stoned absorption, I'd overlooked my hunger until it gnawed at me, and now the odor of food wafting from the cheap eateries on Avenue A made my stomach rumble.

The restaurants lining the street were always crowded, saunas of boiling food and mingled breath that left condensation on the plateglass windows. Usually, I'd sit at the counter, devour overdone meat and potatoes, cabbage or sauerkraut, flaccid vegetables, and mop up the gravy with a piece of stale bread. A great meal, hungry as I was, not having eaten all day. I'd reemerge on the street renewed, energized, and turning up my collar to ward off the cold, begin walking to nowhere in particular, keeping to the wider, brighter streets, burning fuel.

Except now I went the other way, to see my dealer, because I was almost out of grass.

The people who congregated at Tom's pad unnerved me. There was an attitude about them, and either they hardly noticed me when I entered or dismissed me after a cursory glance. Except for Tom, who was neutral but at least didn't judge me.

Anticipating the crowd inside, I hesitated at the green door before knocking. I heard, "Come in," Tom's gruff voice, and pushed inside. To my relief, he was alone.

It was a basement flat with concrete walls and a low ceiling. The narrow front room contained dilapidated soft chairs, a sofa, and wooden crates that served as end tables for jar-lid ashtrays. To the rear, a doorway led to a tiny bathroom and, beyond that, a bedroom cell with a glimpse of paintings, canvases of what seemed jungle scenes. They'd been done by Lila, Tom's girlfriend, and I was relieved that she wasn't there either; just Tom, sitting at his spot behind the table cluttered with books and notebooks, rock samples, stray test tubes and vials.

His long hair, pulled back and tied in a ponytail, accentuated his severe face as he regarded me over thin-rimmed glasses. But as I approached, his usual detached scrutiny was chased by what seemed a smile. "I got it," he said.

I thought I knew what he meant, but the unfamiliar smile and the lilt to his voice left me at a momentary loss. "You mean . . . ?"

"Yes," he said, and unfurling himself with surprising grace, he glided, long and lanky, from the table to the refrigerator, where he removed a tinfoil packet from the freezer. He unwrapped it, plucked two capsules from among two dozen or so, and dropped them in my palm.

I'd heard a lot about this drug and was looking forward to taking it, but the capsules were ordinary, like those for sinus congestion. I stared at them, looking for more than met the eye.

"They just came in this afternoon," he said. "From Czechoslovakia."

Czechoslovakia!

The word exploded in my head, stranding the two of us in America, the wrong side of the Iron Curtain, where it seemed these capsules had been smuggled from so we could be free too.

I closed my fist around them, said, "I'm going to my place to take them right now."

Tom followed me to the door, said, "There'll be some people here later . . ."

I thought about them, the people I never got a good look at and whose indifference always left me uneasy, self-conscious. "Uh-huh," I said.

But he wouldn't let me go, leaned close, said again, "We'll be here later," to make sure I understood.

"Okay," I replied, and hurried out, clutching the capsules in a fist.

Back in my apartment, I swallowed the capsules then arranged the candle, incense, and other things I had on hand when stoned: yellow writing pad, pens, a pack of cigarettes, matches, rolling paper, and the tin canister where I stored marijuana. They were on the steamer trunk, within easy reach. Then I lit the candle and turned off the overhead light. Now there was nothing to do but wait.

But wait for what? How can we imagine what we don't know? I thought about that as the time passed and nothing out of the ordinary happened. Impatient, I considered writing a poem about knowing and not knowing, though given my usual routine, that would have meant smoking a joint first, which might alter whatever it was that hadn't happened yet, though now I wondered if in fact it would . . . and then, after another bout of anticipation, I was sure it wouldn't, sat back and lit a cigarette, exhaling in a long sigh of disappointment . . .

. . . and sometime later realized I was staring at a halo around the glowing tip.

Bemused, I looked at the room, and my mouth fell open in amazement.

The walls were breathing!

It couldn't be (I told myself). It was my heart, beating, pumping blood to the brain . . . projected out, onto the walls . . . which only seemed to be breathing . . .

Each thought evaporated before the next popped up, hovering like smoke over my forehead. *Evanescent* . . . Yes, that was the word! And then that was gone too, leaving a ghostly residue. But it was okay. I didn't mind.

Mind . . .

What did it mean? To mind? To have a mind?

I jumped up, or thought I did, but my body responded in slow motion, unwound, floated out of the chair beneath the balloon that was my head. I could feel my legs, lacking bones, straightening, then moving down there, following my impetus across the floor. Latching onto my coat along the way, I lurched out the door and giddily negotiated the hallway, bouncing gently off the walls. Drunk! I thought. But I knew I wasn't, except as metaphor: drunk on the moldy smell, the rickety banister, the dingy landings as I rushed downstairs into—

The Street!

The reality of it overwhelmed me.

The Street! Civilization! Where everything of importance occurred!

I skimmed above the pavement, looking this way and that, reaching the corner, where jukebox music, laughter and conversation, tinkling glasses, curled out of doors . . . and I wondered why I'd never noticed this *fecundity* before. I'd never truly understood the word until now, and wanted to explore it further, to duck into the corner bar and delve into the source of its vitality. But I was too hyped up, too jazzed, too fecund myself, and I couldn't help but keep moving.

A red light at another corner stopped me. I shifted restlessly at the curb, waiting impatiently for traffic to pass and the light to change, then burst forward in joyous release.

I had no idea where I was going, the scene brighter each time I blinked, and the world even livelier now, with people and traffic, the streets brimming with life, pulsing with excitement! A dozen clichés came to mind, only they weren't clichés, but perfect summations, unique discoveries catalyzed by the scene I was witnessing.

Never in my life had I felt so good!

I could handle whole thoughts now, emotive bursts.

The Revolution is coming!

By which I meant something more than politics, though that was part of it. I meant the resolution of everything, all at once. Belief and actuality. The past and the present. All of it. Right now. Right here. Bursting. At this moment.

Wedged into the walking, talking, gesturing crowd, I thought:

The Revolution is over! And we won!

And, nearly delirious with joy, turning a corner, a neon sign caught my eye: THE EIGHTH WONDER. No doubt put there to celebrate the Revolution.

I rushed across the street, stopping abruptly beneath the striped awning, where a man in a tuxedo barred the entrance. He was short and brawny, black hair slicked back on his scalp, his clean-shaven face marked with a bluish shadow. He stood with arms crossed, blocking the open doorway as music wafted out.

"Two bucks," he said, holding out his palm.

I was dumbfounded. You had to *pay* to celebrate the Revolution? How could that be? I searched his face for an explanation.

At my amazed look, his hard expression dissolved and he frowned; at himself, it seemed. I'd shamed him. He averted his eyes, said apologetically, "Sorry . . . It's the management."

Yes . . . the Management. It hovered there between us, an invisible presence.

"But it gets you two free drinks," he added, cheering up.

His camaraderie despite the situation touched me. I took a jumble of bills from my pocket, stared at the green paper a moment, handed him two singles, asked if that was correct, then entered the club, sidestepping my way through chaos to the bar.

Despite the crush, the bartender spotted me right away. "What'll it be?" he shouted over the din.

"Scotch on the rocks!" I shouted back, having heard the expression before.

I waited, in a bubble of sorts amidst the crowd, until he placed it on the bar. Grasping the glass of amber liquid, I brought it to my lips and drank. It scorched my throat, brought me to my senses. Soberly, I put it down and looked around.

The place was jammed, and no one was still. They fingered their faces and hair, sipped and swizzled their drinks, and in an adjacent room, beyond an arch, sweat-sheened people were dancing in a frenzy beneath cages where women in glitter suits and fishnet stockings contorted themselves to the music, which was so loud it shook the walls and rattled the bottles behind the bar.

I'd often been in such places before, in college, on Friday and Saturday nights. I'd even looked forward to it. Now, I wondered why. The posturing and preening was bizarre, the mood desperate with the compulsion to have a good time. Separate bodies, individuals, were lost in a mindless whole as they drowned themselves in sound and movement.

I pushed my way out.

The crisp cold air was a benison. I stepped into the sidewalk traffic and was borne along by the flow, down the street, back the way I'd come. It was not unpleasant. Calmer now, I noticed details that hadn't registered before: steam rising from gratings in the street, lights mirrored in shop windows, people huddled inside winter coats, the collective mumble of conversation as they moved along the sidewalk.

And I was part of the stir and mumble. It was our custom to go out on a Friday night, to mix, to mingle . . .

This thing we all shared brought tears to my eyes.

Then I recalled the Eighth Wonder, and knew it wasn't true. Though we were together, we were alone, within our own skin.

I stopped at a corner and saw a woman hailing a cab; a couple arm in arm, laughing; an old man, holding a dog by its leash. It seemed cruel, the way he was yanking it into the street. It caught my eye, and I watched as the dog squatted in the gutter, shitting . . .

I was an animal!

It struck me with stunning force, and for a while I couldn't move.

The sidewalk crowd moved around me, and when I resumed walking, it was more slowly than before. We were animals. Of course, I'd known as much before, but as abstraction. And now . . . I was no different than a dog. We all were no different.

Then, abruptly, the implication of that similarity imploded in me:

I would die!

I stopped dead, my breath caught in my throat. Around me, people were walking and talking, moving this way and that, dodging traffic, talking to each other, laughing and gesturing. It was outrageous! How could they be so unconcerned? We were all going to die!

But then, what could they do about it?

What could I do about it?

I sighed heavily and set off again, even more slowly than before.

I would die, I would die, I would die . . .

I couldn't get over it:

I would die.

At First Avenue, I waited for the light, though no cars were in sight, then crossed quickly, as if one might suddenly appear and run me over, then fell back into my lugubrious pace on the other side.

I would die, I would die, I would die . . .

It was a dirge, and I walked to its rhythm, the street meeting my feet with gravity. I was back in my neighborhood now, the streets nearly empty, and each time I blinked, the air appeared darker. Never had I felt so alone. If I could find others—not an Eighth Wonder, but a place with people like me, who knew they were going to die—that would be something, at least. We could commune in our common fate. Find solace in each other's company.

As if in response, I turned a corner and saw the lights of the Forum a few blocks away. In a rush of exaltation I hurried toward it.

There was no thick wooden door, no sense of aged solidity, as I would have liked. And when I pushed inside, the tables, though wooden, weren't as substantial as my mood required. And how could I have forgotten how glaringly bright it was? But there were people there, fellow animals gathered in each other's presence, existing together. That was the important thing.

Then I spotted Mark, and shouting his name, rushed toward him, pushing chairs aside, reaching out and clutching his shoulder in heartfelt solidarity. My old friend! My compatriot!

"Something amazing's happened! Everything's different now!" Though we'd seen less of each other recently, our differences were insignificant now, because we were animals, and we would die.

I stood over him, about to blurt my great discovery, but Mark spoke first, in a loud whisper: "Sit down and lower your voice!"

I sat down, annoyed, but instantly shrugged it off. After all, what's annoyance compared to death? Squinting against the light, I gathered myself, in order to begin again, to explain, but the waitress appeared and instead I gave her my order. When she was gone, I leaned forward and earnestly told Mark that I'd taken a drug and walked halfway across Manhattan, an epic trek bursting with discoveries. And then, on the way back, I saw a dog shitting in the street and realized that I was an animal! That we were animals. Not theoretically, but actually!

Abruptly, I saw that his eyes were roaming the room. I'd been about to tell him about death. But it was too important, too monumental, to just toss out when he wasn't even paying attention. I sat back then, and said nothing. He was my best friend, and I couldn't tell him the most important thing I'd ever discovered. A sad moment; a great loss. Gripping the mug that had been placed in front of me, I brought it to my lips and sipped. I'd ordered hot chocolate, channeled it from childhood. It was sweet and cloying, like syrup. I pushed it aside.

There was a jukebox against a wall, a dozen tables, and a few people in the room. There was a plateglass window in front, reflecting the long room. To the rear, through a doorway, an old man stirred a pot on a stove. The waitress, looking bored, leaned against a wall.

There was nothing there for me.

I stood up and headed for the door.

Mark sat up then, said, "Where're you going?"

I didn't answer. I kept walking. Where was there to go to?

Outside, head down, I turned the corner onto Eleventh Street. The side streets had always made me nervous at night, the tenements looming on either side, but now I hardly noticed, didn't care. I was alone, doomed to a solitary existence while awaiting death.

It took me a moment to realize I'd stopped moving. My feet had brought me to a door. Green, as in the song:

> Green door, what's that secret you're keeping?
> Green door, while the morning comes creeping,
> Green door . . .

I reached out, touched it with my fingertips, and it swung slowly open, revealing a group of people gathered around a dazzling candle. They looked up, curious, and as if expecting me, widened the circle, made room.

The air was liquid, the candle flame rippling in gentle, concentric waves, conveying particles out toward the end of the aura. Waves and particles simultaneously, the conundrum of modern physics, resolved by the dilated eye. The luminous glow filled the room, anointed the atmosphere, which was occasionally punctuated by a laugh, which spread from one to another, for no apparent reason. From a far corner, violins and cellos provided rhythmic counterpoint, solid sound, channeling elation, transmuting it into harmony.

Bliss.

Another word I'd of course heard, but never experienced. A quiet ecstasy that went on and on and on . . .

And then change burst in the door, babbling, gesturing, wildly roiling the flame, as we sat agape, dispossessed of our former certainty, the intruder our new focus.

Tom, whom I'd only peripherally noticed before, emerged from the circle to meet this challenge. "What's up, Myron?" he asked.

"It's Leo," Myron replied. "You got to see it! He's dancing on a table at the Blind Justice, singing at the top of his lungs!"

Tom took in our puzzlement, seemed to weigh it against the imploring intruder. Perhaps Leo, in the coffeehouse, also weighed on his thoughts—which were suddenly resolved. He stood up and flicked a switch, the brilliance of a bare bulb transforming the cozy enclosure with its warm shadows into a light-blasted room. He crossed the narrow aisle to the pile of clothes in the corner and pulled on a coat, and taking their cue from him, the others were now on their feet too, retrieving coats, putting them on, filing outside.

I watched all this tumult without moving.

Tom stopped at the door and looked at me. "You don't want to come?" he asked.

"No," I replied. "I've already been out there."

He regarded me for a long moment, said, "We'll be back soon," and was gone.

Alone, I gazed at the room, brightly lit now, marveling in the sudden privacy. The radio was squawking news, and I got up, turned it off, and sat back down in a different chair, changing my point of view. The concrete aspect of the concept made me smile. From that new angle, I took in the things on a wooden crate: a pack of cigarettes, book of matches, jar lid containing butts, glass of water, pen, notebook; insignificant objects, yet with a solidity to them that made me take them seriously.

I picked up the notebook, opened it, and took pen in hand, gripping it with pleasant familiarity between thumb and fingers, as if my hand were an appendage of my thoughts. I expected a torrent of creativity, but no words came as I stared at the lined page. It was puzzling. I felt better than I ever had before. How could I have nothing to say?

Concentrating on the cigarettes, matches, ashtray, and glass of water, I willed them to provide meaning, an explanation for their astonishing voluminousness. Again, nothing. And then, abruptly, I was writing:

The glass is a cylinder three-fourths filled with water.
It rests on a rectangular crate of wood. The person in the room is
writing in a notebook propped against his thigh . . .

I paused, read this clinical description, and added:

What more can one write than what one sees?

It was all I could come up with, and the finality of it precluded further effort. I put the notebook aside and looked around for something else to do. For a while I thumbed through a *Scientific American*, but had a hard time focusing on the words, which were a wavering blur. I put it back on a stack of magazines and a map caught my eye. I'd always enjoyed looking at maps, and now unfolded this one with pleasure, a map of the city. Bronx, Brooklyn, Queens, Jackson Heights . . . The words jumped out at me, some bigger and bolder, some uppercase, others not. But like the objects on the crate, the words evoked nothing, not affluence, poverty, ethnicity, politics, religion . . . not even more personal memory, at the names of places I'd lived and been. I took a cigarette from the pack, lit it and blew smoke, staring at the unraveling tendrils, telling myself I lacked imagination, and yet imagining myself Camus's dispassionate stranger.

In truth, I was restless, at a loss. When the cigarette burned down, I tamped it out as if killing it was a profound activity. What was there to do, anyway? But despite my evident boredom, the rattling doorknob annoyed me, interrupted my solitude, which now seemed preferable to anything else. Then the door opened and Tom stood there, looking at me as if unsure what he'd find. I looked back at him without expression, was about to tell him to close the door, that he was letting the cold air in, but something in his look stopped me; his concern for my well-being.

He might have smiled then, a slight movement of his lips as he took off his coat. Turning back to me, he said, "Let's move next door. Some of the others are there."

Why go anywhere? I wondered. What difference does it make? "I'll stay here," I replied.

The answer appeared to annoy him, though it was hard to tell, since his expressions fell in a narrow range. But when he repeated himself, I didn't argue. Why not go next door? What difference did it make? I got my coat and followed him out.

It was an identical basement flat, but without pipes at the ceiling. A few people were asleep on mattresses toward the front. Farther back, a bare bulb shone over a round wooden table in a kitchen alcove, and someone in black, whom I recognized from next door, sat reading a book. Tom leaned against a cabinet along one wall and began to read too, one of his scientific magazines. I pushed some coats off a settee, lay down on my side, propped my head up with a hand and stared at the room. After what I'd witnessed that night, I assumed this new scene would absorb me. But I soon lost interest, picked up one of the comic books scattered on the floor beneath me and flipped through it insouciantly, as though an unseen observer might pass judgment on my low-brow taste. It was something I could have written about, had that occurred to me, and if I'd had paper and pen: the dichotomy between the real and the imaginary, and why I told myself I was not so much reading a comic book as making a point—that reality was all of a piece and on the same level.

But soon enough I lost that self-consciousness, the comic enveloping me with its clever, hidden meaning; the multiheaded sea monster rising from cartoon depths to menace the ship of explorers charting unknown waters on a strange planet. Yes, of course; I knew that monster, the explorers, the lure of the unknown. I finished one and began another.

By the time I'd read them all, Tom was asleep, standing up with his chin on his chest. And the guy in black at the kitchen table had folded his head in his hands, asleep. The room was now infused with gray light filtering through slats in the bamboo shade above my head. Quietly, I got up and left, closing the door softly behind me.

Outside, the morning sun glared off damp pavement. I turned the corner and saw the whirling brushes of a sanitation truck cleaning the cobbles on the avenue. A shopkeeper was cranking an awning open. On the next block, the supermarket had just opened. I went inside and walked down the empty aisles, which brought on an infusion of wonderment: the invisible alliance of farmer, teamster, and grocer that had stocked the fulsome shelves on my behalf. The girl at the cash register, though part of this food chain, appeared bored, and it surprised me that she could be unmoved by the generous scheme in which she played a part. Mechanically, she rang up my purchases and bagged them.

Back at my apartment, I unpacked the groceries and, for the first time since moving in, made breakfast. It was a significant ceremony, welcoming the new day. It was a memorable meal, the eggs real, the rough texture of toasted bread perfectly complementing the smooth butter—I'd never realized how well they went together.

Then I sat in the front room with a book of poetry, verses about death and dying. Ferlinghetti, Ginsberg, Dylan Thomas . . . Of course, what else was there to write about? I'd have to reread everything I'd read before, now that I knew what was important. And yet, despite my absorption, I eventually yawned, put the book aside, tired but still not sleepy. Again I wondered what to do next, and a curious hollow feeling came over me. That my life would be this way from now on. You shop, you eat, you read . . . and eventually you die. What did any of it mean, anyway?

Absently, I turned on the radio, and a tune came on.

It was nothing special, a simple thing, but before I knew it I was on my feet, shuffling around the room, dancing.

In the Realm of Mythunderstanding

Borne aloft by the body, my head floated down hallway and stairwell past gray-bearded patriarchs, cobblers and revolutionaries, pushcart peddlers and their families. On the fourth floor, hearing a soft tap-tap-tap at one end of the hall, I pictured my grandfather, a shoemaker, tapping away. Like the others, he dwelled behind closed doors on each landing, given life by the dilapidated age of the tenement building. The children of these émigrés from the Russian Pale, my parents, aunts, and uncles, came to mind too, scattered over decades, in housing projects built in the fifties, in tidy private houses in borough neighborhoods, and in suburban tracts where some of them eventually found themselves, to reside in a different sort of ghetto.

Past and present mingled in my personal stratosphere six feet above the ground, in scenes I either knew or had read or heard about. The mildew and half-light of the dingy stairwell, the crumbling plaster and watermarked ceiling—history incarnate—rendered me a participant, an immigrant myself, my own descendant.

And then the glass-paneled doors clattered shut behind me, trapping the past in the past as I blinked at the eye-watering daylight of the street, that past at my back, the passage from dark to light an astonishing historical leap from limitation to spaciousness, from old world poverty to the shining hope of a brighter future . . .

I blinked again, and entered this particular future, which curled around me as I bopped up the street, a hipster on his way from here to there, past the local hang-about the cats who lingered beneath a sign on the brick wall: EZ CREDIT, CHECKS CASHED HERE. They smoked cigarettes, shifted from foot to foot, eyed me with the transparent surreptitiousness of neighborhood idlers who'd been at it too long. Unaware of their transparency, they sized me up as I breezed down the block, feeling superior for having seen through them. But I was only vaguely cognizant of my momentary place in the world too, bopping along the sidewalk with a loose gait that gave no hint to the complexity of my particular self.

Then that was gone too, out of sight and mind as I paused at the grand corner intersection of compass points on the planet. I looked north, to check out traffic, a gust of arctic air slapping me in the face with the breath of ice floes and frozen tundra. Ducking my head against the arctic chill, burrowing chin into chest, I crossed that planetary landmark and headed into the tenement shade on the next block.

As I passed the narrow stone church, a semblance of awesome respect rose within me like a genuflection. Not that religion mattered. It was the aesthetics of the slim Gothic structure that moved me, the striving built into the brick, the faith that erected it. It said: *There's something more.* Which stirred me because I had no clear idea what that something was.

Twenty or so feet beyond, I'd push into Arnie Glick's pad.

Up front, three recognizable figures were in a huddle, casting larger-than-life shadows on the wall behind them as they hovered over a joint. I thought of Plato and his cave, though I'd never quite grasped the metaphorical meaning of that required reading in college. Farther back, beneath the suspended light in the kitchen alcove, a woman stood at the stove, stirring a pot, the hem of her peasant dress brushing the floor. And beneath the archetypal table, in its shadow, a dog lay snoring softly; trusty guardian of the hut.

At the edge of the Platonic huddle now, a joint was thrust in my direction, brusquely welcoming me to the order of stoned disciples of the weed. I took a drag and passed it on, to Arnie Glick, the short, balding innkeeper of this establishment, the iron bars on the solitary street-side window a decorative grating, and no less so for being a prosaic defense against thieves. Arnie was out of Dickens, an exaggerated character, wiry and suspicious, his flitting eyes ferreting for interlopers. He wore a leather vest, upon which my impression was built, which all but obscured the ordinary button-down shirt whose sleeves were rolled up fraternity style.

He passed the joint to Leo, compact, well-proportioned. An important person, I'd come to understand, though the respectful silence when I first heard Leo speak had been puzzling, the shards and fragments of nearly incomprehensible sentences and gestures eliciting a collective sigh of satisfaction when he finally, excruciatingly, concluded his thoughts. But now his status was confirmed in the way he brought the joint to his lips and inhaled with Levantine facility, an economy of movement, my initial reaction to his faltering speech, splayed fingers, and shrugged shoulders a misconception of my own, dependent as it was on a different notion of intelligence. Clearly, Leo was beyond the judgment I attached to words; leader of the caravan trade operating out of an exotic Flatbush, from where he trafficked in all kinds and varieties of this and that.

Emery, Leo's chemist, took the proffered joint from him with skeletal fingers. Ghostly pale skin stretched over bone, accentuated by black-framed glasses and black clothing from collar to boots, his narrow lips turned bloodless as he sucked in the smoke and held his breath.

Without looking, he passed the joint to me, and in moving to take it, I stared into eyes magnified by the thick lenses, the dilated pupils empty pits. I'd gone blank before, looking into them, and quickly averted my eyes. Emery gave me the shivers; an emaciated Baron von Frankenstein working on his own monster, a bomb sight he tinkered with next door, in Tom's pad.

"To blow the White House to smithereens," he'd told me gleefully.

Abruptly, with an involuntary twitch of associative reflexes, my emotions might flare, as they often did. We were smoking grass, after all, which was illegal, *underground*, as the word so aptly captured the basement pad, with its shadowy figures on the walls. Then Rose, the domestic peasant in the kitchen, became Rosie the moll, cooking up a roadhouse stew, each new arrival an unknown and suspect character. And since I was there too, my imagination propelled by adrenaline, I'd wonder if the others had their own doubts about me. The circumstantial evidence was overwhelming: I was a newcomer, uttering prevalent slang that sounded false even to me. And my hair . . . it was growing, but not fast enough; despite its dishevelment, I stuck out, a sore thumb.

Music would usually save me: Mozart, Telemann, Bach, Vivaldi . . . The classic orderliness put my mind at ease. I would eventually discover that the playlist had been improvised by Rose, the peasant moll as disc jockey, doing late twentieth century work. If the setting was heating up, the mood a fricassee of unspoken fantasy and unreality, she might go with a cool Miles Davis on the turntable. Or if it was too quiet, verging on the morose, she'd spin, say, uptempo boogie-woogie. Or piano rags to further lubricate the pleasant hum of talk, the place a warm speakeasy as joints and pipes moved from hand to hand.

An unseen muse, Rose would observe the results from the alcove.

Had I known she was the spinner, I no doubt would have considered her psychic, that she'd knowingly played the blues to accentuate my lovelorn admiration for Emily, who rarely spoke and with whom I was infatuated. She was a goddess herself, or close to it, with a doleful gaze that said she pined for someone who wasn't there, a should-be me, though I lacked the nerve to introduce my sensitive secret self. In my absence Emily was courted by Don Juan Goldberg, who hovered over her, laying down a seductive, sorrowful riff. It was a relief that she appeared uninterested, but overhearing his low-toned lament, I could not be sure she wouldn't eventually give in. Speaking softly, beneath the declarations of Mississippi John Hurt, the bus or train that would take him away to Canada to courageously escape the draft was convincing: Who could deny Don Juan his final wish: To spend his last heroic night memorably?

At some point, as the evening heated up, Richie Klein would burst in on stick figure legs, a speed freak among acid heads, and override the music and the talk with a shouted encomium to his latest mind-blowing discovery.

"Einstein! Relativity! Time is space, man! Time *is* space!"

He'd meanwhile pace back and forth in a tight line, declaiming in spasms, pivoting on high-heeled boots. Amphetamine-driven, manically, wildly askew, the madman as genius was his voluble excuse for obtrusiveness, his every shouted conviction irrefutable. And then, before anyone could pin him down, Richie would bolt back out into the night.

Charlie Wu would pop in too, but without flare, on his way home from the nine-to-five job he despised, wearing a cheap, rumpled suit, his tie a loosened noose.

Arnie always greeted him as a special guest, to demonstrate, it seemed, that it was more than okay with him that Charlie was Chinese. "Wu!" he'd shout across the room. "What're you up to?"

A vision of tired normalcy, the sardonic Wu would stand near the door shaking his head, clearing it of the fumes on a midtown street at rush hour. Snatching the joint held out to him, he'd smoke it like a cigarette, puffing away. But instead of smoothing his worry lines, the grass would set him off.

"The city sucks!" he'd begin, and from there escalate his rant against the world, indicting everyone in the room with his anger: "You lazy fuckers! You lay around, smoking dope, contemplating your navels, blathering about the meaning of reality . . . You don't know shit about reality! *I'll* tell you about reality . . ." And he'd spout the story of his day, a trudging tale of a Pavlovian dog responding to an alarm, putting on a uniform, dashing through streets filled with other dogs in order to shoehorn itself into a crowded train so he could get to a desk and sit there hour after hour, doing meaningless paperwork. They let him eat lunch, the bastards, but the food was lousy no matter where you went, processed shit, and after sitting on his ass all day, it congealed in his stomach, which accounted for his chronic constipation. Or else, what with all the coffee he drank to stay awake, he'd have a case of the watery shits.

Once, driving himself to a delirious peak as the daily story built to a crescendo, Wu broke off, turned the radio on full blast and stomped out.

It was the news in full throat. Casualties in Indochina, an explosion in London, a stabbing in the Bronx. The room sat stunned. This was the other world, whose reality depended upon acquiescence. A shared revulsion rippled within the concrete walls of our cloistered shelter. And then someone turned it off, for why would anyone want to know what was happening out there? What was the benefit of it?

There was a television too, but out of sight, beyond the Day-Glo bathroom, in a back room cell just large enough to contain a mound of moldy mattresses and the glowing set. The fluorescent dungeon was the domain of Myron, a rarely seen creature who seemed oblivious to the smell of mildew and stale cigarettes as he stared at the black and white screen. Now and then, between shows, he'd leave his cell, for a food run to the corner bodega, or when the vibrating music from up front, calamitous rock and roll, screaming guitars, a booming bass, told him that Ray from L.A. had taken control of the record player, which meant that Pauline had also arrived. Then Myron would emerge, squinting into the unaccustomed world of color, looking for her red hair, and spotting Pauline, move in her direction, stopping a few feet away to gawk.

Pauline was flattered. It might have only been Myron, but it was admiration. She'd meet his bloodshot eyes, hold them a beat or two longer than mere curiosity could explain, then say something like, "Well, what'd you know." And then avert her gaze, feigning embarrassment at having revealed too much of herself, and bring it back with a tilt of the head and fluttering lashes, coquette pantomime choreographed by the *Kama Sutra*, "On Titillating a Sudra."

A fat cigarette stuck between his lips, Myron would ask, "Got a light?" by which he meant to say more, attempting the unimaginable: fulfillment of the kind of dream that regularly bore fruition on the tube.

Flicking her slim lighter, she'd light him up, Myron bobbing the cigarette through the flame, up and down, up and down, an excited penis, a Sudra for sure, not from a thousand-year-old book, but from Bensonhurst, with its own teenage word-of-mouth primer, tips guaranteed to turn the girls on. Bobbing, bobbing, lighting the cigarette long after it was actually lit and Pauline had lost interest. In fact, she'd lost it soon after confirming the pedestal on which she stood, and now, bored, flicked the lighter shut and turned away. Myron took it well. He had little in the way of ego, was nearly immune to slights and snubs. And anyway, by then the commercial was over, and without a backward glance he'd head back through the Day-Glo bathroom to catch the rest of the show in his asylum.

L.A. Ray, with his glib self-confidence, was amused by this interplay. Hedonism has its own logic; and for Hollywood Ray, appearances were everything. It flattered him that other men would find his chick attractive.

But with the nightly shift next door, to Tom's, Ray found himself trapped in his own paradigm.

Holding back till nearly everyone had regathered, he'd make a grand entrance, sweeping in, a rock star undoing his ponytail and shaking his hair out, announcing himself: Ray is here! Cool Ray! Hoo-Ray! He'd plunk down on in a chair, his long legs extended, crossed at the ankles, arms folded with self-satisfaction on his chest, and then he was through, a blank look on his face, because for Ray everything was appearance; he had nothing more to show.

He'd gone next door because that's what came next, but he was lost there, with no record player to appropriate and none of the noise and hoopla of Arnie's pad. Rather, it was a salon of discrete conversation, and trying to put his two cents in, to earn his way in the new setting, he'd pipe up from his chair, insert himself with needy urgency. It was embarrassing to see how badly Ray wanted to be taken seriously. Soon enough he would flee, slip quietly out, back to what was left at Arnie's, and to Pauline, who was more important to him than he knew, could be counted on to restore his self-esteem.

Rose, on the other hand, became more prominent next door. Sitting in a soft chair, crocheting, she'd follow the ebb and flow of words, and hearing something to remark upon, would peer over her sewing pince-nez and address herself to no one and everyone in particular, phrases that fell smoothly into place, a proverb or aphorism from a book of quotations, though likely it was her own concoction. Her remarks instantly transformed the place into a drawing room scene whose actors improvised a script on the manners and morals of contemporary life, with Rose as omniscient narrator. A harmless world, of human flaws and foibles, petty vanities and whimsical misunderstandings, and somehow comforting for its lack of deeper meaning.

And then there was Lila, who was rarely seen at Arnie's, yet held court at Tom's. Lounging on a long couch, a queen to Rose's lady in waiting, she smiled with superior amusement at the comings and goings her attitude seemed to preside over. Her arm, bent at the elbow, like that of a naked maja muraled in a bar, pillowed her head in a languorous pose, an abundance of thick, golden hair falling in waves to her shoulders. The stoned vibes in the narrow concrete room gave the scene a watery, impressionistic cast, a veil of sensuousness, rendering her Cleopatra reclining in the Nile delta.

Lila hardly took active part in conversation. But she'd listen, and at times, in a husky voice, deign to offer a disinterested observation, and a while later offer another; non sequiturs, it seemed, but she was working on a strand of underlying meaning and with a certain end in mind, which would slowly crystallize. Astute, and often cruel, she'd carve from the general to the specific, sharpening it to a point, then stick it in with a biting conclusion.

I steered clear of her.

"Doesn't Emily look lovely?" she said to Rose one night, an aside intended to be overheard throughout the room.

Emery sat on the floor, a precocious, malevolent child in black, toying with his bomb sight. Tom was at his usual spot behind the cluttered table, reading. Patrick Malone, in his plaid workman's shirt, had come in from the cold after chopping wood for an unseen fireplace whose logic was the presence of a group of strangers dressed in Siberian fur hats and pelt overcoats. Emily sat in a corner, where I kept an eye on her.

It was a distinct contrast: Lila, regally sprawled on her couch, blond, voluptuous; Emily, dark-haired, slim, hands folded modestly in her lap.

" . . . But then, in her particular way," Lila went on, "Emily always looks lovely."

Behind his table, Tom looked up.

Lila turned to Patrick. "Enlighten us, Brother Malone. You should know something about the worship of a virgin. What is there about them that is so appealing?"

"You're speaking to an apostate," Patrick replied, joking, but uncomfortable.

"Then speak as a man," Lila retorted. "The *idea* of the unsullied virgin, the demure woman, cloaked in modesty . . . It turns men on, doesn't it?"

Patrick was not one to play the foil. He didn't reply.

"Women think they want romance, and men want something else," Lila went on, looking across the room at Emily. "They want it until they get it, and then they lose interest."

Emily stood up then, to fumble through the pile of coats near the door. All eyes went to her, and her evident distress. At last she found the coat and pulled it on, aware of the attention, face flushed, fingers fumbling with the buttons.

Then, from the rear, Tom's gruff voice cracked the silence. "Where're you going?" he asked her.

Lila's head snapped around and she glared at him as he gazed across the room, seemingly oblivious to her, his eyes locked with Emily's; a visual triangle that told me all at once what I'd somehow missed.

Without a word, Emily turned and left, the door clicking gently shut behind her.

And in the startled aftermath, I recalled that the gods on Olympus had not been perfect. They were human, after all.

Trew Love

Modest, seemingly shy, even reticent, whenever Emily came within a few feet of me, lithe, thin, with heart-shaped face and long dark hair, I was tongue-tied, speechless. But in the privacy of my apartment I spoke to her all the time, wrote perfervid poems extolling her perfection, impassioned words that would ignite and bind her to me.

When I finally did speak aloud to her, however, it was not at all as I'd composed it.

It happened early one evening when I entered Tom's pad, expecting to join the gang, and stopped just inside the door. No one was there but Tom and Emily, sitting next to each other on the couch. I stood with one hand on the knob, the other holding a cigar, which I'd treated myself to that day; three for a quarter at the shop off Astor Place where two Cubans hand-rolled tobacco behind the dusty plateglass.

Startled, I said, "Oh! Sorry! I didn't realize . . ." sure that this cozy scene was not one I was meant to see.

But Tom appeared unconcerned at being discovered, nor did my secret belle dame seem fazed. The two of them merely looked at me as I stood there, adrift in misgivings; Tom with his usual matter-of-fact lack of expression; Emily curious, and perhaps amused by my double take as I took a step back, intending to flee.

"Come in, come in," Tom said, beckoning.

Still, I hesitated, the triangle that had jolted me a few nights ago posing a moral Euclidean question: In entering, would I be choosing sides for Tom and Emily against Lila? Thinking fast, I held up the cigar, said, "I shouldn't . . . the odor," ducked my head in an apologetic nod and turned toward the door.

"It doesn't bother me," Tom said.

"Me neither," Emily said.

So I turned back, went in and sat down in a chair, at odds with myself now for turning away in the first place, embarrassed about my reflexive belief in the rectitude of sexual loyalty, which I was sure they had both interpreted from my behavior. What an uptight, bourgeois specimen I was! And crafty as well, to use the cigar as a ruse to extricate myself; which itself was an embarrassment—a notion of propriety that led me to apologize for a smell.

To make amends I fell back on craftiness again, a distractive impulse, held up the cigar and said, "A lot of people stare at me when I smoke these." And then, realizing that my ploy also happened to be true, that it did indeed bother me, I added, "I mean, I know what they're thinking, the stereotype that pops into their heads, the knee-jerk reaction . . . If I were smoking a pipe instead, they'd react to a different reflex—that I was an intellectual—and then the exact same words that came out of my mouth would sound different to them. But since I'm smoking a cigar, they assume I'm uneducated, crude, a lout not even worth listening to, a lowlife gangster of sorts, out of an old black and white movie—"

Emily laughed, bringing me back to earth; a musical ripple that made me look at her instead of the tip of my stogie, which I'd been staring at to avoid looking at the two of them, side by side on the couch. Now, I saw the long, smooth fall of black hair framing her face, her alabaster complexion, the pronounced nose and lips, so precise and fine; and the belladonna eyes, the wide black pupils, unreadable, mysterious, intently focused on mine, on me . . .

"I like it," Tom said.

I noticed that he'd untied his ponytail, his hair cascading over his shoulders and down his back. I hadn't realized how long it was. He probably hadn't cut it in years.

"It's distinctive."

What was he talking about?

"You don't see men smoking them anymore," Emily said.

I looked at the tip again, noticed it had gone out.

"We have to be ourselves!" Tom declared. "We can't let them keep us down!"

"Who?" I asked.

"*You* know," Emily said softly, chiding me.

I looked at her again, thinking that I should know. But I didn't.

"Those who see you as a lowlife gangster because you smoke them," she said.

Yes. Of course. I relit the cigar, a revolutionary gesture befitting Fidel himself, and blew smoke toward the ceiling in a bravura exhalation, proudly signaling my independence, my uniqueness. And then, catching that self-congratulatory pose, I swung the other way: I hadn't lit up for myself, but for

Emily. It was artifice. Exhaling on a sigh, I looked at her again, and saw her looking at Tom, and he at her. They only had eyes for each other, as the saying went. I was suddenly superfluous.

Abruptly, I stood up, said, "I'm gonna split . . ."

Tom looked at me and nodded. "See you later," he said.

But it was Emily's soft, lilting "Good-bye" that I took with me . . .

That sweet farewell, embellished with details overheard and overseen—it was what I thought of as poetry. But if, aside from sentiment, I wasn't much of a poet, I had a poet's self-absorbed egocentricity. The world gravitated around me. And for the rest of the evening I recalled how lovely she was, how pale, how ethereal, and once again became the shy knight, the Lochinvar who would eventually claim her. Exactly what I might say to win her over was obscured by the cannabis that fueled my Camelot, a mist in which the dragon of inexperience gnawed at me. I'd never done it. I was a virgin. Heavy baggage to carry, containing a load of upbringing I'd yet to examine; an anachronism in Camelot, where chivalry and romance, purity of intent, and a true heart could transform the dross of base desire to admirable gold.

I put down my pen at three or four in the morning. As usual, my intensity had brailled the surface of the cheap yellow paper. I left the ream lying on the steamer trunk, along with the grass, the candle, and the rest, parted the curtain to the closet of a room where I slept, took off my clothes, and fell exhausted onto the mattress, where my custom was to sleep until three or so in the afternoon and wake up with a headache.

So I was only half conscious when a knock woke me a few hours later. Blearily, my head clogged, I stumbled off the mattress and into the kitchen. Wrapped in a blanket, holding the ends together at my chest like a toga, I opened the door—

"Hi," she said, smiling.

Did I mention that when Emily smiled, her lips formed a perfect moue?

My own mouth, parched after chain smoking all night while composing sonnets to her beauty, confessions and proclamations of true love and adoration, gaped open in flabbergasted amazement.

"Oh, I'm sorry," she said. "I woke you . . ."

"Uh, no," I replied. "It's all right. I was just getting up anyway."

I stepped back, and she glided inside and stopped a few feet away, scanning the place, her gaze taking in the marked-up pages on the trunk in the other room. I had to hide them, I thought, then realized she couldn't possibly see what I'd written from where she stood.

Emily turned back to me, said, "I could make us breakfast while you get dressed."

A contagion of dust motes gave shape to the swath of sunlight that angled from the front windows, across the stained linoleum floor, and came to rest on the sinkful of dirty dishes next to her. In my glance, the funky sink was a perverse shrine to slobbery. I couldn't imagine Emily delving in, her delicate hands touching the green and purple mold as she scrubbed pans, dishes, knives and forks. And having woken up another degree by then, I noticed too that she wore an elegant coat with a fur collar, and that I was barefoot, wrapped in a fraying blanket.

"No, don't do that," I said.

"It's no trouble."

"No, no . . ."

She seemed disappointed. That little moue creased her mouth.

"It takes me a while to wake up," I said, trying to explain.

But she misunderstood, said, "Maybe I should go," softly, regretfully, and turned away.

I almost reached out, to haul her back.

And then she was in the hallway, turning as I stood at the open door, saying, "Maybe I'll see you at Arnie's this evening . . ."

Afterward, I derided myself for being the stupidest person alive. But as I shaved, and admired the smooth face in the tilted, distorting mirror over the bathtub, I doted on that *maybe*. She'd said it with a lilt, as if saying *I hope . . .*

I hope I'll see you at Arnie's . . .

The more I thought about it, the more convinced I was that she looked forward to seeing me. And I thought about it all day, worked myself into a beehive of anticipation, could hardly wait for twilight, when she'd surely be waiting for me at Arnie Glick's.

In my eagerness, I was the first to arrive that evening, and sat down awkwardly to wait.

Rose came in, and a while later Leo, with Emery. Joints were passed, and Patrick showed up, to hit Leo up for a capsule or two. Then Ray and Pauline, with Richie Klein in tow, crashing and ill-tempered, where the day before he'd been ebullient. I noticed Gazi, who'd found a quiet corner, and would emerging from the shadows to grip a proffered joint with the same dextrous certainty as Leo. By then it was snowing outside, people stamping it from their feet when they arrived, brushing it off their coats, the pad brimming with the mysterious energy of winter. Rose was back to the blues, and it filled the room, but I was already down, the lyrics of lost love deepening my funk.

Emily wasn't there . . . hadn't come . . . probably wouldn't. *I lost her this morning, by turning her away,* I wrote in tiny script inside a matchbook. And when the door opened, I looked up, then down again, and added another lament: *Everyone who enters makes it all too clear she's not here.* And then, the inside of the matchbook nearly covered with scribbles, the door swung open and there she was—

My heart leapt into my throat.

I wrote that down too, and looking up again, saw Don Juan Goldberg follow her in.

My heart broke.

I'd just squeezed that in when a shadow fell across me. It was her. She was smiling, or maybe not; the bare bulb behind her, a halo around her head, shaded her face.

"Hi," she said.

And I blurted, "I've been waiting for you!"

She moved to one side, and I could see that she was indeed smiling, in her endearingly modest way. "It's so noisy in here," she said, leaning down so I could better hear her. "Why don't we go for a walk?"

"What about Don?" I asked.

"Don?"

"Didn't you come with him?"

I cringed, hearing myself. My face flamed and I expected her to laugh at me, bourgeois creature that I was.

Instead, she said, "Don Goldberg's a pain," annoyed. "He followed me here."

A pain?

I was glad to hear it, but also surprised. The offhand dismissal was not what I expected from my belle dame. Pushing it aside, I found my coat and, pulling it on, hurried to catch up.

She was waiting outside, on the sidewalk, where I stood a moment, discombobulated, wasted by the pot. She slipped an arm through mine and, with slight pressure, moved me along, the two of us walking slowly . . . so slowly it was a wonder I kept my balance. Emily didn't have that problem. I marveled at her gracefulness as she placed one foot in front of the other, managing to get from here to there without stumbling or falling, while I plodded along on the slippery, snow-slick sidewalk, heart pounding.

A picturesque scene, the snow swirling hypnotically toward us, parting magically as we perambulated arm in arm up the block. Actually, it was too picturesque. It was unbelievable. And with Emily next to me, nearly unbearable. It was beyond me how I could possibly continue to function.

My mouth took over, as it tends to when I'm unnerved, and I heard myself say, "This is really something." The soporific utterance hung there, suspended in the snow swirl, melting in the vapor it had produced.

"Yes, it's beautiful," Emily replied, as if I'd made a profound observation.

Yes, exactly! We'd both seen it. The gentle flakes, coating parked cars, filming the sidewalk, transforming fire escapes into delicate filigree as she held my arm and leaned against me. The unreality of it nearly made me scream.

Up ahead, people were waiting for the light to change, laughing. Woodenly, having rehearsed the line as we walked, I said, "Everyone seems in a good mood when it snows."

"That's because it transforms everything," Emily replied.

"You think that's it?"

She tilted her head questioningly from within her fur-lined hood, scattered fetchingly with snow. "Don't you think so?"

"I don't know," I said. "I've been trying not to find reasons for everything." I might have been a corpse, stiff as a board, speaking about myself as an archeological find. As she continued to look at me with a puzzled expression, I quickly added, "I do too much of that. I'm always asking myself why things are the way they are. I'm always looking for explanations instead of just accepting things as they are."

"But I like that about you," she said.

I was flummoxed. "You do?"

"Yes."

"But . . . why?"

"Because it's thoughtful . . . I'd like to be more that way."

Thoughtful.

The word implied restraint and self-control, not obsession. I liked it.

"What you said last night," she went on, "the way you spoke, the way you observe things and consider them . . ."

What had I said?

" . . . You're not like the others. They're all so . . ." She groped for the words, frowned, tilted her head, impatient with herself. "I wish I could express myself like you do. Maybe if I hadn't dropped out of college . . ."

Her words plunged me into distress. Fervently defending her, I said, "But college just . . . I mean, it's intellectual, but it has nothing to do with intelligence. I couldn't wait to get out . . ." I sighed up a cloud of vapor. "What I mean is, it's hard to get *over* the habits I have, which college only accentuated . . . The need, y'know, to categorize everything, to look for a cause, for a meaning. The need to . . . explain things rather than act on them . . ."

I finally fell silent, and as we walked without speaking, I worried, against the sound of our footfalls, that I'd disappointed her because she liked me for reasons I didn't.

Emily gently tugged my arm, guiding us down Seventh Street, and for the first time I wondered where we were going. As preoccupied as I'd been with walking and talking, I hadn't given it any thought. And then, in the middle of the block, she leaned into me, guiding us toward the Paradox. I knew that place, with its tiny tables and clientele that sipped tea and ate brown rice and seemed to belong to a club that excluded me. I'd never felt comfortable there.

"Don't you just love it here?" she asked after we entered and stood inside, gazing at the crowded room, looking for an open table.

And I agreed, though I felt claustrophobic, standing there, and confused as we jostled through the close-knit klatches to the only vacant table and sat down. My pupils bounced around as I tried to focus, to find a fixed point and stare at it, so I might affect a neutral indifference to the noisy scene.

Emily startled me, reaching across the small tabletop and resting a hand on mine. "Don't you just love observing people?" she asked, perhaps assuming that I was taking them in, instead of trying to locate myself.

"Uh, yeah," I replied.

"But you're still wearing your coat." She'd shrugged out of hers.

"It's cold in here," I replied.

She withdrew her hand.

It seemed a rebuke. To redeem myself, I concentrated on the busy room, trying to find something likable to comment on. But the waitress came and went and came back again with a pot of tea and dainty cups, and still my pupils bounced all over the place as I raked it for something piquant, amusing, charming. It didn't help that Emily turned to me now and then to remark upon something she'd noticed, her confiding tone implying that we had seen it together and come to the same conclusion. But then, I was nodding in agreement, as if we were indeed in harmony, which only compounded my estrangement as I went back to examining the dizzying room in order to offer her some tidbit as proof of my sensitivity.

Then, out of nowhere, Don Juan Goldberg appeared at the table, looking down at Emily, fingering the pretentious mustache he'd recently cultivated. He stood between us, but ignored me as he leaned down to speak to her. I almost pushed him away, since his ass was practically in my face. But I restrained myself, because I was too polite, and because I saw Emily eyeing me across the table, her lips a knowing Mona Lisa slight smile, telling me, it seemed, that we once more shared the same moment and viewpoint.

She said to him, "Won't you join us?"

And he replied, "I'd like that very much."

Astounded, I watched as he yanked a vacant chair from an adjacent table and pulled it over. Straddling it, he reached for the teapot, poured tea into her cup, and having inclined toward her, remained there, draped over the small table, hovering a few inches away, speaking softly, earnestly. I couldn't see her face, only the back of his head, but she didn't push him away. Had she grown tired of my awkwardness, and inferred how inexperienced I was? It bedeviled me as I stared into the dizzying room, feigning indifference.

It didn't matter, I decided, suddenly angry. She was with me, or was supposed to be.

And then I was on my feet, glaring down at her, announcing, "I'm leaving."

Emily looked up at me, bewildered. "But I thought . . ."

But already I was moving away, through the off-putting crowd, to the door and out.

I was halfway up the block, walking fiercely, when I recalled Tom and Emily next to each other on the couch as she stared into my eyes, and then, minutes later, staring into Tom's eyes with the same intensity. The two of them, together, and me, odd man out.

The recollection left me feeling foolish, naive, a boy in a grown-up world where men and women played a mating game that had nothing to do with knights and maidens and ethereal love. Last night I'd gone back to my pad, and Emily was with Tom. And tonight she would have been with me, had I played the game instead of hurrying away in a snit, snowflakes melting on my burning face.

You Can't Call Home Again

I hadn't seen Mark in a while the day I spotted him across the street, shuffling along with his eyes on the sidewalk, his hands thrust into baggy corduroy pants. I was about to call out, wondered if I wanted to get into the old stuff again, the politics and social commentary, and between the old and the new, our past friendship and recent estrangement, the old won out. He looked up when I shouted, and, similarly ambivalent, waited on me with a forced smile as I crossed the street to join him.

Mark and I went back a long way: to high school, college, and now here, in the renascent tenements, where for a while we'd been near constant companions. My Czechoslovak awakening, and the society of acidheads that came with it, had changed things between us. But the personal past is not easy to discount, and shrugging off his visible reluctance to put aside the misgivings I also felt, I mounted the curb with an eagerness that caught me by surprise.

At once he launched into one of his halting, elliptical discourses, fueled by nervousness more than a need to share his latest insight. I'd forgotten how long-winded he could be, and, not for the first time, wondered if his stammering delivery wasn't a ploy to preclude interruption, or even to elicit agreement when he finally made his point. Perhaps sensing my antipathy, he dropped whatever he'd been discoursing upon and abruptly asked if I was still heavily involved with drugs.

I said, "I don't know if I'd call it 'heavily'—"

But he had his own answer in mind, having asked in order to tell me what he thought, and jumped in before I could finish. Everyone was obsessed with drugs now, he said, and that bothered him. It was an escape from social issues, civil rights, the war, the threat of nuclear obliteration, at a time when it was more crucial than ever that we all had to stand up for what we believed in. He spoke in generalities, but I knew he was obliquely speaking to me, accusing me of turning my back on the important things. Then, out of nowhere, now that he'd established his commitment to the bona fides, he said was considering taking acid himself.

"As an experiment," he explained.

"An experiment?"

"That's how Tom put it," he said. "He pointed out that if something, y'know, happened, he'd be right there to help me."

Mark knew Tom from college, where political and bohemian circles had overlapped. In fact, it was Mark who'd given me Tom's address when I moved to the city, and at a pad Tom had on the west side at the time, I scored an ounce of grass from him. It made sense that he wanted Tom to guide him, but this too was a hidden message: that since I'd recently turned my back on him, he would now enter my world without me.

It didn't matter to me. In fact, Tom was a better choice. I'd come to rely upon him myself, to be there, unruffled, when everyone was stoned and the old verities provided no support. And yet it was the past itself, which I'd shared with Mark, that made me glad when he indeed showed up at the basement pad on the appointed night. He was my bridge to a world I didn't want to leave entirely behind.

I could tell he was glad to see me there too, though he was a bundle of nerves as he flounced onto the chair next to mine with a heavy sigh.

"Don't worry," I told him. "It'll be great. You'll see."

Unconvinced, he said, "Maybe I should do this another time."

"Why?" I asked.

"This isn't a good night for it."

"Why not?"

"I'm coming down with something, I think." With his stubble beard and haggard look, he did look sick. But no more than usual.

"You're nervous, that's all."

"With good reason," he said.

"Listen, like you said, it's just an experiment," I told him. "If you don't like it, you don't have to do it again." Though I couldn't imagine he wouldn't.

"But what if I change completely?" he said. "How can I go back then?"

"Go back to what?"

"To the way I was."

"I don't understand. If you change, you change . . ."

"But then I wouldn't have control anymore."

"Control of what?"

"And what if something awful, something . . . irrevocable, should happen?"

"Nothing awful is going to happen."

He sat up, spoke urgently: "Did you see the story in yesterday's *Post*? A guy took acid, went up to the roof of his apartment building, believing he could fly, jumped off and died."

Taken by the gruesome image, I didn't know what to say. And then, considering it, I asked, "But if he died, how would anyone know he thought he could fly?"

"That's what the police said."

"But how would they know?"

"What difference does it make? He jumped!"

"Lower your voice," I said, looking around. "You'll freak people out."

In his agitation he might have forgotten where he was. He looked into the narrow room, at the people on the couch, in the chairs, and milling around the table, talking to Tom, who sat at his usual spot. They too were there to get high, but unlike Mark, were in a festive mood that all but precluded a bad result.

Mark turned back, lowered his voice. "Who knows what I might think or do? What if *I* believe I can fly?"

"Tom will keep an eye on you," I said. "And I'm here too."

He ignored that, said, "Isn't it possible that a person on acid might see a *moiré* pattern and lose himself in it?" He carefully enunciated *moiré*, so I could better appreciate his expertise.

"Where'd you hear that?" I asked.

"I mean, losing yourself in a *moiré* pattern, maybe you'd just stand there staring at the headlights while a car came right at you."

I could picture it. It's possible to imagine anything, after all. But I said, "That can't happen."

"Why not?" he demanded.

"Well, you'd have be standing in the middle of the street without realizing it, for one thing, and for another, car lights are harsh and glaring, not hypnotically beautiful, so when—"

"Then you'd be like a deer in the headlights, wouldn't you? No, not *like* a deer in the headlights! You would *be* a deer in the headlights!"

It came back to me then, how Mark never let a conviction die. I'd been the same way, I supposed, the two of us into argumentation for its own sake. And his urgency as he tried to talk his way out of discomfort turned me off. I found myself sorry that he was there.

"I mean, what if that happens?" he was saying. "It could, couldn't it? Of course it could. I mean, the only difference between the street and the sidewalk is a curb. And how big is that? It's not exactly a barrier. What if that happens and I—"

"What if what happens?"

Startled, Mark looked up.

Tom stood there, peering down through bifocals perched on the ridge of bone that was his nose. "What do you think might happen?" he asked.

Suddenly sheepish, Mark said, "That I might I forget where I am . . ."

"You'll be here, with us," Tom replied, and opened a hand, revealing two white pills in his palm.

Mark gingerly took one of them and stared at it a moment. "It's hard to believe this is what all the fuss is about."

"Go on, take it," I said. "It's not poison."

With a shrug, he popped it in his mouth and swallowed, then giggled, though it wasn't clear what he found funny. It might have been an hysterical spasm.

Then I took the other pill, Tom went back to his table, and we settled in to wait.

Soothing classical music coated the room, and a few candles burned on upturned crates that served as tables. It seemed everyone had simultaneously taken acid and were waiting too, the conversation softer now, the mood one of collective anticipation.

Mark hadn't said anything since taking his poison. He slouched in his chair, staring up at the low ceiling, hands clasped behind his head in a posture simulating contentment. But he was hardly at ease. His feet were fidgeting, his tongue bobbing in his cheeks, and then, abruptly, he sat up and snatched a magazine from a stack on the floor, which he went at energetically, turning the glossy pages, snapping them with a crackling sound. It was a *Scientific American*, and I wondered what could possibly interest him as he worked his way through it. The two of us had been into politics, basketball, and poetry; certainly not the sciences. But then, he'd read about moiré patterns somewhere. Maybe he was looking for one now.

As abruptly as he'd picked it up, Mark tossed the magazine aside. Raking his hair with his fingers, he said, "Nothing's happening! I don't feel different at all!"

"It can take a while," I replied.

"Or maybe it won't work!"

"No, it'll come on, but—"

"I'll bet it doesn't! I'll bet nothing happens!"

"It hasn't been that long," I said.

"But it doesn't *always* work, does it?" He said this hopefully, and before I could respond, added, gleefully, "It probably won't! I'm not like other people, y'know. I have an unusual chemical disposition."

I didn't want to argue. We were all going to die eventually. What was the point of arguing? But his full-of-himself assertion annoyed me, and losing the distance I'd so far managed to maintain, I snapped, "What could be so unusual about your chemical disposition?"

"Well, for one thing," he said, "I'm immune to penicillin . . . and also, no matter how much I drink, I never get drunk."

I found it hard to believe he had an iron constitution. Mark was the most psychologically vulnerable person I knew, if not the most contentious.

"I get sleepy instead." He giggled. "Wouldn't that be something? If I just fell asleep . . . and maybe I'd wake up recalling all these great dreams. *Maybe . . .*" he said, drawing out the word, "maybe I'm dreaming all this now," and he gestured at the room with a sweeping arm, from the candles and the now quiet group in back, where violins and cellos wove a lovely, intricate, counterpoint, to the door a few feet away, where his hand lingered, suspended in air. "Or maybe . . . maybe . . ."

He looked at his hand as though he'd never seen it before, and then at me, his face a play of expressions: surprised, pleased, bewildered, concerned . . ."What was I saying . . . ?"

Without thinking, I said, "You're on acid."

I wanted to retrieve those words, which too bluntly announced what he'd most feared, but it was too late. And when he bolted from his chair and out the door, it seemed my doing. A moment later I bolted after him.

Only seconds had elapsed, but as the door closed behind me and I stood on the nighttime street, the sidewalk was empty. Perplexed, I looked up and down the block, my distilled breath in the winter air the essence of mystery. Where had he gone? I heard different, louder music then, from the adjacent basement apartment, and it drew me inside.

I stopped short just within the door. The place was a stew of sensation, the acrid cigarette smoke a shifting haze in the light of the single bare bulb, the vibrating music coursing through me, the raucous proximity of bodies confounding.

Mark!

Recalling why I was there, I plunged into the thick stew with heroic intrepidity, sweeping from the front door through the Day-Glo bathroom to the concrete dungeon in back, where Myron, reclining on his mound of mildewed mattresses, looked up. The television rendered the cell fluorescent gray, and it smelled of marijuana, saltpeter, and fungus. He regarded me blankly, then looked back at the screen, losing interest in me as I stood there, lost.

Mark!

I followed the summons back out, through the garish bathroom and into the bedlam of life and blaring stereo speakers up front, and I glimpsed Mark at the door, where he'd no doubt been all along. I must have stood next to him before embarking on my frazzling mission. Why had I been looking for him? I'd forgotten. Then I recalled how he'd bolted, and my mission to save him from himself. Without me to calm him down, who knew what he'd do?

I called out while lurching through the hubbub, but he didn't see me, turned away, and by the time I got to his spot, he was gone, out the door.

I followed, stood on the sidewalk, saw the door next door swinging shut, and went back inside. He was sitting in the same chair when I entered, and I sat down next to him, as before.

"It's amazing!" he said, bouncing in the chair. "It's amazing!"

"Yes, it is," I said, relieved. He was all right.

But then he jumped up again, yanking at his lips, pacing in the small space near the door. Why couldn't he sit still for two seconds?

"What's wrong?" I asked.

He stopped short, eyes bulging, said, "I have to call my parents!"

"Your parents . . . ?"

"I have to tell them!"

"Tell them what?"

"Everything!" he said. "I have to tell them everything!" And with that, he snatched his coat from the pile in the corner and bolted outside again.

I grabbed my coat and went after him.

I was in pursuit, halfway up the block, exhaling vapor, when Tom appeared next to me. "Where's he going?" he asked.

"To make a phone call," I said.

There was a booth on the corner at the far end of the block, and by the time we got there, Mark had stepped inside and was going through his pockets, looking for change, turning them inside out, dropping bills and scraps of other paper on the ground.

"Here," I said, handing him a dime.

"Thanks! Thanks!" he said, dropped it into the slot and dialed hurriedly, getting it wrong, depressing the hook and starting over. But before he finished, he depressed the hook again and looked at us in alarm. "What should I say?" he asked.

"Who're you calling?" Tom replied.

"My parents."

"Your parents?"

"I know!" Mark shouted, turning back, dialing again. "I'll tell them how amazing it is! That they should come down here! That I discovered a new universe!"

I said, "You can't say that."

He looked at me, the receiver to his ear.

"It's your *parents*," I said. "You can't tell them you discovered a new universe. They'll think you're crazy."

"You're right! They wouldn't understand! Oh no! It's ringing! What should I do?"

"Hang up," Tom said.

Mark slammed the receiver into its cradle, then fell against the side of the booth and exhaled in relief, which his scattering vapor breath transposed to a sorrowful sigh. "I wanted to tell them," he said, forlorn. "I wanted them to know."

It had never occurred to me to call my own parents and tell them that life was amazing, but now I sighed heavily too, for the same reason.

Tom said, to both of us, "Why don't we go back . . ."

"There's a game on tonight!" Mark exclaimed, and looked at me questioningly. "It's Friday, isn't it?" And before I could answer: "Yes, it is! It's Friday! It's Friday!"

I knew the routine, traipsing through the neighborhood looking for a pad to watch the *Game of the Week*. But we'd never been on acid while doing it. I expected Tom to say something, to shoot down the idea, but he didn't. As Mark set off, he followed, and I fell into step beside him. It seemed I should apologize, since the search for a game had been my custom too, but Tom appeared unfazed, and I realized it didn't matter to him; he didn't care.

Which was a revelation: that a person could be indifferent and yet still be guided by concern. I'd wondered about that while reading a book on Buddhism that Patrick Malone had given me. Seeing the resolution of two apparent contradictions momentarily relieved me of the overriding concern that had determined my behavior. It was possible to care without losing your peace of mind. But as we crossed the deserted park, Mark walking quickly, leading the way, the reflexive mechanism of obligation returned, and I lost the implication of that insight and instead worried about what might be out there and what might lie ahead.

I recognized Alfie's building as Mark hurried up the stoop and inside. When Tom and I caught up to him on the third floor he was rapping on the door. Turning to us, he said, "He's not in!" looking from Tom to me and back to Tom again, as uncertain as when he'd found himself in the phone booth, holding the ringing phone. He was chasing down ideas, expecting them to cooperate with reality, and when they didn't, was in a quandary.

"Why don't we go back," Tom said.

"Harold!" Mark shouted, looking at me. "Harold will be home! He always is!"

So we followed that line of thought to another door, and Harold wasn't in either. Mark stood in the hallway, staring at the door.

"Let's go back," Tom said again, more firmly than before. He seemed to have the right tone for every situation.

"Yes," I said, "let's go back."

Half the people were gone when we got there. Tom left us behind, reclaiming his spot at the table, and Mark and I were back in our chairs up front again. But the night had crystallized for me, had its character and theme, and I felt trapped in it. Out of a notion of friendship, I'd tied my fate to that of my old friend. I'd made his movements and tics my concern, anticipated what they might mean and where they might lead. Out the door again? Like ganglia attached to Mark's nervous system, I was jumpy, skittish, keyed to his every movement while keeping a vigilant eye on him. To the rear, I saw people sitting in the spectrum candlelight. They had the anointed porcelain look of serenity, and I envied them.

Mark was subdued the rest of the night. But that bothered me too. It was not like him at all. Perhaps at some point between chasing possibilities he'd realized he would die. But what if he hadn't? How would he react when he did?

At four or so in the morning he told me, calmly, that he was going back to his place.

"You want me to come with you?" I asked.

"No," he said. "I want to think about some things."

But even after he left, I worried. I pictured him on the empty street, saw him climb the stairs toward his pad, then go up one more flight to the roof and jump.

Patrick Malone

At Arnie Glick's one night, someone I'd often seen there beckoned me into Myron's back room, away from the noise up front. For a change, Myron wasn't there. The television was off, and with the light flicked on, the concrete cell was gray instead of blue. The familiar stranger sat down on a stool, the only chair in the tiny room, gestured at the mound of mattresses, and when I was seated, thrust a hand at me.

"Patrick Malone," he said.

"Pete," I replied, nonplused, as we shook, wondering what he wanted.

"Pete?" he said, and leaned back, appraising me. "That's not a name—it's an utterance . . . I'll call you Peter."

His presumptuousness annoyed me. What could be more personal than a name? And by naming me, it seemed he was telling me who I was. But a moment later I felt pleased, at having been recognized as someone in particular. No one at the basement apartments paid much attention to me, though in fact I rarely gave them reason, since I kept to myself and rarely spoke. In naming me, Patrick Malone had rendered me specific, and substantial.

Looking up from my spot on the mattress, I took in his cleft chin and rugged, square face. His nose was not quite straight, looked like it might once have been broken and reset. And his eyes had a spark of amusement as he observed me taking him in.

"You and I should be friends," he said. "I've been watching you sit on the sidelines, saying nothing, observing everything . . . exuding intelligence. In fact, I'd say you're the second most intelligent person here." And he gestured at the open doorway to the bathroom and the door beyond that, and the noisy room up front.

He grinned at my surprise at his outrageous immodesty, and I couldn't help but grin too. It didn't hurt that he'd included me in his exalted self-judgment, and again, after being momentarily put off, I felt pleased.

Patrick leaned forward. "But first," he said, serious now, "I have to know something . . . Are you a cop?"

I recoiled, indignant. "I could never be a cop!"

He continued to look at me, then sat back and nodded. "I didn't think so, but I had to make sure . . ." He tilted his head, added, "But of course you could be a cop. Anyone can be a cop. We all have it in us, to be anything." He chuckled. "Even you."

That made sense. I had opinions, of right and wrong, good and bad. So why couldn't I be a cop? Theoretically, at least.

"And you?" I said. "Are you a cop?"

He considered that a moment, said, "You know, you're the only person here who's ever asked me that point-blank. The others . . ." He gestured toward the front room. "When I showed up, none of them trusted me. They heard I'd been sent to Millbrook to spy on Leary, and they assumed I was sent here to spy on them . . . Some of them still think so."

I shifted uncomfortably on the mattresses. "So," I said, "are you a cop?"

Patrick's eyes widened, at my impertinence.

"You asked me," I said, "so why shouldn't I ask you?"

He nodded, once. "No, I'm not," he said solemnly. "Not anymore." Then added, "Not that I'd tell you if I were, of course."

And having thrown me off balance again, he went back to Millbrook and told me his story, that the FDA had sent him to spy on Leary and his colony, but from the moment he arrived, they all saw through him, knew exactly why he was there. It bothered him, that he was so transparent, and he began to question what he'd been told about LSD—that it brought on fantastic, destructive hallucinations. So when Leary offered him a dose a few days later, he took it, and hadn't been the same since.

"You're looking at a new Patrick Malone," he declared, spreading his hands, encompassing the tiny room and the world beyond its concrete walls. "The old Patrick is dead!"

I'd never heard anything like that before: to look back on what you'd been and triumphantly reject it. I didn't quite believe it.

Sensing my skepticism, he reined himself in, folded his arms on his chest, looked thoughtful. "In some ways," he said, "I think you and I are alike . . . That's why I think we should be friends."

I could see no resemblance between us. Patrick spoke of a life in which danger was meant to be confronted and examined. He was confident, self-assured. And I was usually overwhelmed, awestruck by the mystery of it, a worm of uncertainty gnawing at me.

"We could challenge each other," he went on, "keep each other honest." He leaned forward, tapped my knee. "So I propose a partnership . . . That we agree to be absolutely, brutally truthful with each other . . . that we speak the truth, no matter what."

It was something in tales and fables; knights of a true round table; not the kind of thing that actually happened in real life. But why not? What was to stop us?

"Okay," I said, savoring the idea.

But after we shook on it and left the back room, Patrick told me he'd bought some tablets but didn't know anyone beyond the basement apartments. Would I help him sell them?

"I don't know anybody else either," I said.

"But you might meet people," he replied. "They're five dollars each, and I'll give you one tablet for every tablet you sell."

I said okay to that too. But it clouded my notion of a noble partnership, left me doubting what I'd agreed to. And afterward, discounting it, I didn't think about it again.

So I was surprised when Patrick showed up at my pad the following afternoon, late in the day, toting a rucksack. I didn't remember telling him where I lived, and now he'd walked in as though I'd been expecting him.

He swung the rucksack off his shoulder and took out a brown bottle. "My valuables," he said, holding it up. He opened the bottle, shook out two tablets, and offered me one.

"But I haven't found any customers," I said.

"Consider it at an advance," he replied, and popped the tablet in his mouth. "So?" he said. "What are you waiting for?"

"I, uh, wasn't planning to take acid today."

"Why plan? There's no time but the present."

It was a challenge, and in response I swallowed the tablet and sat down at my usual spot on the couch, at the steamer trunk. All the things I usually put in place before getting high were there: paper and pens, rolling paper and canister of pot, cones of incense in a small brass dish, and of course the massive candle, soldered to the surface in a congealed puddle of wax.

That candle centerpiece would be my undoing.

As twilight came on and objects in the room became less distinct, I grew restless, and it occurred to me to light it. But Patrick had settled on the floor, where he sat cross-legged, and as unnerving as the murky atmosphere was, I hesitated to change it and alter his reality. It was a conundrum, my burdensome social conscience worrying over whether to speak up and ask if he'd mind, and in doing so jar him out of his meditative silence, and while I fretted, the drug hit. Aswirl in sensation, I lost the thread of self-debate—to light or not to light—yet I wouldn't let it go, chased fleeting thoughts, fumbled for the solution to a problem I could now hardly recall. Then my restless body took up the chase, and lurching across the room, I grabbed my coat and bolted from the apartment.

I had no idea where I was going, but in the pink hue of twilight, I was in a hurry to get there. The hint of things not quite seen flitted by as I hurried up the block and across the street, following the same path I'd taken on my first trip, only now nothing was satisfying. Perhaps out of habit, seeking familiar refuge, I burst into Arnie Glick's pad.

It was early, the place nearly empty. Through the gloom I saw Arnie and Ray across the room, sharing a joint. They looked up as I stood just inside the door, regarded me without a word or a nod of recognition, and went back to the joint. It crushed me, reduced me to nothing. To prove to myself that I didn't care, I leaned back against the wall, tapped my foot along to the music on the radio:

> *Good-bye, Ruby Tuesday*
> *Who could hang a name on you?*
> *When you change with every new day*
> *Still I'm gonna miss you . . .*

Standing there, tapping, feigning my own indifference, my charade suddenly obvious, I escaped again, in a flush of humiliation, lurching outside and heading quickly up the block and then up another. Darkness was coming on, and it served to make me more visible. Paranoid, I stayed close to the buildings, so as not to stand out, ducked into a doorway and looked around at the cars, the empty street, a bank of frozen snow caked with soot that lined the sidewalk, and it occurred to me that someone looking out of a window, seeing me there, lurking about, would find it suspicious and call the cops. Spotting a neon beer logo on the next block, I headed that way, and veered into the place, away from the perilous open street.

It was dimly lit inside, which in context was comforting; a recognizable setting, a quiet barroom. I moved to the row of stools and perched on one, feeling grown-up. Then I noticed the chairs upended on the tables and someone mopping the floor. Was the place open? I peered down the bar at two people at the other end, and the bartender on the other side of the counter, talking to them. He glanced at me but made no move in my direction. Did he know that I wasn't truly a customer, but had just come in to get off the street? But then, I *was* a customer, wasn't I? Or at least could act like one by ordering a beer.

I sat perched on the stool for what seemed a long while, waiting in mounting distress for him to come over. I rehearsed what I'd say. Or maybe only a few seconds passed between when I entered and he looked at me. I couldn't tell; my sense of time was askew. And then he looked at me again, and might have been about to move down the bar, but it was all too much for me and I bolted, out the door, back into the street.

It was full dark now, and the streetlights were on, though they seemed to illuminate only the dark places they didn't reach, the lea of buildings and their recessed doorways, as I moved quickly through the streets. I heard distant sirens, more fearsome for being far away, and anticipated their approach, screaming suddenly around corners and into sight. And I felt the ground rumbling and, having forgotten about the subway, imagined tanks rolling down the sudden openness of a cobblestone avenue, an old street conjuring Prague or Warsaw, the frightened populace cowering behind drawn shades. Images of occupation. Thoughts of curfew. I hurried across the avenue, running now, fleeing toward safety . . .

When I burst into my apartment, I was amazed that nothing had changed, except the candle was lit. Patrick still sat cross-legged in the same spot on the floor. He turned his head to look at me, appeared so calm, so placid, I felt foolish for having left.

I collapsed onto the sofa, said the first thing that came to mind: "Is it Tuesday?"

Patrick tilted his head, looked at me, didn't bother to respond.

"It's awful out there," I said after a moment.

"Awful?" he repeated, raising an eyebrow, calling into question everything I'd experienced, or thought I had.

I managed to light a cigarette, blew smoke and watched it scatter. It was quite beautiful; wavy tendrils drifting up, intertwining. "I never should've left," I said.

"Stay where you are," he replied, "and the world will come to you."

I looked at him questioningly.

"Buddhism," he said. "It's something you should look into." He got up, went to his rucksack, handed me a book on his way back to his spot on the floor. *Buddha and the Gospel of Buddhism*, written by Coomaraswami. As I stared at the lettering, which glowed like neon, he said. "You can borrow it . . ."

"Thanks," I replied, grateful.

He looked at me for a long moment, said, "There's something I've been meaning to ask . . . I've been crashing at Arnie's, for the most part, but I don't like the vibes there. It's gotten weird. Can I stay here awhile, until I find my own pad?"

"Sure," I replied, surrendering my privacy without a thought. Only later did I wonder why, and realize I'd been flattered. Patrick was impressive, and it seemed he was saying something about me by wanting to crash in my pad.

He didn't thank me, just nodded, went to his rucksack, took off his utility boots, peeled off the pair of socks he had on, which were plastered to his feet, pulled on a somewhat cleaner pair, and put his utility boots back on. Then he retrieved his overcoat, said, "I've got some things to care of," and split.

I stared at the candle awhile, then opened *Buddha and the Gospel of Buddhism*. The words jumped out at me, a ghostly glow around the print, but with concentration I was able to read. The act of focusing accentuated what I so carefully read, brought the thoughts to life. I'd never read anything like it before. There was no belief system, no claims to righteousness, no dogma. Instead, it was rational, useful, not at all what I thought of as religion. I couldn't put it down.

The sky out the window hinted dawn when Patrick returned. He brought a record player with him and a stack of records, which he put down in the corner, next to the rucksack. Seeing the book in my hands, he said, "You like the Coomaraswami?"

"It's great," I replied. "I've been reading it since you left."

"You can keep it."

"Really?"

"Consider it a gift."

"Gee, thanks . . ."

"And you can have the record player too," he said, gesturing at the corner.

"A record player? Are you sure?"

"And the records."

I was speechless, astonished by his generosity. And then he left again, saying he'd be back in a while. I took out my contact lenses, curled up on the couch, and fell asleep.

He woke me up when he walked in again. Bleary, and without my lenses in, I squinted at him as he crouched down in the corner. "What're you doing?" I asked.

Patrick straightened up. He had the record player under one arm, the records in the other. "I made a deal with Don," he said. "He's giving me four ounces of grass for this."

I sat up. "Four ounces of grass for a record player?"

"And the records," he replied. "Fortunately, Don likes Mahler."

And then he left again. With *my* record player.

But as the door closed behind him, I realized I'd never used it, hadn't even gotten a good look at it. How could I have considered it mine? I had to laugh at my possessiveness.

It was the same with his rucksack. Because it was there, I assumed he'd be back; it was *his,* after all. But Patrick didn't return that day or the next, as if that too was meant to teach me about possessiveness. Reading *Buddha and the Gospel of Buddhism,* I pictured Buddha as Patrick, popping in and out of tenement pads throughout the neighborhood, leaving this, taking that, spreading the gospel of nonattachment.

When Patrick showed up a few days later, he saw the Coomaraswami splayed on the trunk and said, "You read too much, Peter. You should get out, do things, test yourself through active meditation."

"What happened to 'remain where you are and the world will come to you'?" I said.

"'Consistency is the hobgoblin of ordinary minds,'" he replied. "C'mon, there's something I want to show you. I think you'll find it interesting."

"What is it?" I asked, curious.

"You'll see when we get there," he replied, and was out the door.

Intrigued, I grabbed my coat and followed.

He was waiting outside and took off when he saw me. I hurried after him and again asked where we were going, throwing my words at his back, but he deflected my questions until we were in sight of the subway entrance, where he waited for me to catch up; he had no choice, since he had it in mind that we would go to my parents' apartment and borrow a car.

"They live out on Long Island, right?"

"In Queens, actually."

"The monastery is on Long Island," he said. "To get there, we'll need a car . . ."

A monastery.

It conjured spirituality. He'd mentioned it before, told me he'd stayed there sometime before he became a cop, or maybe after; the details hadn't been clear.

He said, "You told me you wanted to see it."

"Yeah . . . sure."

So I guided him through the subway system, though it seemed I was the one following him, on a mission intended for my benefit. Meanwhile, Patrick's militant silence kept me off balance. He said nothing as we waited for the train and as we hurtled underground. He sat erect and stared straight ahead. And when we transferred to an elevated train, the bric-a-brac streets below held no interest for him; nor did the single-family homes, as we sat on the bus, or the red brick garden apartments where we finally got off.

My mother was surprised to see me; I rarely visited and hadn't called beforehand. She made a fuss about the length of my hair, but backed off at my annoyance, and, perhaps to placate me, or in deference to my companion, who stood watching from the open doorway, gave me the keys to the Volkswagen without an argument. And then we were on the road.

Patrick found a pair of goggles in the backseat and took in the scenery through the yellow lenses, the red brick projects and tract houses at the city limits, the suburban homes tucked amidst shrubbery, the shopping centers and gas stations. And all the while, he said nothing, until the silence became a solid thing too daunting to challenge.

Finally, I ventured, "Boring, isn't it?" though it was the silence, not boredom, that unnerved me.

"Driving can be a Zen meditation," he replied.

Refocusing on the road, and myself as the driver, hands on the steering wheel, I stared out the windshield at the cars coming and going on either side of the center guardrail, aware of the bare-branched trees flanking the busy highway, approaching and receding with the lay of the land. Now and then meadows appeared beyond fences, and vegetation that had somehow eluded developers; golf courses with carefully preserved copses, glass and chrome corporate complexes in manicured settings, sprawling white brick schools next to athletic fields marked with splotches of snow, which had all but melted in the city. This was a place unto itself! An all-encompassing reality, a particular world, tamed in a certain way, spiced by the threat of dismemberment or death implicit in the hurtling cars on all sides . . .

We'd long since exited the highway, in a region of cemeteries, and then left them behind too. It was dark when we came to a hamlet of wooden houses gathered around a general store with a gas pump in front; a time warp scene out of a simpler past.

A mile or so farther on, Patrick told me to pull over. In fact, the road had ended; we'd driven as far as we could. I turned off the ignition and cranked open the window. Water lapped at an unseen dock, accentuating the silence.

"It's there," he said, pointing across the road.

I saw a snow-covered incline with a few pine trees below and thicker growth above. "Where?" I asked.

"Up there," he said, getting out. "On top of the hill. I'll be back in a minute," and I watched as he hiked up the slope and disappeared amidst the trees.

I got out of the car and stared at the stars in the ink black nighttime sky, thousands and thousands of them, and thought of Blaise Pascal. I tried to locate constellations, and after a while lost myself in the universe and thought about nothing at all. I didn't hear Patrick return, and when he spoke, he startled me.

"We can go up," he said.

And then, on the hill, as we climbed toward a low-slung wooden building resembling a lodge, he explained that we'd have to wait for the monks to finish the evening meal, which they ate in silence, and then we'd find out if we could have an audience with the abbot.

The abbot?

He hadn't said a word about it before.

But he left it at that, and as I wondered what we'd gotten into, we stepped up to the wooden deck and he rang the bell by the front door. A young man about our age, in a beige habit, opened it after a minute, held a finger to his lips and led us into a small study. He whispered to Patrick, then left us there to wait. It was a friend of his, Patrick said, and sat down, hands flat on his thighs, as on the subway, in the bus, and in the car, drawing a curtain of silence around himself once more.

I suspected now that this was more than a casual visit to the monastery he'd either left or been asked to leave, and that his meditative posture was a preparation. I left him there and went into an adjacent room to examine the shelves. There were some religious and philosophical books, but a few paperback mysteries as well, and the record collection had pop albums, in addition to the requiems I'd expected to find.

Patrick joined me after a bell rang a few rooms away. I pointed out the Beatles albums. "The monks are permitted to bring their personal possessions," he explained, "but they have to leave them in this room."

With the sound of unseen, dispersing footsteps, the young monk returned, said the abbot was waiting for us in the guesthouse, and led us outside. I wanted to ask Patrick about the abbot, but he'd moved ahead, to talk to his friend, and I crunched behind them on the hard snow beneath a billion stars. The cottage appeared in the frigid woods, and then we were at the sturdy front door and stepping out of the star-spangled night, into a bright, wide-open room.

Three monks in beige robes stood up when we entered. The eldest, with a long face and a garland of wispy gray hair framing his bald head, said, "Patrick," in a soft voice, and with a hand gestured at two canvas-backed chairs that faced the monks' small semicircle. Patrick's friend had left as we entered, so it was just the two of us and the three monks.

When we were seated, Patrick said, "I brought a guest, Father . . . His name is Peter."

The old man smiled, not with delight or perfunctory politeness, but something in between, making me feel welcome but hardly honored. Patrick sat straight, hands on his thighs in the Egyptian pharaoh posture he'd been hewing to, and I crossed my legs, for comfort. Before I could fully settle in, however, the abbot asked me what my religion was.

"Jewish," I replied, hoping that would be the end of it.

But he said, "Are you of the Orthodox, Conservative, or Reform sect?"

I'd been so busy thinking *Jewish*, it took me a moment to understand the question. "Branches," a Jew would have said, not "sects." But why not sects? I would no more have gone to an Orthodox synagogue than a Catholic church.

"Reform," I replied, then quickly added, "but I'm not what you'd call a practicing Jew." *Practicing?* What a stupid thing to say. Why would anyone *practice* religion? You either belonged to it or didn't.

But the abbot nodded as though I'd said something sensible, and to my chagrin went on to expostulate on the difference between Judaism and Christianity. I soon lost the train, and listened to the sound of his soft voice until I recognized the lilt of a question, then paid closer attention. He'd asked me about Yom Kippur, likening it to his own ritual of confession. I was at a loss. On that highest of holy days, my family used to leave the neighborhood, so we wouldn't be anathema among our dressed-up neighbors heading to synagogue. We were cultural and political Jews, not religious people. Our philosophical framework had been shaped by pogroms and labor unions, and in more recent times we'd adopted everything about America except, thank God, religion. But I couldn't tell the abbot that Yom Kippur meant driving to a beach, looking for seashells, and skimming rocks into the ocean. So I said something about collective as opposed to individual forgiveness, my solitary voice a noisy scratch in the quiet cottage.

But at least this time when I was through, the abbot didn't pose any more questions. He merely nodded and turned to Patrick. "And what have you been doing since you left us, Patrick?" he asked as I eased back in my chair.

"I'm working, Father," Patrick replied. "I'm working very hard."

"You were always tenacious," the abbot said, perhaps an oblique criticism, given the other qualities he could have cited instead.

"I've never lacked discipline," Patrick said, "just insight."

The old man smiled, slightly. "And now?"

"Now . . . the insight comes more often. It's the work that's difficult."

"You know," the abbot said, "work doesn't have to be difficult, Patrick."

"It's still a struggle for me," Patrick replied. "One moment it seems I'm no further along, and the next, I believe I'm there . . . only to encounter the pride that rises up to disprove it."

It should have been serene in the stillness of that room under the stars in the middle of nowhere. But it wasn't. The air was screaming with tension.

The abbot spoke again, in an even softer voice. I could hardly hear him, the raucous silence all but drowning him out. Yet Patrick managed to answer. And then the abbot came back at him with another question, consisting mainly of sibilants, or perhaps it was an observation; there was no way to know. We were leaning forward in our chairs now, trying to make out the words, our knees nearly on the floor. It was excruciating, and in that supplicating position, I wondered if the abbot was punishing us, in his way. For visiting. For wasting his time.

No, not us: I was the guest. The old man's diminishing voice as we strained to hear him was intended for Patrick.

It wasn't until we were in the car again, driving away, that I pieced it together: that Patrick had enticed me to the monastery because he needed a car to get there, and wanted company when he spoke to the abbot, whom he'd wanted to convince. Of what? I wondered.

I didn't know. But as I drove the dark country roads, he was not quite still, sitting next to me. He was just trying to be. And I knew the encounter had undone his self-assurance, producing a different kind of silence than the one he'd been lording over me all day.

Weird Vibes

I spotted Tom early one evening in the Forum, peering out the plateglass window at the twilight street. Alone in the brightly lit coffeehouse, his pupils darted at movements outside; like an animal in an exhibit, I thought, both frightened and frightening. Still, I'm by nature a friendly sort, and seeing him, I was inclined to go inside and say hello.

But I hesitated in the open doorway at his fierce look.

"Who're you?" he demanded, skewering me with his glare, his voice loud and harsh in the bare room, his face drawn, skin taut over skeletal bones.

How could he not recognize me?

Flustered, I said, "It's me . . . Peter."

He blinked, registering my identity, but that hardly softened him. "What'd you want?" he demanded, his pupils flitting toward a passing movement on the street, then back at me.

"I, uh, just came in to say hello," I replied sheepishly.

He regarded me for a moment, said, "Oh," which signified nothing, then abruptly lost interest, looking back out at the street, his gaunt face reflected in the mirroring glass. He didn't look at me again, and as I slipped away, his bony fingers were drumming on the wooden tabletop, making a racket in that empty place.

He was in his usual spot behind his cluttered table later that night, when I walked in, and Leo was berating him. I sat with others near the front, who were keeping their distance. It was serious business when either one of them got upset.

"It wasn't dangerous," Tom said dismissively.

"How can carbon dioxide not be dangerous?" Leo replied.

"It wasn't carbon dioxide."

"I heard it was."

"You can't inject carbon dioxide," Tom said, as if it should have been obvious.

"Well, whatever it was, you could've, y'know, died."

"Okay," Tom said without agreeing. "I won't do it again." And turned away, ending the conversation.

But when Lila burst into Arnie Glick's pad a few days later, saying she needed help, that Tom was in trouble next door, his distressed appearance in the coffeehouse was the first thing I thought about.

We followed her out, but hung back when Lila rushed inside.

It was an amazing sight. Tom was lurching around the room, bouncing off the sofa and chairs, rolling on the floor as if wrestling with himself. Lila tried to grab him, and he flung her aside. Then Patrick, who'd held back with the rest of us, plunged in, and tried to pin Tom to the floor so he couldn't move. And then we were all on him, falling on his flailing legs, grabbing his arms, holding him down as Lila thrust a spoon into his mouth, to keep him from swallowing his tongue, and I remembered that he was an epileptic. Once, with uncharacteristic pride, he'd announced that since he'd been using LSD, he hadn't had any seizures; that the drug had cured him. Now, he clamped down on the spoon and went rigid, eyes rolling back into his skull, body arching . . . And then, abruptly, he went slack, all the life gone out of him.

It was disturbing, seeing that, and for days afterward the mood in the basement pads was subdued. Though everyone gravitated toward Tom, it had somehow escaped notice that we felt more secure when he was around, a bridge between the known, with its associations, and the unknown, in which even familiar rooms were reduced to mere walls and ceilings, windows and doors. His gruff equanimity seemed to speak to this uncertainty. And now, in the wake of his all too human vulnerability, our brave new world was a more perilous place.

Arnie Glick, who harbored an inexplicable resentment toward Tom, drew me aside to talk about it. Tom was insane, he said, and clearly expected me to agree. Instead, I depicted Tom as an extreme scientist, seeking truth in his own way, and described how, when he visited me one day, he leaned over a flight of stairs until gravity tugged at him, his body accelerating as it moved down from floor to floor, momentum eventually flinging him out into the street. He was like the old alchemists, I explained, dedicated to science, taking part in his own experiments. That same dedication had led him to shoot a homemade drug into his veins: he wanted to see its effects.

"That's what I mean," Arnie said. "He's insane."

Gazi was older than everyone else, and when he spoke—which he did rarely—he sounded like a sage, holding forth in measured encomiums and philosophical generalities. Yet despite his aged appearance, he somehow blended into the scene, all but escaping notice at Arnie Glick's pad, and was never present next door, at Tom's, when the nightly shift to that quieter place occurred.

So I was surprised to see his bald head peer inside one evening.

And it seemed Gazi was surprised as well, when everyone turned all at once to look at him.

In response, he flashed a smile and said, "Any dope around?"

A logical question; nearly everyone who gathered in the basement apartments dealt or was looking for a bit of this or that.

"Not today," someone replied.

And he quickly popped out, closing the door behind him.

Watching this interaction, it struck me that Gazi had assumed no one would be there.

After that, it became Gazi's habit to peer in every night and always ask the same question: "Any dope around?"

"Not tonight."

"Maybe tomorrow."

It was a routine, the kind of thing you don't notice after a while.

But I thought about him right away the day Leo burst into Arnie Glick's and announced that Tom had been robbed.

We piled out and followed him next door, just as we had when his sister had sounded the alarm a few weeks before. Like her, Leo plunged into the basement room, and again the rest of us gathered in the open doorway.

Tom was moving about, throwing cushions off the chairs and sofa, delving into crevices, as Leo, on the floor, searched beneath the furniture.

"What are you looking for?" Rose asked.

She spoke to Tom, but it was Leo who answered. "Tinfoil," he said, and with his hands, gestured a square shape. "A packet."

Then Tom looked at the group clustered in the doorway and said, "Gazi took it."

There was a long silence. No one knew what to say.

His accusation didn't surprise me. It fit with everything I'd noticed about Gazi. But like a child in a grown-up world, ceding judgment to those who are apparently more self-assured, I said nothing. Lack of self-confidence—assuming others know things that you don't—can make you doubt yourself, and now I second-guessed my perceptions.

Gazi was always in Arnie's place, after all, and had been before I ever arrived. Surely Arnie knew more about him than I did. But Arnie looked at Ray, and

Ray looked back at him, silently asking the same question, and in a glance I could see that neither knew Gazi well enough to vouch for him.

Nevertheless, Arnie finally said, "It can't be Gazi."

"Why not?" Tom snapped.

"Well, because . . ." He looked at Ray. "You know him, don't you?"

Ray shrugged, said, "He seems like a nice enough guy to me."

Rose, the calm voice of reason and of avoiding confrontation, asked Tom, "Are you sure you didn't just misplace it?"

The question infuriated him. He strode toward the open door where we lingered, and everyone stepped back, out onto the sidewalk, where he slammed the door in our faces.

Leo rented a pad up the block. He'd just moved in and it contained only a table, chairs, the typical mattress on the floor, a refrigerator, a radio, and fabric that he'd tacked over the front windows facing the street.

The place was meant to be a secret, but Leo told Tom, of course, because he told Tom everything. And his sister Lila, who confided in Rose, who was not good at keeping secrets. And so, only hours after he'd moved into his secret hideaway, Leo had visitors.

Leo liked Patrick, but was not happy to see him. Patrick tried to mollify him, laughed off his secretiveness as paranoia, and then went about trying to cadge something to smoke or swallow that would get him high, which was the point of the visit. He'd brought me along, and while he was palavering, I moved to the window and parted the tacked-up fabric that served as curtains.

"Don't!" Leo shouted, and was at my side a moment later, making sure no light showed where the two halves met.

Then he and Patrick went at it again, one asking for a handout, the other claiming he wanted to comply but couldn't; Patrick's charm versus Leo's resolution, which was at odds with his innate generosity. He'd rented the pad, he said, so Emery could set up a lab and people wouldn't have to buy the unreliable drugs being peddled on the street—or make their own stuff, as Tom had—and then he'd be back in business, with goodies for everyone. Patrick scoffed and countered with flattery, telling Leo that with his contacts and acumen, surely he'd put something aside for his good friends. And eventually Leo gave in. Unwrapping a chunk of hashish in tinfoil, which he claimed was positively all he had, the three of us gathered around the table in the kitchen area to smoke a pipeful.

Afterward, preoccupied, Leo drifted to the window and parted the curtains, eyeing the street below.

"You expecting someone?" Patrick asked.

"No," Leo replied, "but you found me, so . . ."

The remark seemed prescient when he dropped the curtains and jumped back from the window, saying, "It's him!"

"Who?"

Leo didn't say, only gestured us to keep quiet as he moved to the kitchen door and cupped an ear to it. Patrick and I moved behind him, the three of us standing there, silent, listening to the door to the building open downstairs.

"Oh, shit," Leo said.

We heard footsteps come up the stairs and pause on the landing. Then they shuffled down the hall and stopped. I imagined someone checking numbers, working back toward us, where the shuffling stopped, halting just outside.

The sharp rap on the door startled us.

Then, loudly: "I know you're in there, Leo! You can't fool me!"

Leo held a finger to his lips.

The same voice came back, pitched higher and in a mocking singsong: "Let me in, little pig, or I'll bang on your door." And after a second or two of silence, the door rattled with violent pounding that no doubt could be heard throughout the building.

"Okay! Okay!" Leo shouted, and went at the locks.

A moment later he yanked the door open, revealing a wiry character standing in the hallway, grinning like a loon. "Hey, Leo," the loon said, sidling past him into the room. "How you doin'?"

Patrick thrust a shoulder at the newcomer, aggressively knocking him off stride. "What's wrong with you, man?" he said, glaring, as Leo relocked the door. "Are you crazy?"

The loon showed no fear. "Yeah," he said, grinning. "That's me, Crazy Roger. Isn't that right, Leo?" And before Leo could answer: "Just out of Bellevue, and good old Leo here is the first person I came to see . . ."

Leo turned away from the door and frowned at him. "Haven't you done enough already?" he said.

"It's a new day," Roger replied. "Who knows what might happen? But if you don't want me here, I'll just leave . . . as soon as you give me what I came for."

Leo looked at the linoleum floor and shook his head. "You never change," he said. "You think only about yourself. Like the last time, when you—"

"What're you, my mother?" Roger snapped.

It surprised me. I'd never heard anyone speak to Leo without respect. Patrick was startled too, when Leo took a breath, composing himself, instead of lashing out at this sneering character.

He said, "Not this time, Roger. I don't, y'know, have anything for you."

Roger's answer was sudden and unexpected. He dropped to his knees on the floor, clasped his hands in a prayerful posture and pleaded, "Just one dose, Leo! Can't you find it in your magnanimous heart to give me just one dose?" But he was insolent too, speaking with mocking sincerity; a nasty supplicant.

"Get up, Roger!" Leo said, embarrassed by the craven display, overlooking or not noticing its transparency. And reaching down, he tried to pull Roger to his feet. "Stand up!" he demanded. "Act like a man!"

But Roger resisted, stayed put. "I'll be a man, Leo!" he said, looking up at him. "I'll be a dog, or a duck. Quack! Quack! I'll be anything you want! I'll even kiss your feet! Just give me a dose!" and he genuflected toward Leo's shoes.

Leo backed away, and Roger crawled after him on his knees, nose to the floor.

It was too much. Leo cracked. "Okay, okay," he said, "but get up!"

In an instant, Roger was on his feet, smirking.

Later I'd dig into it, ask questions, discover that the two went back a long way, to Flatbush, where they'd been boys and teenagers, a neighborhood connection Roger had consistently drawn upon since. He'd always been a bad seed, I was told, too clever for his own good. And crafty enough to understand that Leo's good nature could be exploited.

Leo went into the back room and returned with a capsule. Patrick was astonished; that Leo could be manipulated by a creep like Roger. His own roguish charm at least offered something, or the appearance of it.

Roger gulped down the tablet, went into the adjacent room and sat cross-legged on the mattress. And now Patrick wanted to leave and it was Leo who implored him to stay, loading another pipe as inducement, the three of us returning to the kitchen to smoke some more, ignoring the miscreant in the other room, who had begun to hum softly to himself, a low, incipherable chant. Perhaps to blot out Roger's presence out, Leo turned on the radio and found a rock station that played old songs. He'd just sat back down when we were surprised to hear Roger singing along to a tune. He had a clear, sweet voice and sang in perfect harmony. It was startling.

> *"Each night I ask the stars up above,*
> *Why must I be a teenager in love . . ."*

Then he flipped out.

Bolting past us, Roger snatched the radio from on top of the refrigerator, yanking the plug from the socket, and raising it over his head, threw it to the floor. It broke into several pieces, yet kept playing, emitting tinny, disembodied sounds. Infuriated, he got down on the floor and went at it again, pounding it on the linoleum, smashing it, killing the sound, no doubt reducing the radio to broken tubes and plastic shards—we didn't stay around to see. Leo was already out the door, Patrick and I following him down the stairs, into the street, and up the block.

That night, Roger was at Arnie Glick's. He'd taken off his clothes and stood on a chair in the front room. Grinning, he fondled himself and watched the reaction of those who entered, a clarion of his own perverse tough-minded world in which everything was permissible and anyone who thought otherwise, who had notions or standards about how one should act, fell short of his standards. Most of those who walked in, walked right out. Rose stuck around awhile and tried to talk him off the chair, and Arnie sat with his nose in a book, pretending not to care. But soon enough he left too.

Alone, Roger's apparent disdain for the modern world found another outlet. The pad, like Tom's, was a converted basement, and it contained the fuse box for the building. He found it and killed the electricity.

A Con Ed van with flashing blue lights showed up first, and soon afterward, the police with their red lights. In the confusion, the cops happened upon an abusive naked man who seemed out of his mind, so they made a call and another official vehicle arrived, bringing the men in white who took Roger back to the asylum from which he'd so recently escaped.

In his back room cell, Myron had little contact with what went on up front. But when the electricity went off, and the television along with it, he knew something was wrong. Hoisting the set to his shoulder, he found his way out through the pitch-black, headed down Eleventh Street, and somehow showed up at my place.

I didn't know that Myron knew who I was, much less where I lived. He asked if he could stay awhile, and I gave him my reflexive answer: "Sure." He repositioned the steamer trunk so it sat against a wall with a socket, put the set on top and plugged it in, then flopped onto the couch to watch. What with commercials and station breaks, he might not have even missed a show.

Cartoons, movies, *Star Trek,* whatever it happened to be, Myron got lost in it. After a few days, when he showed no inclination to move, or turn it off,

I wondered what I'd gotten myself into. With the set always on, I stayed away as much as I could. It was on when I woke up in the afternoon, and at night, when I returned. To escape its squawking voices and blue glare, I retreated into the closet-size cell, where I'd only slept until then, and tried to read a book. I hadn't attempted that since putting down *Buddha and the Gospel of Buddhism* weeks before. Maybe that's what I picked up again, but with the voices penetrating the curtain that separated my little room from the rest of the apartment, I couldn't concentrate. Putting whatever it was down, I went into the fluorescent room to tell Myron to lower the sound.

When I was a boy, I sat on the floor, inches from a primitive six-inch screen set in a massive cabinet in the living room. As a teenager, in a bigger apartment, my brother and I shared a room and a larger set, and I'd watched as much as the typical American boy. But I lost the habit in college, and now stood staring at the screen . . . and then, dallying longer than mere curiosity could justify, sat down on the armrest of the couch and watched with sociological interest, a school assignment, doing research on an exotic local custom . . . and then, drawn further in, losing all sense of discrimination, and the need to justify my interest, I just watched. One program ended and another began, Myron and I now side by side on the couch, staring at the screen.

The days and nights to come were a blur. The two of us communicated the essentials, took turns going to the grocery store, ate baloney sandwiches, drank soda, smoked cigarettes, and watched. I never quite lost sight of the fact that I'd turned simpleminded. But there was something appealingly vacuous about sitting there, accepting everything, expecting nothing.

Others, soured on the basement apartments, experienced the same appeal. At first they dropped by to catch a late night movie, and then more often, the apartment full, people perched on the couch, the mattress, and sitting on the floor, the room a blue-gray haze of cigarette smoke, smelling of saltpeter and pot, reminiscent of Myron's old dungeon. Arnie was usually there, and Pauline, Richie Klein, and L.A. Ray almost as often. Tom and Emily came by once, and Patrick too, to scoff. But he lingered to watch, and like the rest, was glued to the screen when *The Thief of Baghdad* ended, laughing out loud at the closing line, "And the hair on my chin will continue to grow," which he declared psychedelic.

The next night, however, he came back in a different mood. Planting himself in front of the screen, he said to the four of five of us who were watching, "Look at yourselves, sitting here hour after hour. Where's your self-respect? Don't you think it's time to rejoin the living?"

"Get outta the way, Patrick," Myron said.

"Television's a narcotic," he went on. "The more you watch, the more difficult it is to break the habit. It's turning you into zombies."

"C'mon, c'mon," Myron said impatiently. "Get outta the way."

But Patrick stood his ground. "When I was a boy, my father came home from work one evening and saw me and my sister staring at the set. He spoke to us, but we didn't pay attention. So he walked right past us and put his foot through the screen—just kicked it in."

"Touch that set," Myron warned, "and I'll kick your *head* in!"

And someone else said: "Have some consideration, man. We're trying to watch."

So he left.

But he might have made his point, since only Arnie showed up the next night, and the night after that it was just Myron and me again, watching the *Late Show,* the *Late Late Show,* and falling asleep during the show after that, as the sky brightened out the window.

Then Emery walked in. For a change the set wasn't on; one of us had woken up and turned it off. Emery stood over his brother, who was sitting up, rubbing his eyes, and shouted at him, "Why aren't you out collecting?" He was referring to the gummy gel in the jar that Myron kept in the refrigerator, a drug Emery had recently concocted.

"I was about to," Myron replied, fearfully regarding his bespectacled brother.

Emery leaned toward him, got right in his face, his eyes magnified by the thick lenses. "You been busy, huh?"

"Yeah . . . I haven't got around to it. I'll do it today."

A bone-thin arm shot out from Emery's bat cloak, his long, thin fingers clamping on Myron's neck.

I was shocked . . . but also fascinated. The solid, barrel-chested guy terrified of a pale, emaciated guy. I looked from Myron to Emery, wondering what he'd do next. But though I was watching, saw him release his brother's throat, saw Myron's hand go to his neck and massage it, I couldn't quite believe it. And when I heard the sharp *crack!* I had to backtrack, replay the hand sweeping like a scythe, the palm smacking a cheek. It hardly seemed real. And then Myron falling back on the couch, in slow motion, his forearm coming up, too late, in a protective gesture.

Horrified, but enthralled, I waited. What would happen next?

Myron stood up, went to the refrigerator and retrieved the jar, and without a word followed his brother out of the apartment.

He would not return.

* * *

Leo was on a mission. The vibes were weird, things weren't what they should have been, the right kind of drugs were not available. He'd set up a lab for Emery someplace, but not much had come of that, so he went out to the coast, where all things seemed possible, and was due back that night. It was all very hush-hush, but as usual, everyone knew it about it, and a crowd had gathered in anticipation.

It seemed like old times; only it wasn't. Arnie's speakeasy, where no one actually spoke much, was frenetic, people straining to resurrect happier days. And then, after the shift to Tom's, to a setting where it seemed there was a point to getting high, a higher plane to be attained, the old distinction between the two places was lost, the mood hardly different. It was just as chaotic and noisy as it had been next door.

The narrow room, resplendent in drugged memory with liquefied candlelight, was ablaze with harsh bare-bulb light. The thick pipe running the length of the low ceiling, the concrete walls, the overstuffed furniture that cluttered the front room, the people crammed from the front to the table in back, gave the basement pad the aspect of a crazed bomb shelter. Only Tom, sitting behind his table, appeared unaffected by the mood. Too much so, in fact. He seemed to inhabit a world apart, disconnected from the rest of us. Amidst the tumult, was he actually reading the magazine hiding his face? Or was he just hiding behind it?

Don Juan had wedged Emily into a corner, where she appeared discomforted by his persistence but unable to extricate herself. On the floor next to the refrigerator, Emery tinkered with his bombsight. Across the room, Richie Klein was pitching himself to Pauline, quoting romantic poetry in a loud, braying voice, egged on by the coy tilt of her head and her fluttering lids. Seeing what he wanted to see, Richie missed her amused asides to Ray, who was watching, reveling in the power of her betrayal in his favor. Patrick was there too, looking dour, interrogating a stranger he was sure had to be a cop and who either proved as much by squirming under his third degree or suspected Patrick of the same crime.

"You are," I heard Patrick say.

"Am not," his suspect replied.

"Are."

"Am not."

Then the lights went out, the sudden pitch-black stunning the room to silence.

Light and dark. Locks and keys. Doors open or closed. The great issues of the day. Seeing and not seeing. Freedom, security, and fear. The stuff of dreams gripped the room.

Out of the darkness, Tom's disembodied voice announced, "We're having a black mass."

A frisson of uncertainty swept through the room. What did he mean? Someone giggled nervously, others tittered, and then people began standing up, shuffling around, bumping into things, tripping over each other as they headed in the direction of the door and the visible world outside.

In the confusion, someone shouted, "Turn on the light!"

And at nearly the same moment, a match was struck, a tiny glow that hovered a moment, then floated toward what remained of a candle encrusted to a wooden crate. It touched the wick, the teardrop flaring into fuller flame. It illuminated Patrick, holding the smoking match, glaring defiantly at Tom, who glared back.

They remained frozen in mutual hostility for a long moment, then Tom shot to his feet and shouted, *"Get out! All of you, get out!"*

Tom had always been a fearsome character. It was perhaps the secret to his influence that his behavior only hinted at his possibilities, which were subtext to the respect he inspired. He could be irritable and sarcastic, and he'd certainly been angry. But no one had ever seen him as furious before, and now he erupted, emerging from behind his table, scaring people toward the door, which wouldn't open; the police lock had slipped when someone yanked at the knob in the dark and now was jammed. The crush built as Tom bore down on the mass, pushing with stiff arms, as if no one individual was distinct from another.

The lock was finally disengaged and the door yanked open, cold air flowing in as people stumbled out into the night. But Tom kept pushing—they couldn't leave fast enough for him—until someone there for the first time turned on him and said, "What's wrong with you, man? Can't you see we're going?"

He stepped back, startled. Had he suddenly seen himself as others saw him?

The place emptied quickly, and seconds later, as I stood with the others on the sidewalk, Tom emerged too, to stand among the milling group he'd just expelled, looking around as if wondering where he was, as people shied away from him.

Had he freaked himself out and fled his pad to escape the out-of-control self he'd so sharply encountered? Or was he just confused, oblivious to the scene he'd wrought, standing there without a coat, looking left and right, at a loss?

He bolted then, ran across the street and away in long, loping strides, and veered into a building up the block.

A musician he knew lived there. Tom spent the night in his pad, was left alone to play the guitar he found, his long fingers attacking the strings, plucking them hard, wringing out every bit of sound they might contain. He played for hours, finally collapsing on his back, exhausted, the guitar on his chest . . .

. . . While the candle in his basement pad burned down to a puddle on the crate, where the flame went to work on the wood.

A burnt odor permeated the street when I walked up the block that morning. There were fire trucks in front of the building, thick hoses snaking between cars and across the sidewalk. The firemen were still moving in and out of the charred apartment, and I spotted Tom nearby, with the crates and plants he'd managed to retrieve before being restrained. I thought to cross the street and speak to him, but seeing him there, staring at the gutted, smoldering scene, with who knows what in mind, I kept to my side and walked quickly past.

Mark Greenbaum's Last Trip

Mark was hesitant about taking acid again.

"Why?" I asked. "What're you afraid of?"

"That I'll change," he replied. "That I won't feel the same way about things."

"But people change all the time," I said. "If you see things differently, it's only natural you'll adapt to your new viewpoint and change."

"But what if what I see differently isn't real?"

I laughed. "How can what you perceive not be real?"

"Maybe," he said, "it would be the drug."

"The drug doesn't see for you. It just provides a different lens."

"Maybe," he said. "But what if I see then isn't true? And thinking it is, I change and I'm not myself anymore? Then where would I be?"

"How can you not be yourself?"

"Well, maybe I won't believe the same things."

"Okay, but why hang on to something that no longer makes sense? I mean, if your beliefs change—"

"Who am I if not my beliefs?" he said.

"'I think, therefore I am,'" I replied, "doesn't mean you are what you think, although I can see how you might think so. I mean—"

"But I *am* what I think!"

"Are you?"

We could have gone on that way for a while. But I didn't want him to dig in and become even more adamant. As difficult as he could be, Mark and I had been through a lot together. We had a history. And that meant something to me.

"What really worries me," he said, "is that I'll become like the people who hang out at Tom's and the place next door, who think that . . . that because they take a certain drug, they see more than anyone else . . . that they're better . . . and that I'll begin to believe that too, and act like I'm superior . . . like I belong to some kind of exclusive club."

"You think I'm that way?"

"Well . . ." he said, hesitant. We'd often disagreed, but rarely criticized each other personally. But since I'd asked, he went on, "You've changed . . . and for the better, mostly," he added quickly. "You seem more confident now . . . more sure of yourself. But . . ."

"Go on," I said. "I can take it."

"Well, I wonder if you're not losing your ideals."

My ideals.

I understood. Just the day before, Mark had gone downtown to the courthouse with me, where I was on trial with eleven other people. We'd staged a sit-in at draft board headquarters on Forty-second Street, protesting the war. It lasted all of twenty minutes, before the cops showed up and we peacefully followed them downstairs, into a paddy wagon, and down to the Tombs, where we spent a night in jail. Since then we were required to appear once a month, for six months now, and listen to the prosecutors and our lawyers argue about one thing or another, with a break for lunch. Our act of conscience had become a charge of trespassing, the why of it irrelevant and immaterial to the judicial process. Worn down by the wheels of justice, I'd come to the conclusion that symbolic protest was not worth the effort.

But in the meanwhile, life had gone on for those of us who'd gotten arrested on principle. We'd been changing, and now showed up at the courthouse wearing beads and bandannas, with longer hair and a patois of newly discovered slang. We'd hang out in the courtroom and the hallway, exchanging information on the latest drugs, and even duck into a stairwell to share a quick joint, though the place was crawling with cops. I lined up my first deals there, for marijuana and hashish, and more recently had become a celebrity of sorts because I could procure LSD, which my fellow protestors were eager to try.

Mark would get up early to come with me. He never missed a session, boring as they were, out of solidarity, I supposed, and perhaps because he'd held back on that fateful day when I impulsively left the picket line and gotten arrested.

Now, as we stood in the street, he said to me, "What bothers me is, what if a person changes because they get high all the time, and your friends, let's say—and your family—no longer think the way you do? You see what I mean? It's not the different *opinions* that bother me—well, it's not *just* that—but what if whatever connects us to the people we know disappears? What then?"

I didn't have a ready answer. The same line of possibility had also occurred to me, and I'd wondered where the disconnection would lead. But my concern was more than balanced by how good I felt. In the expansive apolitical world I inhabited, old friends and acquaintances I ran across appeared crimped, with their tedious jobs and predictable opinions. They seemed burdened by their identities, their speech punctuated with apologies and disclaimers for saying this or that, as if merely acknowledging doubt was evidence of humility, proof that they were thoughtful and honorable, though in fact they were not truly questioning themselves but hedging against being caught out and thought wrong.

Not that I often ran across anyone from my former life, except for Mark. But when I did, it was usually because of him. Like when he convinced me to host a reunion of a few of our mutual college buddies; guys we'd worked with on the school newspaper. His pad, he explained, was too small; he didn't even have chairs, just the mattress in the middle room. So I agreed.

The three guys showed up at the same time one evening. They might have met after work, or waited for each other at the subway entrance, so they'd have company while walking the ghetto streets. Or so it seemed as they warily entered and suspiciously eyed the bathtub in the kitchen. Mark, who wasn't an observant type, didn't notice their nervousness. Greeting them euphorically, he ushered them in as if it was his pad, not mine, and with a curious possessive attitude that seemed to say that these were his people, not mine. And yet, in our dishevelment, Mark and I resembled each other, not our old newspaper colleagues. Though we'd all been out of college no more than a year or so, the three had a grown-up look, having not only been employed since then, but working to leave their looser, more playful younger selves behind.

I served tea, and we sat around awhile, recalling those good old days, which made Mark restless, possibly because much of it smacked of false sentiment. But then, he'd been the office rebel back then, and with his stuttering sense of righteousness, was admired for his apparent rectitude. He liked that, and at times played it to his advantage. Except now as he reprised that old Billy Budd role, bringing up the war, stumbling to express his thoughts as they formed, his guests were restless, impatient. Cutting him short, they quickly agreed with his woolly diathesis and brought the conversation back to the topic that truly interested them: themselves. Mark didn't see it, and tried to squeeze in, blurting remarks, creating awkward pauses before the three moved on again, precluding his usual rambling observations.

It didn't help that I rolled a few joints, to be hospitable, and briefly wondered, when eyes turned toward me, if I hadn't instead offended the guests. I couldn't have been more wrong. Right away I could see that smoking dope was their weekend ritual. They inhaled and held it in with practiced patience, and soon enough were giggling and pursuing non sequiturs as if each sudden thought was a grand idea, and then they began to focus and unknowingly turned competitive, each one trying to prove himself and outdo the others.

The reporter, with the easy cynicism of those who learn to skate on the surface of things, where motive consists of technique and strategy, rather than philosophy, psychology, poetry, sociology, history, myth and mythology, and the rest, which more contemplative types turn to for meaning, breezily dropped the names of the well-known and well-connected he'd come across, names with a significance in and of themselves. He knew how to begin a story—the who, what, where, and when of it—but was not much of a finisher, concluding his tale of a mafia don on trial for extortion—a nice guy, actually—by admitting that in fact he hadn't met the mafioso face-to-face since there'd been a misunderstanding with the doorman of a high-rise building when he tried to talk his way in. Then rolling up his sleeve in search of a last second denouement, he displayed the fading smudge marks of bruises he'd gotten while being forcibly evicted, putting his anecdote to bed.

The advertising copywriter revealed a tricky turn of mind, launching a preemptive attack on those who considered his a dishonest profession. (He well knew that on the old college newspaper, no one would have approved of his career.) You find good and bad people in all lines of work, he argued—though no one in the room had said otherwise—and when he went on too long, protesting too much, digging his own hole, embarrassing himself, until the newspaperman, displaying an unexpected streak of compassion, bailed him out by asking the ad man he'd done recently. The copywriter perked up, and with the eagerness of the student he'd been not too long ago, recalled a jingle he'd had a part in producing, a cute play on words, but one that hardly restored his diminished stature.

The teacher, aware that his profession was considered more selfless than that of his peers, compensated with self-deprecation. After all, he had no need to brag; his job did it for him. But by now he was wasted, and it's difficult to be humble on pot when its influence is channeled into vanity. He soon lost himself in extolling the gratifying rewards of instructing others, without mentioning the kids themselves, but only the hours he invested on their behalf—grading papers, making lesson plans—and then, turning bitter, his hassles with the principal, the vice principal, his fellow teachers, and, worst of all, the parents, whose interference was the bane of his existence.

By then Mark had stopped trying to make himself heard. He sat in a protective posture against a wall, knees drawn up, hands clasped around his legs. But he was nothing if not loyal to old friends, and when the others stood up to leave, he stood too, and suggested that we reconvene in a coffeehouse to talk some more. Again he was rebuffed by his guests, as they gathered up their coats, offering the excuse that they had work the next day and had to get up early. Mark would follow them out anyway, and all the way up to the subway stop at Fourteenth.

But to my astonishment, before leaving, each of the three paused to shake my hand, one at a time, and thank me for inviting them, though it had been Mark's idea and invitation. One of them even hung back to apologize for the way he'd treated me in the past—not for anything in particular, from what I could make of it, but for not recognizing me back then for who I was.

Who did he think I was?

Once, he'd considered me nothing special. But he now knew better.

I decided afterward that it was my silence that had impressed him.

Mark was alone the last time he dropped acid, in his own apartment. He assumed he'd feel secure in that familiar setting. But like me, he was a restless type, and for some reason, perhaps the azure sky above the roof line of the adjacent building, beckoning him, he left his pad before the rush came on and headed for the park.

It was an early spring day, after a long winter, with some actual warmth to the air, rather than the absence of a chill. The sun must have felt good as he sat on a bench, but then the drug hit and someone sat down a few feet away. Tottering to his feet, Mark looked for a more private spot. Except his head was spinning now, and he couldn't find the exact right spot. Before he knew it he'd wandered out of the park and into the streets . . .

He was in distress when he showed up at my door, babbling. I guided him in and spoke reassuringly, though I had no idea what to do for him. He paced back and forth in the kitchen, tripping over his words as he described finding himself on the street among people who would have noticed him if he hadn't kept moving. I asked a few questions, but he was too overwrought and hardly heard me.

Taking charge, or rather, falling back on what I knew about him, I guided him into the front room, saying, "Don't worry. You're here now. No one will bother you. You'll be all right."

Myron's television set was still there. I moved the chair in front of it, sat Mark down, turned on the TV, and found the sports channel as it warmed up. The picture blossomed onto the screen a moment later.

"*College Game of the Week!*" Mark shouted. "Is it Saturday?" And before I could answer, "Yes it is! It has to be Saturday! The game is on!"

I said, "It's the NCAA playoffs, I think."

"Yes! Yes, it is!" he replied, excited, his hands on the armrests as he bounced up and down in the chair. "It's the NCAA playoffs!" He pulled the chair forward and leaned toward the set, his face inches from the screen. "It's Jimmy Walker! I'd know him anywhere! It's him, I'm sure of it!" Nevertheless, he looked to me for confirmation.

"It's him, all right," I said.

He turned back and stared at the screen. "This is *just* what I need," he exclaimed. "This is *just* what I need. I'll be all right now! I know it!"

I wasn't so sure. I sat down behind him, on the couch, and tried to watch the game too, but couldn't concentrate, not with Mark jiggling in the chair. From what I did see, it was close and well-played, with few mistakes; the kind of game you remember years later. But afterward I would only recall Jimmy Walker, and Mark bouncing in his chair, blurting, "This is what I need! This is just what I need!"

A second game immediately followed the first. I'd seen enough, but sat there, keeping an eye on him. He was motionless now as he stared at the screen, and then surprised me by flicking the set off and sitting back. He sat there awhile, neither moving nor speaking, as if the game were still on. I often stared at nothing in particular myself, but this was Mark Greenbaum, and quiet contemplation was not his usual state.

I wondered what to do, what to say, and then he turned the chair around, so we were facing each other, and said, "Throughout history there have always been people who thought they were different . . . people who didn't fit in, who didn't feel like everyone else, who didn't feel they belonged . . . Even when we lived in caves there were people who felt that way. I'm sure of it . . . There have always been, and there will always be, people who know they're different."

He spoke solemnly, letting his thoughts come to him, rather than chasing them. Stopping, he raked his fingers through his hair, an old habit, then caught himself, clasped his hands at his waist, and leaned back.

"I've always believed," he said, "I mean, I always *wanted* to believe, that nothing could make people conform to what others expected of them if they truly didn't want to . . . But the truth is, I wasn't sure it was true . . . and actually, I was afraid it wasn't . . . You were right about that: there's a difference between believing something and seeing it, perceiving it . . . And now I know.

We are what we are, and no one can change that . . . Of course, we might have to temper how we appear, so we don't scare society, but within ourselves, we can *always* be who we are. *Always.* That can never be taken from us."

I expected him to continue, because that's the way Mark was. When he started to talk, he'd only stop after he squeezed out every bit of meaning and then repeated it once or twice. But then, I'd never heard him speak so calmly before, and now when he stopped, the expanding silence didn't seem to bother him, didn't goad him into filling it. His pause went on and on, until I wondered whether he'd forgotten I was in the room with him. His gaze had shifted to the window, and he stared out at the rooftops and the city beyond. And that too was different. I'd never seen him sit and just look at the world around him. Even more than me, Mark Greenbaum lived life in his head.

When he finally did speak again, the silence had gone on so long that his voice startled me.

"I won't take acid anymore," he said. "I'm not sorry I did . . . I've had insights . . . about how life can be when we stop everything, even stop thinking about ourselves—*especially* stop thinking about ourselves. But I've seen things that terrified me.

"Like today . . . the broken glass on the street, the foil and gum wrappers glittering like cheap tinsel, the garbage no one bothered to pick up . . . The world looked so cheap and . . . *sordid.* The women wore junk jewelry and painted their faces, which looked like garish masks . . . and the men with their hair greased back and plastered to their heads, to their skulls. None of it seemed real . . . and everywhere I looked, it was the same. Everything was garbage and pretense. And worst of all, I knew no one could see it but me . . . and I was afraid if they saw me standing there, noticing them, they'd know I wasn't like them—and hate me for it.

"I understood then how people can take each other's lives. How they can . . . kill each other. I've always been against the death penalty. You know that. But until today, I could never understand how anyone actually *could* kill another person . . . and now I know. It's because they don't see them as people. That's why they can do it. They see someone as different . . . as not even human anymore. I mean, I saw it that way too. That the people on the street were . . . I don't know, not really human. And when I realized that, I began to tremble uncontrollably . . . And then I saw someone staring at me, in this world where anyone could commit murder—an *insane* world—I don't like that word, because it's used to describe someone who doesn't matter anymore, but I knew then what it was like to be truly insane—to live in a world where everything is make-believe, a world where you can commit murder . . ."

The gravity of his remarks seemed to weigh on him, and he fell silent again, but then abruptly sat up and blurted: "But I knew I could come here! I knew I'd be all right if I came here!" Just like that, he was in a different mood altogether; excited, ebullient. "That's the thing! That's what keeps us *sane* no matter how crazy the world might seem—the people we know, the people we trust, the people who accept us as we are!"

I was touched that he thought of me that way and wanted to respond, but didn't know what to say, so I just nodded.

He sat back then, and I sat back too, and for a long time neither of us spoke.

Noises wafted up from the street as evening came on, and it seemed we were floating in the thick silence that filled the room like ether.

In the fading light, crow's-feet appeared around Mark's eyes and his blond stubble filled in. It was an hallucination, seeing him age, becoming an older version of himself, becoming the person who had spoken with profound seriousness. But it was of course real too. We all get old. And a sadness came over me, as if I were old myself and looking back, recalling this moment when my old friend's path veered from mine and led him elsewhere.

The Eighth Street Commune

After the fire, the group that hung out at the basements scattered, and with no agora, no communal marketplace, people drifted here and there. It bothered Leo, and being who he was, he took it upon himself to find a new place for the gang to gather. He applied himself to this mission while staying ahead of the cops, or his suspicions, as he bought this and sold that. But eventually he had the cash and rented a large flat on Eighth Street, east of Avenue B.

He would have liked to christen the pad with psychedelics, but the good stuff was scarce, what with the cops making life difficult for hippie entrepreneurs, so he fell back on the uppers and downers he'd peddled as a teenager: prescription drugs to mute or exaggerate, numb or excite, disorient or bring on a laserlike focus.

With the generosity for which he was known, he distributed them as people arrived, colorful pills and capsules, reds and blackies and all sorts of whatnots in between. The pad quickly filled up with bodies and cigarette smoke, which hovered at the ceiling and became a lowering cloud, working its way down as the jumbled contact high of different points of view and inclinations textured the atmosphere and screeching guitars and a throbbing bass beat vibrated the walls.

In the kitchen, a subculture of speedballers spent the hours talking, talking, talking, striving for the absolute last word to a topic that sprouted new limbs as they gabbed on and on, the next thought and a new last word rendering everything that had been said before irrelevant, forgotten. Around the corner, in the long middle room, a smorgasbord of potato chips and pretzels, Cheezits and Snackos and inedible dips, were gobbled up like manna, the telephone spool table Leo's teenage lieutenants had lugged in a traffic circle for movement back and forth, in and out, past the dazed and dissociated who reclined on a bank of mattresses pushed against one wall. Behind tacked-up curtains of the small rear room and a walk-in closet, beneath the loud music, groans and moans of sexual ecstasy, or maybe agony, signified that something in the place, at least, was coming to a conclusion, or not. And yet there was a surprising ordinariness to this variegated scene, like the found objects with which the place was furnished, and eventually the much ado dissipated and transpired from simple exhaustion.

By then Leo had moved on, as he always did before the events he set into motion played out: the place littered with detritus, empty bottles and cans, cigarette packages and spent butts, a tacky legacy for the bodies sprawled in stupor on the mattresses and floor.

Patrick had been in the kitchen the night before, with the manic philosophizers, and left when he caught himself shouting to be heard. Now, only Rose was awake, and she let him in. In one of his silent moods, he moved down the gloomy hallway and eyed the debauched scene in the main room. Stepping over and around the scattered bodies, he went to a window and opened a shade, suddenly flooding the place with light, then forced the window open. Fresh air wafted in, somewhat diluting the stale cigarette odor. Still without a word, he walked back to the kitchen, rummaged through the cupboards and closet, returned with a broom and dustpan.

"If we're to live here," he told Rose, who stood by, watching, "it has to be livable."

When he began picking things up and throwing them in a trash bag he'd found, she took the broom and began sweeping the floor.

Later, in her trip book, Rose would render Patrick with a fuchsia aura, and in verse liken his labor to that of Hercules, cleaning the Augean stables.

People began to stir as the two of them moved about. Most retrieved their coats and left; they'd come to party, after all, not to tidy up. But others stuck around, helped clean the place, went out to buy necessities: food and toilet paper, incense and candles. A drape was hung, creating two rooms where there'd been one, and mattresses rearranged, so those who wanted to sleep at night wouldn't be bothered by those who preferred to stay up, and rules were set— though no one called them that—about when the record player would be off limits and when not.

Taking pride in the transformation, Patrick later claimed that his silence had been strategic; his dour behavior intended to scare the slackers off right away, since they'd only undermine the workings of a commune.

A commune . . .

I thought I'd sworn off politics, but the notion stirred up old ideals, and though accustomed to my privacy, it would be my custom to gravitate to Eighth Street, to hang out and observe the noble experiment, which I called the Eighth Street Commune.

I was there the morning Louis, one of Leo's teenagers—who collected front money when he needed it and distributed drugs when he had them—showed up with a hundred doses of beautifully buffered pills. Patrick, with the wariness of a former cop, told him he couldn't keep them there, where their discovery might endanger others, so Louis distributed some samples, rolled the rest into a tinfoil ball the size of a grapefruit, and tossed it onto a pile of rubbish in the ground-floor stairwell. A perfect hiding place, he boasted: out in plain sight, where no one would ever notice it.

But later that day, as I went upstairs, I noticed that the tinfoil ball was gone, and when I walked in, Louis broke out of a huddle in the front room and accused me of stealing the silver ball.

"I'm not surprised it's gone," I told him.

"Because you took it!" he said, incensed, pushing up to me.

"No, because it stuck out," I explained, "a shiny object sitting on a pile of garbage. Maybe some kid in the building took it . . ."

We were standing face-to-face now, the other teenagers watching, and several others drawn to the room by the raised voices.

"You took it!" Louis said, spearing my chest with a finger.

Then Patrick was on him, clamping a hand to his shoulder, turning him halfway around. "If Peter says he didn't take your pills," he said, "then he didn't take them."

"I saw how he looked at them!" Louis shot back. "He wasn't satisfied with just one! He wanted it all!"

"I know Peter," Patrick said in a low rumble, "and he's no thief."

I spoke up then, saying, "I know I didn't take his pills, Patrick, so it doesn't matter to me what he thinks."

"But it matters to me!" Patrick snapped, suddenly as angry with me as with my accuser, and turning back, said to the teenager, "When you accuse Peter of stealing, you accuse me too . . ."

"But—"

"And then you'd have to leave . . . or be thrown out."

Louis glared at him, and Patrick glared back, implacable, and after a long moment, the kid lost his nerve and stormed out.

Leo showed up a few days later. He hadn't been there since the housewarming party, and when he walked in, everyone gathered around the spool table to greet him. Leo was an important person, and he reveled in attention. But he wasn't in his usual effusive mood. He gestured inarticulately, made circles with a hand, finally said, "I came here, y'know, to talk," looked at Patrick and quickly away, then spoke to the tabletop. "I got to say, I'm disappointed . . . in all of you . . . I told Louis, and the others, they would be among friends here . . . that this place . . ." He gestured at the room. " . . . that we all share whatever we have." Finally, he forced himself to look at Patrick. "So I don't understand why you'd tell him to leave . . ."

Patrick replied, "We welcomed Louis like we welcome everyone you send here, Leo. We treat them with respect, and we expect the same from them . . . I didn't tell Louis to leave. I told him he'd have to leave if he didn't show respect for us."

"He said he was robbed."

"Not by anyone here . . ."

Leo looked doubtful.

Then Rose spoke up, saying, "He accused Peter of being a thief."

Leo looked at her, surprised, as I stood on the periphery, wondering whether he knew who I was without someone pointing me out.

Then Gary, who'd moved into the small back room, said, "We're a family, Leo, and no family can endure without trust."

And then Ray spoke up, saying, "Louis went too far."

Leo distrusted talk, and disagreement unnerved him. But this gathering where no voice had been raised, where people had the nerve to respectfully disagree with him, made an impression, and as he scanned the faces around the spool table and surrendered to perception, he understood that there was more to the story than he'd heard before. And that something special was going on here, in this pad he'd rented and bequeathed to whoever chose to live there. Out of that, he settled on a different point of view, and in surrendering to what he beheld, took proprietary pride in what it seemed he'd accomplished.

"Maybe I misjudged," he said. "After what I heard, I thought maybe Tom didn't come here because, y'know, of what he heard . . ."

"If Tom comes here, we'll welcome him," Patrick said.

"I was worried about that . . ."

"Rest assured, Leo," Patrick said. "There's always a mattress here for Tom, if he wants it, and for you too, if you decide to settle down."

Patrick was kidding. Of course Leo was welcome. He was the candyman, after all, and more than that, everyone's benefactor. But Leo wasn't much for irony, and the offer choked him up. "I wish I could," he said, "but . . ." He gestured toward the door. "There's things I got to take care of . . . But when I come again, I promise to stay awhile . . ."

It had never been my way to wake up instantly, eager to meet the new day, but now when I opened my eyes to the strip of sunlight on the wall, I swept the blanket aside and bounced off the mattress. In seconds I was dressed and in the kitchen, stuffing the coins and bills on the table into a pocket. Seeing the early sunlight slanting across the tenement rooftops out the window, I crossed to the soft chair, sat down and took in the scene.

The quilt of tenements filled the foreground at uneven heights, stretching to the red brick border of Stuyvesant Town at Fourteenth Street. To the west, in the distance, the Empire State and a jumble of skyscrapers marked the business district. To the east, thin streams of white smoke rose from the Con Ed smokestacks next to the sluggish East River between Manhattan island and the squat warehouses and factories lining the Brooklyn shoreline. Farther north, the span of the Queensboro Bridge seemed an erector set construction. And around everything, the entire panorama, the ochre smudge of pollution . . .

It took my breath away.

Then the toilet flushed, and I snapped out of the trance.

The first time it flushed by itself, I was tripping, at night. Alarmed, I'd stared at the door to the water closet in the kitchen, and thought a thief had climbed into the narrow window facing the air shaft. He would have had to scale the walls of the building, squeeze in, and then announce it by pulling the chain that flushed the toilet from an overhead tank. It made no sense at all. But I didn't think it out, or couldn't, and the sound of the flush drove me from the apartment. Returning in the morning, emboldened by daylight, I peered into the pebbled glass window, trying to see inside, and then, with a frying pan as a weapon, yanked the door open. Of course, there was no one there.

Later, Tom told me it had something to do with water pressure and hydraulics, but the science of it could never be as appealing as the cosmic joke I took it as—the flushing toilet punctuating thought, snapping me back to the present and throwing my musings into perspective. Whenever it happened, I couldn't help but laugh, for it was uncanny, interrupting me at what always seemed the right moment. Clearly, there was no such thing as a thought worth dwelling upon.

Now, when the flush caught me staring out the window as I marveled at the cityscape and its pollution, I had to laugh, and pushing myself out of the chair, snatched up a flannel shirt and raced downstairs.

It was spring, finally, but the six-story buildings blocked the sunlight, shading the street, so I cantered through the chill to the corner, where light spilled down Avenue B. There, I basked in the warmth, gazing toward the haze of buds on trees in the park a block away. But instead of heading in that attractive direction, I continued up Eleventh, past the burned-out basement apartment across the street, still with a charred smell, all these weeks later, and halfway up the block, where I veered into a building. Only then, in the dank, moldy hallway, did I realize where I was headed: to Arnie Glick's. And then I almost turned around and left.

Since he'd moved, after the fire, Arnie was rarely seen or even mentioned, and when he was no one had anything good to say about him. Though I had nothing against Arnie, I'd only visited him once, perhaps influenced by the prevailing opinion. Maybe I was feeling bad about it that morning. At any rate, finding myself there, in his building, and trusting in the impulse that had brought me—as I'd come to follow all my impulses—I took the worn steps to his floor and rapped on the door.

A few seconds elapsed before I heard his strained, high-pitched voice: "Who is it?"

"It's me, Peter . . ."

"Who?"

"Peter."

He must have had at least three locks. I stood in the hallway as he undid them and wondered about his mental state. What was he afraid of? Who was he locking out? And then he only opened the door the length of a chain lock and eyed me through the narrow gap.

"Open up," I said, impatient. "It's just me."

He undid that last lock and pulled the door open. I entered the murky kitchen and waited as he reattached the chain and relatched the other locks. The green shades covering the windows gave the room a bilious hue. It seemed Arnie was in hibernation.

In fact, I'd woken him. He turned to me, rubbing his stubble beard with one hand while holding his terry-cloth robe closed with the other. "What time is it?" he asked.

"Oh . . . yeah," I said. "It's probably early."

Grumpily, he said, "How early?"

"I don't know, but I usually get up later."

He scratched his balding head, garlanded with wispy flurries of hair, as I grinned, amused by my own generalities. Then Arnie grinned too. "You know, Weissman," he said, "I remember when you were a sensible sort . . . and now look at you. You're just like everyone else."

I gestured at the room. "You should get out, y'know. The sun's shining, there're buds on the trees . . . spring is here."

He stared at me for a long moment as his mind worked, weighing things, no doubt, calculating—Arnie often had that look—then he said, "Wait here while I get dressed, okay?" and without expecting a response, went into his bedroom and closed the door.

I sat down. Cerebus, the German shepherd, was beneath the table. He nudged me, and when I petted him, licked my fingers. He'd been under the table at the basement pad too, the rollicking inn. And now that Arnie lived in relative seclusion, it seemed the dog was his only companion.

"It's a good thing you dropped by," Arnie said, opening the bedroom door. "There's something I've been meaning to do, and this seems a good day to do it."

"Do what?"

"I've been thinking about going over to Leo's pad . . . on Eighth Street? You want to go with me?"

I'd never heard it described that way before: Leo's pad. "Yeah, sure," I said after a moment. "You haven't been there yet?"

"No, but I've been meaning to drop in."

He strode back in wearing corduroy pants and a blue button-down shirt that he might have worn to an office in his previous life. He'd been in the navy—he'd said so once—and had a job of some sort afterward. He looked presentable enough to me, but it wasn't good enough for him. He said he wanted to shave first, and flicking on the bare, overhead bulb, crossed to the small sink and turned on the faucet.

"You hear about Eckhart?" he asked, leaning down to see himself in the mirror propped over the sink as he applied shaving cream.

"Tom?"

"Yeah . . . that he stole Rose's car?"

I said, "He didn't steal it, Arnie. Rose drove it down and—"

"Well, that's what I heard . . . He's crazy, y'know." He looked across the room at me, half his face covered in foam. "He's out of his mind."

I'd had that conversation with him before, and could think of nothing to add.

He turned back to the mirror, continued shaving. "You seen Patrick recently?"

"Yeah . . ."

"I hear he's been telling everyone I burned him . . ."

"I don't know anything about it," I replied.

"Y'see, the thing about Patrick is, he has no head for business. None whatever. Believe me, there's no worse person to bring into a deal . . . I fronted him two hundred bucks for a kilo, and he bought a pound instead. Can you believe it? I told him the going price for a pound was only a hundred twenty-five, and you know what he said?"

"That it was grown in some exotic place and was so powerful that one pound of it equals two or more pounds of anything else."

"Yeah, pretty much . . ."

I laughed.

"It's not funny. I had to pay for the loss."

After a while he turned off the faucet, wiped his face with a dish towel, went back into the bedroom and reemerged pulling on a suede jacket. "Let's go," he said to me; and to his dog, "C'mon, Cerebus! We're going for a walk!"

Downstairs, as we walked up the block, Arnie absently slapped the curled-up leash against his thigh, the dog trotting ahead. Around the corner, on Avenue B, he stopped in front a bakery that was just opening, asked me to wait and went inside.

I gazed at the cakes in the window awhile, and then, impatient, went inside. He was having a hard time making up his mind. "What'd you think of that one?" he asked, pointing at a cake in the display case. It was massive, with marble icing.

"Is it someone's birthday?" I asked.

"No, no, it's just a little something. But you're right," he said, "it's too fancy," and he pointed to a plainer cake, with a thin layer of milky frosting. "How 'bout this one? Looks nice enough, doesn't it?"

"Yeah, sure," I said, if only to move on. But it seemed odd, peculiarly formal; the kind of cake my parents used to buy when we visited my grandparents. Considering we were going to Eighth Street, a loaf of bread would have made more sense.

And then we set off again, and it appeared odder still, Arnie holding the cardboard-boxed cake in front of him, following it down the street. I gazed at the park, with its pastel buds, a vision of freedom beyond the iron-ribbed fence.

Rose opened the door, and Cerebus did an excited dance around her. She crouched and ruffled the dog's fur, saying what a good boy he was and how much she'd missed him, all but ignoring Arnie as she led us down the hallway to the main room.

Ray, reclining on a mattress, managed a hello for Arnie, and then he too sat up and gave the dog the same warm welcome Rose had given it. Patrick, on another mattress, said nothing at all as Arnie set the cake box down on the spool table, opened it, and backed up to a wall. Rose sat down in a chair and picked up her knitting, the dog curling up on the floor nearby as the clicking needles became the only sound in the room, the cake on the table the focus of attention. Its milky icing drew two flies, orbiting wildly. One finally landed, then the other. Emily peered out of the doorway to the walk-in closet and quickly ducked back inside.

In the throes of this silent treatment, Arnie took off his jacket and folded it over an arm. Droplets of perspiration appeared on his forehead. He brushed them off with the fingers of one hand, rubbed his hands together, and resumed his stance against the wall as the excruciating silence went on and on. Finally, he pushed away from the wall, parted the curtain and entered the other room. A few seconds later, perhaps out of respect for his endurance, I followed him in.

Sunlight poured through a window at one end, the room warm. Arnie draped his jacket over an armrest, sat down on the couch, and crossed his legs, looking awkward and out of place as he stared at the heavy curtain. I sat down a few feet away, heard them talking on the other side of the thick curtain, a garble of indistinct comments until Patrick raised his voice, saying, angrily, "He's got some nerve!"

Arnie didn't react. He continued to stare at the curtain, ignoring the more and less audible talk, until it stopped altogether. Then he stood up, carefully pulled his jacket back on, and looked down at me.

"You coming?" he asked.

His voice had a disembodied, grating quality in that brilliant room.

"No," I replied, and hearing myself, then watching him part the curtain and leave, I knew it was the wrong answer.

School of Existential Being

After the fire, Tom found a pad on Seventh Street, between C and D. He'd managed to save plants, books, notebooks, and other stuff from the old apartment, before the firemen restrained him, though not the iguana that roamed among the ceiling pipes and had likely perished in the blaze. And with this salvage and other odds and ends he found or people gave him, he quickly transformed the new place.

It was a cozy cloister when I dropped by, the smell of incense permeating the rooms, paisley fabric tacked to the walls and over the windows. A comfortable place to live in urban retirement, I thought, though Tom, despite his aged appearance, was not that much older than anyone else.

You usually had to initiate conversation before Tom would talk, and then he'd respond prosaically, with a few words. He was more forthcoming when asked a question, but even then, I found talking to him was often excruciating. In fact, it forced me to think about what I was saying, and as a result, afterward the self-examination these pause-laden conversations engendered gave them the aspect of an audience with a sage.

So it came as a surprise that he was in a rare, talkative mood the first time I dropped into his new pad. Picking up on this, I brought up the commuter college we'd both gone to, and he told me he quit after his freshman year, deciding to pursue his own studies without the hassle of showing up every day, attending classes and taking tests. He would have dropped out sooner, he said, if not for the chemistry laboratories, where he spent most of his time. But then, you could only use them at specified periods, and he decided it wasn't worth the hassle.

He'd grown up not far from where I had, in Queens, and I told him a few things about growing up out there as a teenager. The landmarks I mentioned triggered his memory, calling forth his own experiences, which he recalled with a faraway look on his face, as if channeling another lifetime.

He'd been in a gang that rumbled with other gangs. Pretending to grip a chain in his fist, he swung it in a wide arc, laughing; I'd never heard him laugh outright before. He drove a souped-up car, he said, and tied his girlfriend's kerchief around his neck before heading into battle; a leather-jacketed knight wearing his lady's colors.

As always, he paused often, between discrete blocks of thought, but instead of the usual blank ellipses that discomforted me, he now reacted to his own words as revelation, astonished at what he'd once done. Interpretation would have connected the past to the present, explaining it, but Tom was a detached narrator, and he spoke of the person he'd been as a different character altogether. With that same detachment, he recalled his buddies back then, some of whom were in jail now; one for armed robbery, another for murder. Nor was description his thing. It was up to me to picture them in jail cells as he shook his head in bemusement at a turn of affairs that was beyond him.

I knew he was still seeing Emily, but she was staying uptown, in a coterie around a young millionaire into drugs and wild parties. A social register scandal that made tabloid gossip columns: bizarre characters traipsing into a grand old building in Gramercy Park, ferried upstairs to the penthouse by a uniformed attendant in a plush elevator; a running story about the debasement of the jaded rich.

When I asked Tom about her, his details were sketchy, and again I filled in the blanks—the high ceilings, the thick-pile carpets and gleaming parquet floors. And when he mentioned the things she brought him—a silk shirt with French cuffs, a leather belt, and even an ascot—I imagined she enjoyed pilfering from a walk-in closet bigger than most tenement rooms, got off on the outlaw gallantry of stealing from a dilettante lover, who kept a harem, and bringing the spoils to her impoverished paramour. It was my fantasy, not his, reflecting my take on Emily: that she lived for aesthetic pleasure.

I'd seen for myself that Emily's own fantasies could be demanding, but never considered it from her point of view. While visiting Eighth Street, I had a glimpse of it, through Rose, who was a storyteller, or at least a purveyor of snippets. Emily had confided in her that Tom put on the fancy silk shirt, then tossed it aside, because it was too slippery. She thought him ungrateful.

Of course, I thought. Its provenance would have meant nothing to him. His intuition bypassed explanation and precluded anything that wasn't practical.

And then there were the drugs. Always, there were the drugs. No history of that time can be understood without them, as influence and obsession.

To Emily, taking acid with someone was the essence of intimacy; and afterward, the memory of that perfection was a template for what should be. With psychedelics scarce, during one of the periodic droughts, Emily still managed to cop capsules for the two of them; the rich can always get what they wanted, whatever the market's condition. Recalling the past, she might have envisioned a night of candlelight ecstasy, a seamless. unending series of perfect moments as they stared into each other's eyes, communing soul-to-soul. Or her vision was less specific: an atmosphere, a mood . . .

It's hard to live up to the past. It never was quite what we think. And times change, rendering exact repetition impossible. The air itself has a different quality from day to day, from hour to hour, brings out this instead of that. And people are never the same, though we fix them at a point in time and in a set of circumstances and situations through which we define who they are.

Tom, it turned out, was not the person Emily thought he was and expected him to be. Showing up at Eighth Street one morning after taking acid with him the night before, she told Rose about it, as if betrayed by his behavior. He'd been detached, she said, uncaring, brutal.

She was through with him.

Rose commiserated, as was her way, but Emily's confession gave her ideas of her own. Despite her easy affability, which was taken for granted, she had dreams too, and desires. I'd seen as much in the basement hangout, when she'd pause over her knitting to make a cogent observation, a portion of her glance lingering on Tom, sitting behind his table, to see if he was listening and to gauge his reaction.

She did not reveal more than that peripheral look. He was living with Lila, after all, and though Emily had turned his head, Rose was a supportive type, a homebuilder, not a home wrecker. But now that Lila was in Europe and Emily was out of the picture, it seemed to her that Tom might welcome the attention and care she could offer.

That same afternoon, she showed up at his pad with a bag of groceries. It was food, after all. How could he refuse? She made an omelet for dinner, then served tea and biscuits. And as in a salon, a setting she knew how to operate within, she told him stories about Eighth Street, things she'd recorded in her trip book, with titles to match: Patrick's Herculean Labor, The Stolen Tinfoil Ball, Arnie Glick's Gooey Cake . . .

Tom was a good listener, and Rose could tell a story. There was a match in that. In the crucible of his undivided attention, she might well have been inspired, brilliant. Not that he asked her to stay; but then, he didn't tell her to leave. And when she spooned up next to him on the mattress that evening, he didn't push her off either.

I'd heard they were living together, and when I dropped in one afternoon, Rose opened the door and welcomed me in, the gracious lady of the house. I followed her through the kitchen to the front room, where Tom was reclining on a mattress, his shoes off. Rose sat down at the spot she'd left, picked up one of his bare feet and went back to gouging a splinter from his sole with a needle.

"Now that Peter's here," she said to him in soothing tones, "it won't hurt as much."

"It has nothing to do with who's here," he replied, annoyed. "It's pain."

"Now Tom, don't be a baby," she chided, and went at him with the needle as he leaned back on a cushion, hands clasped behind his head, looking disgusted.

I'd noticed a calendar in the kitchen; a Van Gogh burning sky, a landscape with psychedelic waves surrounding a blazing yellow sun; done at an asylum, according to the caption. A testament to Rose's good taste. In art. But why would anyone want to know what numbered day it was? Not too many months ago I'd occasionally consulted a calendar, and even worn a watch. Now that seemed an odd obsession. What was the point of knowing what day or time it was? And there were notes in a few of the squares, in Rose's handwriting, to do this or that. Were they reminders to herself or to Tom? Was it an attempt to put his life in order?

When the splinter was removed, Tom gestured me into another room and closed the door, shutting Rose out, though she made no move to follow. His furtiveness surprised me, as did the room itself. It seemed it was where he truly lived, that the rest of the pad was extraneous. All his old things were there: the science magazines and rock samples, the books and beacons and test tubes. Was he making his own drugs? And testing them on himself?

At Eighth Street, where Rose now hung out most days, she'd confided to whomever was around that Tom was even stranger than she had assumed. He'd hidden the calendar she bought. And though he complained about the cockroaches, he wouldn't let her use spray, attacking them with a broom instead; to give them a fighting chance, he said. And often, for no reason that she could see, he'd abruptly go into his room and close the door, and stay in there for hours. In fact he'd become sedentary, uninterested in the out-of doors, and hardly left the pad at all anymore.

If Rose took any of this personally, it didn't show. Like a social worker on a case, she had his welfare in mind. She went up to Westchester to get her sports car, garaged at her grandmother's house, drove it down to Seventh Street and parked it in front of Tom's building. It was for him to do with as he liked, she explained. He could go to the botanical garden in Brooklyn and steal leaves off the cacao plants if it pleased him. Or take a drive upstate and commune with nature. She'd go with him if he wanted, but if not, he should get away by himself. A change of scenery might do him good. And handing him the keys to the car, she left, staying at Eighth Street that day and night, removing herself as a possible influence on the well-intended therapy.

When she went back the next morning, the door was locked and Tom didn't answer. Assuming he wasn't in, she returned that afternoon, and again in the evening, with the same result. He'd never given her a key, so she had no choice but to return to Eighth Street and try again the next day. Before knocking, she heard him moving around inside, but again he didn't answer, though he stopped moving about, as if hiding the fact that he was there.

Worried, she returned with others, stood in the hallway and spoke to the door, certain he was inside, though he didn't respond. Gary stepped forward and tried to coax the invisible man to speak, to at least tell them he was all right. And then Ray gave it a shot, saying, "C'mon, man, talk to me. I know you're in there . . ."

Ray liked to think that he and Tom were special buddies, hipper than anyone else. So he took the silence personally, and stomped out of the hallway and into the street, where he nursed his self-image. "I know he's in there," he said when the others joined him. "He's just being an asshole."

The car, sitting at the curb, was now plastered with parking tickets, an oddity on a block of beat-up jalopies and a dilapidated Buick on cinder blocks, its tires stripped.

On the third or fourth day, Rose went back, saw the car keys on the hallway floor in front of the door, retrieved them and left for good.

I spotted Tom one afternoon on Avenue C, lugging crates to Mark Greenbaum's pad on Thirteenth Street. He told me he'd been evicted and that Mark told him he could stay there until he got back from San Francisco. I offered to help, and the two of us moved the rest of his things in two trips.

Mark and I had killed a lot of time in those tiny, spartan rooms, talking politics and bemoaning the world's condition. But as Tom unpacked and put his things here and there, the place took on a different aspect. He had a knack for transformation, and took to it with the same concentration he had while reading or playing a guitar. The pleasant smell of incense wafted through the small apartment while he worked, pausing to skim through books and magazines before adding them to shelves that contained Mark's chap books and mimeographed poetry collections, which were soon overwhelmed by Tom's more extensive library. He set out jars of herbs, powders, dried flowers, a tray of rock samples, then tacked paisley fabric to the walls and window frames, creating another sanctuary.

I sat smoking for a while, and when he'd put the books away, I browsed through the newly stocked shelves, with their scientific treatises and articles, the textbooks on botany, biology, geology, and chemistry. But what interested me most were the books on Buddhism, the *Bhagavad Gita,* and the *I Ching,* which I took from a shelf and leafed through.

"Do you consult this?" I asked.

He looked up, seemingly surprised I was still there.

"The *I Ching,*" I said, tapping it. "Do you, like, read it as if it were philosophy, or do you toss coins and check out the patterns?"

He didn't answer for several seconds, until I thought he might not answer at all, then said, "Sometimes I toss coins, and sometimes I just read it . . ."

We were back to the long silences, ellipses you could fall into, each one an abyss. And as always, the pauses made me nervous. And when I'm nervous, I usually talk. "Lately," I said, "I haven't had much interest in reading, and yet, ironically, I think a lot about it, about what I might read that would be worth the effort . . ."

Tom didn't respond. But then, I hadn't asked him anything.

"Like, the last time I was on acid," I went on, filling the silence, "I didn't realize how strong the dose was, and took two tablets instead of one—"

"The orange tabs?"

" . . . Yeah. Those. I took two, and I guess I went supernova, or something, because I blanked out for a while . . . When I came to and was cognizant of myself again—of being in my body—I was naked. I didn't remember taking my clothes off—or anything, for that matter—and it was, y'know, like I'd been newly born, stripped bare and starting fresh . . .

"Anyway, without thinking about it, or even aware of the fact that I'd moved, I found myself in the other room, studying my bookshelves . . . standing there, naked, reading the titles. I had to make an effort—the words kept swimming in and out of focus—and then, when I did manage to focus, to understand what they meant. Anyway, when the meaning of a particular phrase or sentence registered, I'd remember the whole book itself, what was inside it, what kind of book it was, and I realized that I'd bought it for a reason, and saved it, as if it were an old friend . . . I went through all of them, but couldn't find the one I wanted—though I didn't know exactly what I was looking for."

I laughed at the absurdity of it, but Tom nodded solemnly.

"I was attracted to *The Stranger,*" I continued. "Camus. My hand moved of its own volition and took it from the shelf. I opened it and read the first sentences:

'Mother died today. Or maybe yesterday; I can't be sure . . .' It knocked me out. Then the rest of the book came back to me, and it was satisfying to recall . . . but I knew it wasn't what I'd been looking for. It was description, and I wanted something else . . . So I put it back, and another book caught my eye, *Time and Free Will,* by Henri Bergson . . ."

"I know it," Tom said.

"I opened it at random, someplace in the middle, and began reading . . . Every sentence was exquisite, a gem, and as I moved from one to another, and they formed paragraphs and then whole sections, the meaning that burst forth as the separate parts meshed knocked me out . . . I mean, the mere act of reading made his point, about perception and cognition, being and becoming . . . But after a while I realized that as beautiful as it was, it was an explanation, and that's not what I was looking for either . . ."

Tom picked up the *I Ching* as I spoke, then put it down, resting the book on a thigh as he gazed out the window, now flanked by paisley curtains, at the brick wall across the air shaft and the swatch of sky above the roofline. I was about to go on, to break the lengthening silence, but recognizing my disquiet, and the habit I had of speaking out of it, I restrained myself.

It was Tom who finally spoke. "When I was living on West Nineteenth Street," he said, "my super ran what he called 'a school of existential being,' which was up the block. There was a sign on the storefront window: 'School of Existential Being.' He lived on the ground floor, and whenever he saw me, he'd tell me to drop in, to meet people or listen to lectures . . . He'd stop me in the hallway and tell me that existentialism was really taking hold, with people protesting against the war and getting arrested, the demonstrations, the marches . . . and when I'd try to say something, he'd start up again. I couldn't get a word in . . . and all I wanted was for him to fix the kitchen sink."

I laughed, but at the same time wondered if he was rebuking me because I talked so much. Or was it a koan on my search for meaning? In either case, taking it as a putdown, I got up to leave.

"You're going?" he said, surprised.

"Yeah," I replied, surprised by his surprise, wondering if I'd jumped to the wrong conclusion.

He followed me to the door; to thank me, I assumed, for helping him move. And since he was still holding the *I Ching,* I thought he might offer to loan it to me. But instead, as he closed the door, he turned away, seemingly having forgotten that I was standing there, or perhaps that I'd even been there at all.

*   *   *

When I came by a week or so later, Tom opened the door a fraction and peered out at me before pulling it open and gesturing me in. He seemed distraught. Except for that night in the coffeehouse, I'd never seen him as nervous. Only now he wasn't fierce, but beside himself, his uncertainty accentuated by the acid he'd taken, the vibes enveloping me as I followed him into the small middle room. The contact high put me on edge as I sat down on the mattress, a few feet from him, any trace of daylight hidden by the curtains, the room illuminated by a burning candle.

Abruptly, Tom said, "Have you seen Arnie Glick?" his sudden, angry expression both fierce and unbelievable; a kabuki mask.

It startled me, and I replied cautiously, "I saw him the other day . . . Why?"

"I hate him!" Tom blurted.

Nothing he could have said would have surprised me more. "You hate him? But why? What'd he do?"

Maybe it was the words repeated back at him. Startled, he shook his head, quickly said, "Never mind," and gestured brusquely with a hand, erasing his thoughts, roiling the flame, tossing shadows.

It alarmed me, seeing him that way, and suddenly I was talking, about I don't know what, but pouring it out, drawing on the thick vibes that filled the room. I was passionate, eloquent, possessed, and I went on and on, embellishing ideas, revisiting them from various angles, interjecting opposing notions, and weaving all this into a narrative of some sort, a great edifice made up of universal notions that I was sure while discoursing a blue streak would have stood the test of all time, though I forgot each elegant notion as soon as I moved on to the next, and forgot all of it, the whole panoply, when I abruptly stopped talking, maybe a half hour later, or as much as two or three. I had no idea. And in all that time, I hardly looked at Tom, only sensed his presence and that I'd captured and held his attention, which I suppose was my driving impetus. Only now, in the silent aftermath of my outburst, wondering what had come over me, did I look at him.

Tom stared at me with gratified wonderment, reached out a hand to grasp my shoulder, squeezed it, then fell back on his heels.

Walking downstairs, I was pleased with myself; I'd done a good deed. But afterward, on the street, I wondered what I'd been so driven to remedy.

When I came by again a week or so later, the wooden door was covered with scrawled notes addressed to Tom, and I knew before knocking that he was gone.

Martha from Minnesota

When I heard him shout and saw Mark across the street, waving, I was glad to see him. Then I spotted Gerry Gornish with him, and waited with mixed feelings for my old buddy to cross to my side. Not that Gerry was pleased to see me either, his gaze shifting away after a perfunctory greeting.

Mark launched into a description of a woman he'd met in California, falling into our old custom, and after the failures and rejections we'd once shared, I momentarily fell back to those days myself, and was happy for him. Not that my reaction mattered. He was enamored, addressing the world through me, calling her the love of his life, or something like that.

"What the hell is she waiting for?" Gerry muttered, gazing back across the street as the three of us stood there.

I saw her then, a bespectacled woman at the opposite curb, teetering there as at the precipice of a raging rapids she couldn't bring herself to cross, though the nearest cars were idling at a light a block away. Then, just as the light changed, she got up the nerve to cross and made a wild dash in our direction, holding her glasses to her nose with a finger, clutching a pocketbook in the other hand. She barreled toward us, leaping the curb and onto the sidewalk as we backed up to get out of her way.

"This is Martha," Gerry said as cars rumbled past behind her. He gestured offhandedly as she stood there, breathing heavily, cheeks flushed. "Martha . . . Peter."

"Pleased to meet you," she said, thrusting a hand at me.

Startled by her formality, I took it and shook. She had a firm grip. "Pleased to meet you too," I replied.

"We were going to the Annex," Mark said. "Why don't you come with us." I didn't care for that place, but I could see that Mark wanted to tell me more about his California woman, and when he added, "My treat," I agreed.

As long as I'd known him, Mark Greenbaum had never offered to buy anything. Even when I was arrested at the draft board sit-in, I had to plead with him—as they loaded us into the paddy wagon—to put up the fifty dollars bail for my release. He agreed, but only with the proviso that I'd pay him back as soon as I could—the next day, in fact, when he waited at the Tombs for my release, and afterward accompanied me to my bank. So it was a big deal that he wanted to buy me a beer.

But I'd soon discover it was not just the woman from California that was on his mind. There was something else afoot.

I watched him take off, to catch up with Gerry, who'd walked off after introducing the woman who now stood next to me.

"What was your name again?" I asked her.

"Martha," she replied, and fell in beside me with a bouncing gait as I began walking.

Jokingly, I said, "You just get off a bus?"

"Why, yes!" she replied, the thick lenses magnifying her surprise as she tilted her head quizzically and looked up at me. "How did you know?"

"Uh . . ." It was her overabundant enthusiasm. But I said, "Your coat . . . It's not that cold." Which was true, I realized, even though evening was coming on.

She took a breath and held it, inflating her cheeks, which I now saw were rosy, not flushed, then exhaling with feeling. "You're very observant," she said, impressed.

"Thank you," I replied.

"Though actually, it wasn't a bus—it was a plane—and I didn't *just* get here—I've been in the city two days already."

She offered these qualifiers with such seriousness, I wondered if she was putting me on. But no. She was in earnest. "Where did you fly in from?" I asked.

"Minnesota!" she said, blurting it, her round, rosy face ballooning next to mine.

I'd been there once, though I hadn't seen anything but a floodlit freight yard at night. I was about to say so, but Martha went on, telling me she'd met Gerry at the university, and he'd told her to look him up if she were ever in New York, so she had, and was staying with him now. Which surprised me. I'd seen the photos of naked women on his wall, and Martha looked too wholesome; I couldn't imagine her joining his gallery.

Indeed, in the bar it seemed Gerry might have come to the same conclusion, for he all but ignored Martha, turning away from her as he drank from his mug, darting glances at the occupied phone booth, as if waiting to make a crucial call that would somehow extricate him from his predicament.

I'd heard the rumors that cocaine dealers frequented the Annex, and with twilight encroaching and the lights not yet turned on, I believed it. The place had a furtive feel, shady-looking characters flitting in and out, from the batwing front door to the phone booth, no doubt arranging deals or pickups.

Mark was still bending my ear about his perfect woman, and having a hard time following him, I slipped into charting his inflections, which I'd been doing more often lately. Gerry had taken out his little black book and was thumbing through it, while still keeping an eye on the booth. Martha, sitting erect, was sipping from her mug, on her best behavior it seemed. And then, the booth free for a moment, Gerry burst from his seat, got there before anyone else, and closed the folding door behind him. Mark got up too, to go to the bathroom, and I found myself alone with Martha.

"So," I said, turning to her, "how do you like New York so far?"

She scraped her chair closer to mine and in a blurted half whisper said, "It's been awful! I hate it! I never should have come!" And then, as if I might be offended, she quickly added, "Not that I don't like New York. Actually, I think I could like it, a lot. But I only came here because I thought Gerry wanted me to visit, as I told you before, only now that I'm here, I can see he doesn't want me to stay with him at all, that he was just being polite. Oh, I know it was a long time ago and the situation was different, but still . . ."

She went on that way awhile, adding some other things I half heard, her magnified eyes blinking distress as I lost the thread and followed the woof and warp of it, until she abruptly stopped speaking. Gerry had left the booth, looking dissatisfied. As he approached, Martha gripped her half-empty mug and looked into it, escaping there, and took a tiny sip. Then Mark sat back down, and we were in limbo again, four people in separate worlds, in that miserable place.

I knew the sensible thing was to split, but when I opened my mouth to make an excuse of some sort, I heard myself saying instead, "Martha can stay with me if she wants . . ."

In an instant the mood changed. Gerry was elated, though he tried to hide it. And Martha seemed shell-shocked.

"Would that be all right, do you think?" she said to him, politely, uncertainly.

"I don't see why not," he replied, as though it didn't matter to him one way or the other. But he couldn't restrain his true feelings, and with a sweeping gesture offered to buy everyone another round.

"Not for me," I said.

"Me neither," Mark said.

And that quickly, the false good cheer routed by the underlying truth, everyone was eager to move on.

It all happened so fast, I was bewildered as I stood on the sidewalk outside, in the blue-gray twilight, watching Mark and Gerry move up the block, and once again wondered what my old pal saw in his opportunistic companion.

Martha said something, snapping me out of it, and I looked at her. "What?" I asked her.

"I *said*, where do you live, and when will you be there, so I can come over?"

I recited the address and told her she could come any time she wanted.

"But how will I get in if you're not there?"

"The door's open," I replied, and took a backward step, wanting to get away, to let the restless evening take me where it would.

"You don't have a key?" she said, drawing me back.

"No. There is no key. The door's always open."

She regarded me without comprehension in the gathering dark.

"I've been robbed a few times," I explained. "My radio, my typewriter, my record player . . . there's nothing left, and the lock was busted the last time. So I didn't see the point, y'know, of fixing it . . ." I sighed, feeling put out. It was such an effort to explain things.

She continued to look at me, then said, "I want to thank you again, Peter. You're really, really helping me out of a jam."

"That's okay," I replied, only now realizing what I'd offered, and that it might affect my life. And that made me even more eager to be on my way, to move, to feel the world fall away around me.

Martha nodded, releasing me, and I took off.

It was dark when I returned to the building the next day and took the stairs to the sixth floor two at a time, wondering if she'd be there. Out of breath, I pushed the door open—and stood there in the hallway, gaping.

The overhead light, which I never turned on, made the brilliant room, shimmering before me, almost painful to look at. The formica table, which had been in a corner next to the door, repository for loose change, matchbooks, slips with scrawled names and numbers, and anything else in my pockets, was now at the center of the linoleum floor. On it was a familiar display of forks, knives, spoons, napkins, glasses, and plates, arranged in two place settings, with a long, tapered, unlit candle between them.

Hesitant, I stepped inside, a primitive being entering civilization.

"Oh, there you are!"

I saw Martha then, in the front room, sitting in my window chair, regarding me over the edge of a book. She put the book aside and entered the kitchen as I stood there, rooted to my spot. She looked as she had the day before, only more so in a white blouse and a pleated dress, her hair combed neatly and falling nearly to her shoulders, where it bobbed up at the ends; the Little Dutch Girl, I thought, recalling an old TV advertisement. Her cheeks were full and rosy, and when she spoke, her voice had a singsong lilt: "Did something happen? I thought you'd be home by now."

"What's this?" I said stupidly, gesturing at the table.

"Oh. I thought it would be nice if I made dinner my first night here."

I didn't know what to say. "Good idea," I finally replied, and pulling a chair out from beneath the table, sat down before one of the place settings.

"Only I was so famished," she said, "I already ate . . . I'm sorry, I couldn't help myself."

"Oh . . . Okay . . . But then why are there two settings?"

"For symmetry," she said, and laughed.

I supposed that made sense.

"But I haven't had dessert yet," she added quickly, "so we can at least eat that together."

"Good," I said, though that was one more imponderable. What did she have in mind? Cake? Ice cream?

"Should I light the candle?" she asked.

"Yeah," I said quickly, "good idea . . . light the candle, and I'll turn off the light."

Which was an improvement. I didn't care for bright light. Now, with the fancy candle burning, I eased back in the chair, an honored guest at a special occasion.

"Look what I bought!" Martha said, and yanked open the refrigerator door.

The shock of light shattered the restful semidark, the boxy interior an illuminated shrine of shapes and colors. Where before there had been an empty container or two of spoiled orange juice and sour milk, the shelves were now jammed with bottles, jars, and packages. Martha stood beside the open door as though presenting a modern appliance, while I peered at the contents, recognizing pickle relish, chocolate syrup, salad dressing, maraschino cherries, aerosol whipped cream, margarine, skim milk, soda, olives—

She closed the door as abruptly as she'd opened it, plunging the room into relative darkness. It was taxing, how energetic she was. And not for the first time, it occurred to me that she seemed oblivious to the environment she so offhandedly altered.

"The food is warming in the oven," she said. "Why don't you wash your hands?"

It had been a while since I'd done that, and when I stood up and turned around, I was surprised to see that the dishes and glasses that had always been in the sink, coated with a green and purple film of mold, were no longer there, but clean and stacked in a plastic dish drainer, leaving the porcelain sink glaringly empty. I splashed water on my hands, dried them on a dish towel, and sat back down to still another incongruity.

A folded newspaper sat next to my place setting; the husband home from work after a long day at the office. I flipped it open to a jumble of headlines on the front page, too much to take in at once, from Washington, Saigon, Albany . . . Bringing the paper close to my eyes, to bring it into focus, I noticed that the weather was a problem in Texas and the stock market had gone up. I was examining a photograph of a soldier pointing a machine gun at a Vietnamese whose hands were clasped behind his head when a plate of pork chops, baked potato, and peas was placed in front of me. Nonplused, I put the paper aside and began to eat.

I hadn't known I was hungry, but now went at the food like a starving animal, which I might well have been, shoveling it into my mouth, hardly taking the time to chew before swallowing as Martha sat across the way, watching me.

"Oh, I almost forgot to tell you!" she said. "Patrick was here!" Her sentences were declarations, urgent announcements.

I kept eating. "What did he want?"

"He told me to tell you he had something for you, and when I told him you'd be back in the evening, he said he'd probably run into you before then."

"Uh-huh . . ."

"Did you?"

"Did I what?"

"Run into him?"

"Uh, no . . ." I was having trouble with the pork chop. Either the knife was too dull, the meat was too tough, or I'd forgotten how to properly eat.

"He seems like a very interesting person," she said.

"Who?"

"Patrick, silly . . . What does he do?"

I stopped eating and looked up. "I don't know . . . I mean, what does anyone do?"

"Don't be silly," she said. "People do all sorts of things. They have jobs, or go to school, or stay home taking care of children—"

Chided, I said, "I guess you could say he deals drugs, when he's not taking them. But if you asked him, he would probably tell you he's studying . . . that he's a student of life."

Martha tapped the slight cleft in her chin; a pondering gesture. "That's interesting, isn't it? To say you're studying when you're not in school . . . I like that—a lot. In fact, you might say it's why I'm here now . . ."

I was confused. Wasn't she with me to get away from Gerry?

But she meant something else, went on, "It's the reason Eric and I broke up. He wanted to get married right away, and I wanted to take some time off, to collect myself . . . to find my way, so to speak."

"Eric?" I said, inclining back to the food.

"I mentioned him yesterday," she said with a hint of reprimand, "in the bar. Remember? That Eric and I talked about buying a farm?"

A farm.

I didn't remember, and looked up at her. It was an arresting concept.

"Only I wasn't ready to plunge right in after finishing school—to marriage and all that—even if we could have afforded it, which I'm sure we couldn't. And it's hard work, you know. It's a full-time undertaking, to say the least . . . And as I said, I wanted to do a few other things first . . . like see New York City. *Everyone* is *always* talking about New York City . . ."

I looked back down at the food. It seemed I'd been eating for a long time, but most of it was still on the plate, including an untouched pork chop. I put down the fork and knife and leaned back.

"You don't like it?" Martha asked, nodding at the uneaten pork chop.

"No, it's fine."

"The pork chops weren't too dry?"

"Dry? . . . No."

"They might have been in the oven too long . . ."

"I'm just full, is all."

" . . . because I did expect you earlier."

The accusation hung between us.

"Martha," I said, "maybe I should explain . . . I lead what you might call an irregular life, so it might be better if you didn't plan on me for dinner anymore . . ."

"If you could just tell me when you'll be coming home," she said, apologetic, "I'm sure I can do better."

"It's not a matter of doing better . . . Actually, you did a lot more than you had to—"

"I *am* a guest here," she said, suddenly annoyed. Which gave way as abruptly to another emotion, her lip quivering as she held back tears and lowered her head.

In an instant I began to talk. I hardly ever ate in the apartment, I told her, so the meal she'd made was a real treat. And I wasn't much of a cook when I'd actually tried. When I first moved in the extent of my efforts had been to heat up soup in a can. Then, ambitious, I went to the supermarket for a chicken, but bought squab instead, because it was more exotic than chicken, used the oven for the first time and overcooked the two tiny birds until they nearly disappeared. A while later I attempted a lamb stew, but drowned it in oregano, or maybe nutmeg; I couldn't remember which. It was awful. Even my scrambled eggs turned out rubbery, and I couldn't seem to fry an egg without breaking the yolk, though that was the only part of the egg I liked . . .

It was all true, but as I got into it, I made myself sound as ridiculous as possible, and finally got her to laugh.

"You *did* like the food, then?" she asked.

"Oh, yeah," I replied, smacking my bloated stomach with the palm of a hand.

"You're not just saying that?"

"No, no. I wish I could return the favor."

"Well, as I said, you are letting me stay here, so it wasn't a favor."

"Well, yeah—"

"But there *is* something you could do for me," she said, her tone surprisingly assertive.

"What?"

"I want you to turn me on."

I stared at her. "You mean . . ."

"You know, turn me on," she said. "Isn't that what Patrick means when he says he's 'studying'?"

Truths and Gambits

Martha sat erect as the rush abated and the recognizable world returned. Not the reality she was accustomed to, however, but one with a shimmer of energy outlining objects, and the air itself refulgent, an ether of animation. So who could say that the ordinary rules of nature still applied? And so, as when visiting acquaintances one doesn't know well, she appeared on her best behavior, with feet together and hands flat on her thighs; a portrait of propriety. Except her eyes were wide as she goggled at the scene.

A rap on the front door jolted her out of this credulous trance, her eyes darting toward the sound. Seeing it as she might have, I noted that the candle flame on the steamer trunk played tricks on the adjacent room. The table, which had been pushed back against a wall, the appliances, the bathtub, were ambiguous objects. And the knock had been sharp, demanding, a more pointed uncertainty. Martha's eyes shifted to me, looking for guidance.

"I'm coming," I said toward the door, and aware of her eyes following me, crossed the kitchen and opened it.

The crew from Sunnyside stood in the hallway. I'd seen them that afternoon, while delivering a batch of the drug Martha and I had just taken. As always, they'd welcomed me with food and with drugs of their own. No cache of hashish or pot was held back when the candyman showed up. The royal treatment discomforted me, but I understood and appreciated it. Only now I wasn't pleased to see them, not with Martha on her first trip, watching from her spot, wondering what was going on. And by the look of them, the Sunnyside crew would complicate things.

Tony stood in the doorway, Sal and Ernie behind him. Apologetic, he said, "Sorry to bother you, Pete, but we have a little problem," and he rolled his eyes toward Ernie, tallest of the three, whose pupils tick-tocked in his horselike face, a human bomb timed to explode.

They'd been to my pad before, but when I nodded them in now, they milled uncertainly in the kitchen, staring into the candlelit room where Martha sat on the couch, regarding them through her magnifying lenses. Seeing her,

Tony stiffened, a response that communicated a lifetime of masculine conditioning passed from generation to generation, an unwritten rule with the force of taboo: the implication of a man and a woman, alone together.

I knew it myself, and recognizing it, said, "It's all right," and with an arm to his shoulder, guided him toward the front room, the others following.

Martha seemed more curious than afraid now, as they sat down: Tony in the window chair, Sal and Ernie next to each other on the couch, keeping space between themselves and Martha. Without moving his head, just his pupils, Ernie glanced at her once, then not again. Sal, in contrast, looked at Martha with blatant curiosity, then spotted the pot among the other things on the trunk and leaned forward to examine it more closely.

Only Tony, now that he'd been given dispensation to ignore the taboo about intruding on another man's woman, knew what the situation called for, and smiling at Martha, the scar on his cheek creasing, becoming a long dimple, said, "Hi . . . How're you doin'?"

She beamed back at him, blurted, "I'm stoned!"

He laughed. "Yes, I can see that . . ."

"This is Tony," I said to her, "and this is Sal, and Ernie . . ."

Sal nodded without looking at her, and Ernie didn't look at all. He sat at attention, rigid, staring straight ahead.

"Pleased to meet you," Tony said to her, and gathering himself, said to me, "We took that stuff you brought this afternoon, Pete. It was great . . . better than anything we ever had before. But, uh, Ernie . . . well, he took two of the capsules . . ."

"Two?"

"I know, I know, we should've listened when you said one was enough, but we didn't know, and . . . anyway, since then, well . . . Ernie's been sort of out of it . . ."

I noticed then that his pupils were no longer ticking, but he kept to his immobile posture, as if playing a part, listening while pretending not to.

Sal, meanwhile, had opened the cellophane bag on the trunk and begun rolling a joint with the papers he'd found there.

"You should ask first," Tony said sharply, reprimanding him.

Sal and I had been among the dozen or so who sat in at draft board headquarters, spent a night in jail, and then gathered at the courthouse once a month, for the tedious trial. It was through him that I'd met Tony. Drawing on that connection now, a fiction in which we were old pals rather than circumstantial cell mates, Sal rolled his eyes and said to me, in a lazy drawl, "Do you mind . . . ?"

There was so much going on all at once, a tableau of discrete parts, each capable of affecting the others. Martha, who was ready to be amused, if only she could see where the possibilities would lead. Tony, who wanted to help his confused pal, but didn't want to hassle me. Ernie, pretending, for some reason, to appear more fucked-up than he was. And Sal, who just wanted to get stoned, and to whom I now said: "Why don't you and Ernie smoke that joint in my bedroom . . . over there, on the other side of the kitchen." I added, "It's Martha's first trip, you know."

"They can stay," she said. "It doesn't bother me."

"It's better this way," I replied. "They'll join us later."

Ernie lumbered to his feet and hesitated a moment, to stay in befuddled character, then followed Sal through the kitchen and into the other room. The light went on behind the curtain, and within minutes they were talking and laughing.

Without Ernie to worry about, Tony began to converse with Martha; and having composed a solution out of the disparate elements, I sat back with relief and listened. He asked her where she was from, and Martha, delighted, regaled him with a recollection of summer storms, clouds that built up to the heavens, rumbled thunder and flashed lightning, then rained down with fury, leaving a placid aftermath. He'd never been farther west than the Hudson River, he told her, and they laughed at that. Then the toilet flushed, and I laughed too.

The universe works in mysterious ways. But the world can be explained. "It's the plumbing," I said. "When the pressure builds, it eventually gets released."

Then Patrick burst in, shattering the equanimity.

He wore a black cape, which he whipped off with the flourish of a superhero, tossing it aside, roiling the candle flame, splashing his acid vibes into the mix. He nodded at Martha, who was pleased to see him, then spotted Tony and froze. The two had met before, briefly, and Patrick had taken an instant dislike to him, assuming he was a narc. In fact, Tony had been a cop for a while, with the NYPD, so they were relatives of a sort. Now, with a meaningful look, Patrick gave me a glimpse of the bottle of pills he'd been hiding in his cape and discreetly slid it toward me across the trunk as he sat down. To appease him, I put it away in a kitchen cupboard. When I returned to my spot, he was sitting with his back to the others, hands resting on his thighs in a Buddha posture.

It was a bizarre juxtaposition: the flamboyant entrance followed by this withdrawn meditative pose. But he was still the elephant in the room, emanating the dose he'd taken, and as with Ernie before him, was a disquieting presence. He hadn't gone so far as to close his eyes, however, and to draw him into the setting, I nodded at the chessboard that sat on the trunk, inviting him to play.

In response, Patrick's lips creased in a slight smile, telling me he found the invitation humorous, beneath him. To play a game—of all things—while on acid?

I replied with a slight smile of my own, saying a game is only a game, after all, and if we recognized as much, what harm could it do?

Then I pushed a pawn.

He pushed one back.

And we were into it.

The game developed around the central squares, his bishops threatening from the corners, my pawns stubborn, my knights well-placed. At some point Sal and Ernie returned to the room, and Patrick looked up and frowned, but I pushed a pawn, bringing him back to the board, and as they sat down against the far wall, and Tony and Martha philosophized in particulars, Patrick and I inhabited a bubble, producing collaborative patterns, our absorption transcending competition.

Then something shifted. Who can know why? Things change—it's a fact of life—and after the fact, it's always possible to come up with explanations. It could have been the moon, the sun, and/or various planets falling out of favor with each other; or a biochemical thing, the unbearable ecstasy that fine-tuned our nervous systems hitting a discordant note. Or indigestion. Whatever the reason, a mocking half-smile now appeared on Patrick's lips after each move he made. And this glitch in the perfection we'd momentarily found affected his play. He pushed too hard, lost a bishop, a rook, and finally his queen.

When the board had been simplified to a dozen pieces, he set the king on its side. "You thrashed me," he said, leaning back, speaking for the first time since we began playing.

"I wouldn't say that," I replied.

"I was too attentive," he said, complimenting himself with his self-critique. "You can't play chess in a state of heightened awareness. To win, you need to concentrate."

"You did all right," I said dryly, "until you moved your bishop."

"Exactly my point."

"Who won?" Martha asked.

With an ironic smile, Patrick looked at me over the board, to see how I'd handle the challenge of acknowledging victory.

"I did," I said, and shaking some cigarettes out of the pack and onto the trunk, pushed one toward him. He raised an eyebrow, and then, though he usually didn't smoke, took it and lit up.

That might have been the end of it, if accepting defeat weren't as difficult as acknowledging victory. "The great chess champions," Patrick declared, holding the cigarette aloft and ostensibly speaking to me, but addressing the room-at-large, "are single-minded . . . They have the ability to *concentrate,* to blot out everything and engage in the limited confines of a game . . . It's what some people call 'genius.'"

He paused and watched the smoke catch in the candle draft and spiral up toward the ceiling. The room was silent, waiting on him.

"The so-called intelligence in game-playing can be *measured* . . . activities that have an end, a goal. But the 'genius' of those who don't play games—the lunatics, the so-called idiots and psychotics—is immeasurable . . . After all, how can you measure a transcendent state of mind? To know nothing and see everything . . . the antithesis of having a goal."

"But that's so extreme, Patrick!" Martha blurted. "Surely we don't have to be psychotic to see what's around us!"

"No," he replied. "But it helps."

Her eyes bulged behind the lenses, and the others regarded him with similar awe or perplexity. "But . . ." She frowned.

He tamped out his cigarette. "By 'psychosis,' I mean a state beyond self, beyond thought. Not *living,* as in 'the good life,' but *existing,* in the moment."

I said, "But we're capable of living in the moment without obliterating memory."

"The past is illusion," he replied.

"Well, yeah, but you can acknowledge it without being controlled by it."

"Can you?"

"Well, yeah. When you exist in the moment, the past is an abstraction, but what we say and do in the moment *becomes* the past, even if we don't see it, or think it . . . It's a reality too."

He didn't answer for a moment, then said, "You've been reading again?"

It was a surprising question; a personal attack. "Actually, no," I replied. "Not recently."

"Bergson," he said. *"Being and Becoming* . . . you made this argument before, when we were debating the difference between truth and fact."

"I'm not arguing," I said, "I'm just trying to make a point—that you can't *choose* between being or becoming. Like waves and particles, they both *are,* simultaneously. Bergson says there's no bridge between them, and he's right. But it's a paradox. We can be in the moment, without a past, and thus a future, and at the same time our actions over successive moments record a personal history. Truth and fact at the same time."

"You read too much," he said bluntly.

I blinked in surprise.

Behind him, Tony said, "How can anyone read too much?"

Patrick threw him a dark glance, but in response spoke to me. "Reading closes the doors of perception. Look around you," he said, spreading his arms, casting a shadow on the far wall and halfway across the ceiling, where it loomed over the room. "The people, the vibes, the odor of incense and cigarettes . . . the candle flame, and what it illuminates, the reflected scene in the window glass, the shadowy shapes outside . . . all of it, here, in this moment. To read about it, to *think* about it—speculating on what it means or why it is—only diminishes what we perceive, reduces it to an *interpretation* . . . obscures reality."

"But everybody looks for meaning, Patrick," Martha said, and at a glance from him, added, with less certainty, "Don't they?"

"No, not everyone," he replied.

I leaned forward and pitched my voice low, to draw Patrick toward me and away from the others: "You're saying that perception is everything . . ."

"That's one way to put it."

"But who's to say that perception doesn't have some of the attributes of thought? I mean, maybe we bring to perception what we've already seen, heard, and sensed . . . This room, for instance. I've been in it often. I'm accustomed to it. Maybe that influences my perception in some subtle way that might not affect anyone else."

"You're saying you have a memory of it.

"Well . . . yeah, I guess."

"Then it's not perception."

"But who's to say that perception itself doesn't have its own memory?"

"You mean associations?"

"I mean, when we see an image on the retina, it's only after it travels to the brain, through neurons, synapses, or whatever—I'm not a scientist—and who's to say that along the way it doesn't pick up tidbits of information from the past that it brings back with it?"

"That just proves my point," he replied. "When you lead a simple life, you don't build an . . . edifice of explanation around perception. You don't *crystallize* reality, or alter it . . . Take Buddhism . . . I assume you're still interested in it . . ."

"Ever since you gave me that book."

"Okay. That's what I mean. For you, seeking nirvana became what you read. The Four Truths, the Eightfold Path, a code of behavior—"

"But . . . no . . ."

"It was probably a mistake, giving you that book. You can't change yourself by reading about what you should or shouldn't do. Reading fosters the illusion that you're getting someplace, but when you put the book down, you're still here, in the same place. Nothing has changed . . ."

Not for the first time, I wondered what Patrick had against reading. I didn't believe it was a spiritual aversion; he was too adamant about it. But then, what did I know about him beyond what he'd chosen to tell me? He'd been in the army, had a hard time following orders in Vietnam and avoided court-martial by agreeing to become an undercover narcotics agent for the federal government. At some point he went to a monastery. And I recalled something about military school. He recounted his past as the making of a legend; a heroic figure, in his own eyes. If he'd also flunked out of school, or barely scraped through, would he have said so? For all I knew, he might have been given the Coomaraswami by his friend at the monastery and had it in his rucksack for weeks because he found reading a chore, and at the first opportunity gave the book away—to me.

I recalled, then, his uncharacteristic uncertainty the day he drew me aside at Eighth Street to show me a poem he'd written. He'd found a typewriter somewhere, and the six lines were neatly centered on the page. He'd stated, with elegant simplicity, that he was not yet ready to die because he hadn't yet discovered the reason he'd been born. I told him I liked it, and he brushed the compliment away, uncomfortable with it, but carefully refolded the page and put it back in his pocket as he moved away.

Now, with the chessboard between us, it struck me that despite what Patrick had said about the deficiency of words and explanations, he was enjoying himself in a way he couldn't at Eighth Street, where talk itself was a shibboleth, a shortcoming; that among those who were more exalted, words were unnecessary.

"What's *rational*," Patrick was saying, "is not the same as what's *objective* . . ." He laughed softly. "Nothing could be further from the truth."

My mind had wandered. I wasn't sure where the conversation had gone. "You're saying that perception is objective?" I asked.

He frowned. Few things bothered Patrick as much as people who didn't pay attention. "Didn't I just say that?"

"But how can you know for sure that something that seems objective to you is objective to someone else?"

"You just *know*," he said. He thought a moment. "Like the night the four of us smoked DMT . . . We all shared the same objective vision . . ."

We were seated around the candle, the pipe passed from one to the other, each of us inhaling deeply. It came around again, more slowly, with ageless, ceremonial gravity. And with that inhalation, the room expanded, yawned outward, the air a pointillistic ether of energy as slowly, ever so slowly, my hand reached for the pipe as it came around once more, an ancient ritual. The ammonia smell was strong as I inhaled, the drug smoldering in the bowl flaring up, the flow of air and what it contained a seemingly solid substance from mouth to lungs, filling cavities, sacs, and capillaries . . . the nervous system, the brain—

The room exploded in light!

It radiated in spokes from the candle's flame, glowing yellow circles extending up and out to the ceiling, spokes of bright yellow orbs in perfect symmetry to the others as they fanned out, and between each, another layer of spokes, green and violet bars . . .

I gaped, incredulous, at this astounding tapestry. It was dazzling, and yet transparent. I could see Patrick opposite me, and the other two on either side. And at the same time, I was gazing down from the ceiling at four bodies seated around a candle . . .

Much later, I would read about a mystical vision of Mohammed, creation in the shape of a peacock formed of white pearls and walled about by veils. And even later, about the purple and green rods and cones in our eyes, the shapes I'd seen that night. But at the time there was just the vision, which I gazed at in astonishment . . . and after a while wondered what I was seeing, and then how it was possible to think while witnessing a miracle. Had Moses wondered about the source of the burning bush after staring at it awhile? My inquisitiveness seemed a sacrilege—the pursuit of knowledge, the original sin—which would surely obliterate the amazing vision, for in questioning it, I was no longer worthy of it. And in fact the marvelous tapestry of light flickered then, and a moment later abruptly vanished.

Now, I said to Patrick, "How can you be sure we were all seeing the same thing?" though I'd never doubted it, and still didn't.

"Because," he replied, "we were in total telepathic contact."

I was startled. "How can you know that?"

"Because . . ." He paused, looking at me. "I read your mind."

"Oh c'mon, Patrick."

"That night, you wavered first . . . You broke the link before the vision disappeared . . . You began to think."

Rattled, I said, "We were on a drug, for chrissake, and it was wearing off! I mean, didn't you eventually begin to think? And the others, didn't they begin to think too?"

I heard myself then, voice raised, and saw the others looking at me. Picking up a cigarette, I lit it, leaned back and exhaled. Looking away, toward the window, I saw the dawning sky outside, the tenement rooftops, the shapes of the city beyond. We'd all been in that room a long time.

Patrick got up and went to the water closet, and I exhaled smoke with a sense of relief. The others seemed relieved too, now that he'd left the room. Remembering something I'd read, I went into my bedroom and found the book, and when Patrick returned, held it toward him, splayed open to the passage. He took it and read to himself:

> When a Buddha becomes conscious of his halo, the halo vanishes.
> Not only does it vanish, but it is apt to harm us in one way or another.
> The halo shines most when we are unconscious of it.

I thought he'd understand, but he hardly took the time to consider it before turning toward the others, saying, "This is what I mean!" drawing everyone's attention, holding it up as though it were evidence in a trial. "A book!"

No one knew what he was talking about. Even if they had, they knew me, not Patrick, and with the loyalty that comes with familiarity, would not have sided with him unless he'd won them over in the course of the long night, which he hadn't. On the contrary, he'd made everyone nervous.

So they turned away, and ignored him as he put on his cape; except for Martha, who called out a cheery good-bye as Patrick closed the door behind him.

Fruit Salad for the Head

At dawn, Martha and I were alone again, the long night behind us, the sky brightening over the nascent city. As we sat in the quiet room, which hummed with energy, her eyes sparkled as she stared at me. Not looking for guidance, but . . . something else. Whatever it was, she was not the same woman who'd been there before.

Truth *is* beauty; and beauty truth. It's no cliché. She'd been ordinary, or just there. And now, in her vivacity, she was not plain and overweight, nor bespectacled and from Minnesota, or from anywhere else in particular, but unique, attractive . . . desirable. How could I not have noticed?

She smiled across the space between us; a smile that shared something with me. What was it? But at the same time, I knew. And it made me nervous, unsure of myself.

She got up from the window chair, unfolding the leg tucked beneath her, moving softly, without effort, glided to the couch and sat down beside me, a foot away. A pas de deux, with me as her partner; only I didn't know the steps. Did she sense that? She appeared careful, muted, so as not to frighten me. Or was I imagining it? Not giving me time to think about it, she reached out and took my hand, squeezed it lightly, and without a word stood up, bringing me with her. I didn't resist, followed her through the kitchen and into the tiny bedroom.

The curtain dropped behind me, and in my uncertainty, I began to imagine things, conflated the chess game with being led, became a pawn. And then my thoughts flipped, around the game theme, and I was a player and Martha the pawn, and I'd been planning this seduction all along, from the moment she'd been in distress in the bar and I invited her to move in with me. It was ridiculous, of course; my mind playing tricks on me. Even I could see that as I excoriated myself. Had I not been overwrought, I might have laughed aloud. But I was literally beside myself, a stranger in my own bedroom, standing in the narrow aisle next to the mattress that nearly filled the room, staring at the rumpled blanket and sheets, pink-hued from the light filtering through the narrow window I'd painted to fancifully simulate stained glass.

How naive I was! How young! No more than a boy, really, as she slipped out of her clothes and onto the mattress, pulling a sheet up so it covered her—not out of shame, but to cover my embarrassment as she smiled, welcoming me, inviting me to join her.

I wanted to smile back, but couldn't. I was too nervous to have a sense of humor. Too much was at stake. But now that I knew it would finally happen—this event I'd thought about for so long—a less innocent mind-set pushed my uncertainty aside, and with a sudden competitive, rapacious urge, I tore off my clothes, dove under the sheet, and went at her like an animal, gripping and groping.

"Slow down," she said gently, but firmly, placing her hands over mine, stilling them. "There's no need to hurry."

It brought me to my senses, and I was so grateful, I could have thanked her. It would have been appropriate. She was tutoring me, after all. We both knew that now. That cat was out of the bag. I knew almost nothing, had no experience. None of my photo fantasies had been real enough to touch, and I'd never had to concern myself with their response. What's more, she deserved my gratefulness for not bruising my pride, which she could have easily shattered.

She took my hands then and guided them here and there, telling me what to do; to stroke, circle, or pat, harder or softer, faster or slower. And I began to catch on, her breath communicating, instead of her words, telling me what she didn't have to say. I responded to each cue, felt empowered by my concrete influence, yet at the same time wasn't in control, but a means to an end. Maybe she sensed as much, as it seemed she'd sensed everything else, because she moved her hand down then and touched my shaft, which was hard, and with a quick shift, drew me on top of her and guided me in.

And just like that, her vagina swallowed me, whole, and I swooned.

Home at last!

The thought popped into my head.

I had no time to think about it, for now she was moving beneath me, thrusting up, falling back, no longer instructing me, but rather, asserting herself, demanding, insisting. It was all I could do to keep up with her. What had happened to the meek woman from Minnesota? How could I have been so wrong about her? And all the other women I'd thought about . . . had I been wrong about them too? And then I forgot about all that and was bumping and grinding, thrusting and parrying, thoroughly losing my head, pumping in and out, in and out, in and out—

"Slow down," she said in my ear, her hands tight on my hips, pushing up. "Don't let yourself get carried away."

"Easy enough for you to say," I replied, and she laughed, which changed everything, reminded me of who and where I was; for a while, I'd forgotten.

Slower now, I felt the length of me sliding in and out, in and out, each stroke a long caress, a loving gift, it seemed, until I began to tingle and grew so hard I thought my brain would burst as her cushy, soft walls tightened, gripped me, her thrusts more strenuous, tossing me up on a trapeze, until, in delirium, I lost my mind in a maelstrom of incomplete stray thoughts, as Martha lost it too, rocking and rolling, no longer restraining me, sighing a long *"Aaaaaaah"* just as I exploded in stars and fireworks, then spasmed again and once more, and again, in diminishing aftershocks, before running out of gas.

And then it was over, though energy still pulsed in my cock as I lay on top of her, trembling. Had I left her behind? Or was that the *aaaaaaah*?

She spread her hands on my back, said, as an offhand suggestion, "We can do it again in a while, if you like."

"Yes," I replied, a boy once more, and grateful again, that she'd said the right thing.

We might have talked then. But I was distracted and couldn't focus. And after a while I went into the other room for my cigarettes, where the scene out the window caught my attention, the bric-a-brac rooftops and buildings, the skyscrapers and bridges. Smoking, I sat down in the chair and took it all in, expecting the scene to somehow look different. I thought it should, now that this long anticipated thing had finally happened to me. But nothing had changed. That bothered me, and trying to join the scene, I told myself that I now belonged to it in a way I hadn't before. But still, it was what it was, which itself became the basis for the change I wanted to see. In an instant I became jaded, assumed an attitude as I watched the cigarette smoke scatter.

With cocky indifference I tamped out the cigarette and, a worker at the end of a coffee break, went back to finish the job.

But when I pushed the curtain aside, Martha was snoring lightly, asleep.

Nor did anything change between us afterward. Or maybe it was just me, reverting to where I'd been when I walked in and found dinner on the table. It bothered me that I found Martha clunky and uncool after what we'd shared, but my sense of superiority persisted, and was reinforced whenever I got high and she didn't. I even found myself wishing that she'd move out, which also bothered me, put me in league with Gerry Gornish, the pornographer. Like him, I'd asked her to come, and now I had no use for her anymore.

We didn't sleep together again, and in fact didn't even see that much of each other. Martha made her bed in the front room and was gone when I woke up in the afternoon; looking for work, she told me. I'd see her there when I came in at night, usually asleep, or reading by the light of a lamp she'd set on the floor; Coomaraswami, I realized, examining the small pile of books beside the mattress one afternoon, along with several by modern authors I didn't know. Nor did she make dinner for me again. But she must have cooked for herself, since the stuff in the refrigerator dwindled until the shelves were almost as barren as before she'd arrived. And she washed her dishes, stacking them in the drainer next to the sink, which was always spotless.

One day, she told me she'd found a job and would be renting her own place soon.

"You can stay as long as you like," I told her.

She regarded me without expression for several seconds, the thick lenses, as always, giving her an ingenuous look. But I knew her better now. She was merely observing me. "Thank you, but no," she said, pursing her lips.

I was abashed that she'd seen through my insincere offer, but also impressed. There was something dignified about Martha, sleeping on her mattress on the floor without complaint, keeping her own hours, cooking her own food, reading her books, leaving the apartment and going to work . . . I might even have envied her, hewing, as she did, to her own purpose, with no encouragement or support from me.

We were all but strangers, living separate lives. So it came as a surprise to her, a few days before she was to move out, when I told her I had tickets to a rock concert and asked if she wanted to go. "To, y'know, sort of say goodbye . . ."

She was sitting in the window seat, an open book in her lap. "How great!" she said, lighting up, all rosy cheeks and wide eyes, having just gotten off the plane, when everything new elicited an exclamation. "I've never been to one before!"

But the night of the concert, I knew right away that I'd made a mistake.

She'd pinned her hair up in a coil atop her head, accentuating the fullness of her face, and put on a metallic-looking dress that might have once been fashionable, or maybe still was, somewhere. "What do you think?" she said, pirouetting.

"You look nice," I replied.

And then my suburban drug customer, a friend of a friend, showed up with the tickets and his entourage, and I cringed at the looks they gave her, though I'd felt the same way. The two guys were overly polite, condescending, and their dates, who had a cultivated hippie look, could barely contain their disdain. Clearly, Martha was an oddity.

They wanted to smoke DMT before we left for the concert, so I filled the pipe and we gathered around the trunk. Martha declined, setting her further apart, and as the pipe went around, she bustled in the kitchen in her shiny dress. We were already stoned when she brought a large bowl of fruit salad into the room, along with smaller bowls and spoons, and set it down on the trunk. No one knew what to say. We all just stared at the cut-up fruit.

"It's fresh," she said. "I made it myself. Help yourselves."

Again no one spoke, though speech would have been difficult even without the wholesome anomaly in that room pungent with ammonia.

Finally, I managed to say, "Not for me, Martha."

There were head shakes and grunts from the others.

The pipe went around again, and she receded to the periphery, outside our instant, close-knit network, and she remained there, apart, when we left the pad, zombies moving down the stairs and up the block, heading for the Fillmore, a half-dozen blocks away.

The side streets were never well lit, but with our capillaries engorged, they were a bright stage setting, the street lamps perfectly aligned on each block, spotlights for a Broadway play with song and dance routines on the mock-up sidewalk, leaps and twirls up convincingly constructed stoops and around garbage cans charmingly clustered by the curb. We moved through this scenery with heavy heads and unintentional deliberation, the act of walking momentous, one step following another. Closer to the theater, others appeared, walking too, but curiously without weight, inflated balloons bobbing along, loosely moored to the sidewalk; like Martha, who drifted beside me, a loose buoy, hardly there at all.

At our approach, the crowd gathered in front parted, in reflexive deference to our stoned monumentality; heads turning, eyes lingering, as we entered the vestibule, presented our certifications of privilege, and moved on through a barrier of glass doors and into a splendid lobby. It had been dilapidated when I'd last been there, and seemingly renovated since, the ornate friezes and flourishes a throwback in time. Klatches of people were scattered about, multiplied in the polished mirrors of the grand salon. They lingered on the red carpet, beneath dazzling chandeliers suspended from the high ceiling, leaned against the mirror walls, were propped up on banisters, inhabited the space with stylish insouciance, wisps of cigarette smoke rising here and there. Their languid indifference was amusing. A transparent pretense. For how could anyone be jaded in such awesome surroundings?

The two couples had tickets down below, so Martha I continued alone up the opulent staircase toward the highest level; an exaltation, it seemed, though the uppermost seats were the cheapest. Then inside the auditorium, we groped toward our seats, the darkened theater illuminated from the light on stage far below, where a band was playing.

It was wild up there, in the balcony. An electric bass throbbed, vibrating the walls, and a squealing guitar sent ripples through the collective nervous system of the amorphous crowd, limbs and heads responding to the booms and shrieks, the bass, treble, and percussion that swept up from below in a surf of energy that washed over the rows, rippling the human stalks, hitting the rear wall and ricocheting back down, where it met the next wave, the collision a roiling surf that eddied, frothed, agitated the contact high stew of bodies crammed between sloping walls.

Beside me, Martha gripped her armrest tightly.

Then a beam of light thrown from a projector high up behind us filled a screen on stage, above the minuscule band, a whirling pattern of changing color that was thrown back at the crowd-creature, whose eyes were focused on the midpoint of a relentless, hypnotic, centrifugal spinning wheel as mammoth amplifiers saturated the place with sound.

Martha sat at stiff attention.

"It's just a rock concert," I managed to say, and she nodded stiffly, her face a frozen mask as she stared bug-eyed at the whirling wheel.

But I sensed the raw power of the mindless crowd, and understood her terror. One could drown in it, which no doubt was the point.

"Let's leave," I said.

She looked at me with surprise. "Leave . . . ?"

"Let's get out of here."

She was relieved, but said, "Are you sure?"

"Yeah," I replied, and led her down the row, up the crowded aisle, down the curved staircase, outside.

We walked awhile without speaking. I couldn't have said much anyway, my body drifting along beneath my head; the two of us a mismatched couple, Martha earthbound, walking a straight line, eyes fixed on the sidewalk.

Then she said, "I'm sorry . . . I ruined everything."

"Nothing's ruined," I replied.

"You left because you knew I wanted to, didn't you?"

"It doesn't matter," I said.

"Well, I think you're very sweet for doing it anyway."

She was walking faster than me. "Slow down," I said, and she fell back, consciously matching her pace to my floating amble.

"Do you remember when I told you I can be anything I want?" she asked. "The night we took acid?"

"Uh-huh," I said, vaguely recalling something of the sort.

"I was feeling pretty good, of course . . . No, I was feeling great! I could see that we don't have to be confined to what we know, that there's a world of possibilities if we just open our eyes . . . Patrick was right about that."

"Uh-huh." She was excited, and walking faster again. She couldn't help herself. And I was having a hard time keeping up with her words too, what with one phrase leading to another and then somewhere else.

"Tonight I realized—*again*," she said, chastising herself, "that I can't be *anything*. I mean, it would be nice to think so. But there are some things that don't suit me . . . personally, I mean. That whoever it is that I *am*—"

"Slow down," I said.

"Oh, sorry," and she fell back again. "Are you still high?"

" . . . Very."

She considered this a moment, while deliberately keeping pace with me. "I was afraid," she said. "That's why I wanted to leave. The music was so loud, and that swirling target, and the people, so excited . . . out of their minds, you might say . . . It made me realize that I *can't* be anything I want, that there are things I'd rather not do . . . that I just don't like."

We stopped at a corner to wait for the light, and I laughed. Martha looked at me curiously, her head tilted. "It's funny," I said. "The way you put it . . . so . . . adamantly."

The light changed and we resumed walking, crossing the street.

"You think that's okay, then?" she asked.

"Of course . . . Why wouldn't it be?"

"Because I know what it means to make excuses . . . to find reasons not to do things, to explain away a . . . greater fear."

I momentarily grasped her meaning, then lost it. For a moment I'd known exactly what she was talking about. "Greater fear?" I repeated.

"Yes. I think a person can sincerely dislike something, and it doesn't have to mean they're just afraid of experiencing it. I mean, there are little fears— fears about little things . . . what we call 'worries,' or 'troubles'—and they don't mean much, when you really think about it. They come and go, and they always will. If we don't dote on them, they're harmless . . . They don't tell us anything significant about who we are . . . And then there are the big fears, what I call the greater fears, and that's a different story altogether . . ."

"Yes," I said, trying to hold on to her words long enough to respond. "But we always know what's true. It's there, in the front of your mind, before it slips away . . ."

"Yes, I know what you mean," she said, excited. "We do know the truth, if only for a moment, and then we wonder if it really *was* the truth, and maybe we want to convince ourselves that it wasn't . . . to make excuses, to overlook it and go on without having to act on it . . . The trick then—though of course it's much more than a trick—it might be the most important thing we ever do—is to just listen to ourselves . . . to our truer selves."

I'd followed most of what she'd said, gotten lost, but reconnected at the satisfying conclusion, but could only say, "Yes."

We'd stopped at another light, and for some reason it occurred to me I'd remember that corner when Martha was gone. She was honest, considerate, *real.*

What I didn't know, of course, was how much I'd miss that sense of reality in the difficult days to come.

Trouble Walks in the Door . . .

I hadn't thought about him in weeks, maybe months, and now here he was, standing in the hall, smiling at me as if no time had passed at all. Our final meeting came to mind, our friendship abruptly cut short by an argument over the layout of a news page. He had been the managing editor, and I was in charge of the sports page.

I have a good memory, ruminate over details from years ago that could have occurred just the other day. But the grudges and resentments almost always evaporate out of their context, or at least fade, as they did now, seeing my old friend in the flesh, taking in the familiar spatulate nose and brillo-curled brown hair.

His broad smile faltered as I took him in, the breakup perhaps occurring to him too, before I absolved him, saying, merely, "Michael."

He reacted as though it was a hearty welcome, thrusting a hand at me and shaking, his smile restored, the two of us long-lost buddies reunited. It rekindled a time when we indeed had been pals, and I responded with a firm handshake, collaborating in his enthusiasm.

It was a warm day, yet Michael wore a tweed sport jacket, a sheen of sweat on his broad forehead as I led him into the front room and he sat down on the couch.

I took the chair by the window, which was open to catch a nonexistent breeze. "You must be hot," I said. "Why don't you take off your coat?"

A fleeting, troubled look crossed his face, and like a detective encountering an old, unresolved case, I wondered, not for the first time, what made Michael tick. It had been his custom, for instance, to take the floor and sing bawdy drinking songs, old Irish or Welsh ditties, when the newspaper gang went to McSorley's after putting the paper to bed; which seemed odd, out of character, since Michael never said anything licentious about women, nor did he ever curse, when he and I were alone. And it occurred to me, as it had before, that his off-color songs and Jewish jokes were a camouflage, a front he put on to prove he was a regular guy.

All this came back to me because of his reluctance to take off the sport jacket, which he wore like civilization itself, holding chaos at bay. But it was also civilized to be a proper guest, and I'd suggested that he take it off, so overcoming his reluctance, he did, carefully folding the tweed coat lengthwise and setting it down on the couch next to him.

In his short-sleeve oxford, Michael appeared shrunken, deflated, no longer the cheerful fellow who'd so strenuously pumped my hand at the door.

I noticed too that he showed no curiosity in my apartment or in the panoramic view of the city out the window, though he'd been a voracious collector of information in college. We'd had that in common, the two of us recalling old baseball teams and players, old-time facts and oddities, and his own specialties—defunct newspapers and their renowned columnists, old comics and comic strips, crime stories about forgery, fraud, and embezzlement. But on second thought, his lack of curiosity now only clarified what we'd chosen to notice then, when we trafficked in facts of a certain sort, remnants of the past, old news, rather than the details of our immediate lives.

The toilet flushed, interrupting thought, and I explained, "It flushes by itself."

He looked at me without comprehension.

"The toilet," I said. "It flushes by itself."

He still had no idea what I was talking about, and then he did, trolling back to the sound, and nodded, incurious, as if it were an ordinary thing. Or perhaps still didn't know what I meant and was just being polite.

"So," I said, moving on, "how've you been?"

A casual question, in response to which he rocked forward, placing his forearms on his thighs, a movement that launched a flood of words that threw me back in my chair, a rush of details about where he'd lived, traveled, and worked, from Queens to Chicago to Culver City, California, somewhere near L.A. He lost me out there, in a neighborhood of bungalows and bougainvillea, and I tuned in again as he began to wind down, with criticisms of the laid-back West Coast lifestyle, which hadn't suited him at all. But then he shifted eras and picked up steam again, throwing up the old college newspaper gang, my old girlfriend, whom he knew had moved to England; the pompous editor-in-chief toward whom he still held a grudge; the reporter, the ad guy, and the disgruntled teacher Mark Greenbaum had invited to my pad . . .

"It was Mark who told me where you live," he said, then shifted gears again, within our mutual past, telling stories, tales of those grand old days, while steering clear of the argument that ended things between us, when he was managing editor and I was in charge of the sports page. Obviously, he wanted me to think well of him. But why? What did he want from me?

And then he stopped altogether, and I paid closer attention. He sat on the edge of the couch, regarding me with the expectant look I'd seen earlier.

"That's why I came here," he said. "I want to try the drugs I've heard so much about."

I didn't know what to say, backtracked to California and the miserable, isolated existence he'd conveyed, to make sense of it.

"Mark told me all about it," he said. "And I can see for myself how much you've changed . . . Your speech, so sparing, only the important things communicated . . . and the way you move, so economically, like the people I saw in the park on my way here, who glide as if in a state of grace, hardly touching the ground . . ."

It was a bit much, but it penetrated my reserve, flattering me, opening a trapdoor through which I fell.

"Okay, Michael," I said. "I'll turn you on."

The words were hardly out when the sheen of perspiration on his forehead again made an impression on me, and alarm bells went off. He dabbed his brow with a white handkerchief, and the proper, gentlemanly gesture confirmed my intuition: that turning him on would be a mistake. But I'm not one to easily admit to a mistake. And through the din of alarm bells I heard myself saying, "Okay, then. Come back Friday night."

When he left, I watched from the window as Michael emerged from the building, the jacket folded over an arm. Heading toward the corner, he passed an open fire hydrant gushing water into the street. Barefoot children were splashing in the curbside current. Up the block, four men were playing dominoes around a sidewalk card table, and a half-dozen others lingered around it in skivvies, drinking out of paper-bagged bottles, fanning themselves, trying to stay cool. Michael walked with head down beneath the lattice of fire escapes, flower pots, people leaning out of open windows, oblivious to the street scene in which he was an unknowing part.

Maybe he was right, I thought later, intent on countering intuition. Maybe if I turned him on, the universe would open up to him as it had for me with that first acid trip. And then, digging deeper into the hole I'd made, I relived that great awakening and vicariously anticipated Michael's upcoming initiation, as if, through him, it would happen to me again.

Only it didn't turn out that way.

When the blizzard of energy abated, the atmosphere was thick and airless, the candle's aura a forlorn beacon of light in the dead room. Those of us gathered around it were now capable of speech, but no one said anything.

Michael stared bleakly at the flame, his face a grim map of mortality. He looked at me from his spot on the couch and in a bleak voice said, "Is this all there is?"

Is this all there is?

The question captured the sense of things, yet nevertheless stunned me. A mechanical universe without an animating spirit. I should have led him to the door, with its hinges, and shown him out. Instead I replied, apologetically, "There are nights like this," doing the inexcusable—excusing reality.

Is this all there is?

It bugged me. And so, following that moribund night, and with the presumptuousness of a spokesman for the universe, I made it my mission to show Michael that life was more, much more, than the nuts and bolts that explained the swinging hinges.

The next time he took acid it was just the two of us, and when the rush ended and we were back in our bodies, I didn't give him a moment to think, to interpret what he might be seeing and come to his own conclusions. Before he could say a word, I began to talk, spouting grand ideas, witty observations, whatever popped into my head. I could be persuasive, and bent on overwhelming whatever gloomy outlook Michael might arrive at without my interlocution, I mesmerized him with my eloquence, gave his mind no opportunity to drift, and in talking ad lib without letup, lost myself in a buzzing hive of my own creation. Michael disappeared to me as well. I barely took notice of him, sitting there. But my bladder was another matter, almost bursting as I strove to finish one point and begin another. When I could bear it no longer, I broke off and hurried to the water closet.

It was a piss that went on forever, and when I returned to the front room, he was gone.

I wondered where he went, and sitting at my perch, gazed out the window, smoking cigarettes. Dawn came and went before Michael finally returned, the fever I'd stoked with incessant talk having long since passed.

"Where'd you go?" I asked.

"Up to the roof," he replied, looking drawn and gray. He splayed open his small spiral notebook and solemnly handed it to me.

I read:

> *With numbèd tongue and fumbling hand*
> *With sorrow's grey ode and heart like stone*
> *With so little joy as*

It ended there.

I took a long, hard look at him then, the first I'd taken in hours. He sat on the couch, head bowed in a defeated posture. Clearly, all my blather had not kept him from himself. I had no idea what to do next.

"'With so little joy as' . . . what?" I asked. "Why didn't you finish it?"

"I couldn't think of anything joyless enough," he replied.

" . . . But why, Michael? I mean, why should you feel so sad?"

"Because I know what awful things I'm capable of."

"Well yeah, of course, we're all capable of awful things, but—"

"Up on the roof, I thought about the people I know, and those I knew— in college, in high school, when I was a boy . . . I thought about the things I've said and done . . . and the things I didn't do, when I could have . . . I thought about the world I created—"

"The world you created?"

He looked at me as if he'd forgotten I was there. "Yes."

"You mean, the influence you've had?"

He clasped his hands between his legs. "It's more than that . . ."

"What're you talking about?" I asked.

He looked up at me, his broad forehead creased with worry lines. "Their fate is in my hands," he said softly.

"Whose fate?" I asked, losing patience.

He gestured at the open window. "All of them . . . The people I knew, and those I know now . . . the people I see in the street, and those I don't see, behind drawn shades—"

"How can you know they're there if you don't see them?"

"Because I do," he replied simply.

"But if you can't see them—"

"If I think about them, they're there."

An icicle of fear skewered me. Then a curtain of guilt fell over me, for turning him on.

What had I done?

"I wish it weren't true," he said in a despairing tone. "But it is."

And suddenly I was furious. "Just because you think something doesn't make it so!" I snapped.

He looked at the floor and shook his head sadly. "If I think something like . . . like . . . I can't say it."

"Don't bother saying it," I said, "just *think* it! According to you, that should be enough, right? Like, for instance, if you thought me dead—"

"Don't say that!" he shouted. "Don't even think it!"

*   *   *

In college, the night before the paper came out, we'd all go to the print shop in lower Manhattan to correct galleys. Often, I went home with Michael afterward, because my parents' place was another hour away. He lived in an apartment in Jackson Heights with his mother, and when we got off the subway at one or two in the morning, we'd take long, rambling walks through the empty residential streets and talk about the Brooklyn Dodgers, A.J. Leibling, and other arcane trivia. Now, Michael took long walks by himself and returned with a different kind of trivia, which he obviously considered meaningful: a comb with broken teeth, an old shoe without laces, a doll with severed limbs, a scrap of tabloid newspaper, an empty pack of latakia, eyeglasses, buttons, pens and pencils, a conk, a yo-yo without string, a cigarette lighter that didn't work, a spool of thread . . . And he brought back descriptions of bums, sleeping in doorways, lying on subway gratings, begging on street corners, and presented these findings to me along with the rest, as a puzzle, as if they'd be comprehensible if only we could put the pieces together, connect objects and people; an amputated finger and a missing button, a remark overheard while waiting for a light to change, a gesture glimpsed or maybe imagined.

He assumed I would know what this disparate catalogue of found objects meant, since I was his guide, after all, having made it my mission to convince him that life has purpose. But I was at a loss. Jokingly, I told him he was looking through the wrong end of a telescope, but he had no sense of humor about his findings, or about anything, for that matter, and I'd stumble around concocting answers, none of which satisfied him. And after a while he became more demanding, and then disdainful.

"He asked for thirty cents!" he repeated when I shrugged. "Now, do you understand?"

"Well," I said, trying to be reasonable, "maybe the bum wanted a cup of coffee and a doughnut. That would add up."

"No! He could have asked for a quarter. A single coin. That would have been logical. But instead he asked for *thirty* cents!"

"Okay, I give up. What do you think it meant?"

"*Thirty pieces of gold!*"

"Oh . . . I see. You felt betrayed."

"No, no! I wasn't *that* one. I was the *other* one!"

"The other one? Oh . . . yeah." Yeah what? What the fuck were we talking about?

He sat down on the couch and in a barely audible voice said, *"He knew."*

I regarded him without comprehension. "Knew what?"

He bolted from the couch, headed for the door.

I followed him, called after him in the hallway. "Knew what, Michael?"

He didn't answer.

I moved to the stairwell and shouted down as he descended, "What did he know?"

He ignored me.

Michael didn't return for a few days, and I assumed he was staying with a guy he'd met in the park, a concentration camp survivor he'd once introduced me to. Or he might have gone to Queens to visit his mother. Meanwhile, I went to the local library, browsed around and checked out a book, *Discontents of the Superego.* It wasn't easy to read, but I wrestled with the convoluted language and managed to slog through two-thirds of it by the time he walked in again.

He paced back and forth in the kitchen, kneading his hands together, waiting for me to ask him what was wrong. From my window perch, I watched him pace, waited for him to acknowledge me before speaking, since I had something important to tell him, and I knew such things should be elicited, not just tossed out. But his nervousness got to me, and I spoke first, saying, "You seem upset, Michael. What's bothering you?"

Indeed, he'd been waiting on me. He entered the front room, sat down on the couch and said, "I was returning from Jackson Heights, and since it was such a beautiful day, I decided to get off at Union Square and walk . . . I came down Fifteenth Street, and the park there looked so pleasant, I walked in to sit awhile . . ."

"Stuyvesant Park," I said. "I know it. It's near my old high school."

He went on as though I hadn't said anything, absently picking at the fraying material on the armrest. "As soon as I entered, I knew someone was watching me, so I walked around the oval to the north side, near the old church, to get away from him . . . but I could feel his eyes on me, and when I sat down, I saw him there, at the other end, staring."

I said, "Who?"

He continued to pick at the armrest. "I don't know. but he resembled *someone* . . . and he thought he knew me, I could see it . . . And then he got up and walked in my direction. I shut my eyes and willed him to disappear, but when I opened them, he was still coming toward me. I looked away, and he sat down, on the same bench . . ." Michael shuddered, looked up at me. "He was grinning, his pebble teeth stained and discolored . . . and there was something . . . depraved about him."

"Depraved?"

"I averted my eyes again," he went on, yanking at the loose strands, "but I could still see him. He had a stubble beard and stringy hair that hadn't been washed in a while . . . And then he began to speak to me—hobo gibberish. I didn't understand it, but I knew he was accusing me of something."

"How did you know that?"

"And then he leaned toward me. I could smell the alcohol on his breath. And he touched me—poked my shoulder with a finger, like this . . ." Michael speared his index finger at me. "And he said something . . . *unclean.* It took me by surprise, and for a moment I wasn't sure he actually said what I thought I heard . . ."

"What did he say?" I asked.

"It was hard to decipher. He said it very fast . . ."

"What do you think he said?"

"It sounded like 'fuckyamotha.'"

"Fuck your mother?"

He recoiled from the words. "That's what I thought he said."

I sat back. "Okay, listen, Michael—"

"Why did he say it to *me?*" he asked plaintively. "There were other people in the park, but he ignored them. He came to *me,* sat down next to *me,* spoke only to *me!*"

"Listen, Michael," I said quickly, before he could continue. "It's not what he said that matters, but your reaction to it. What you think about it. I've been giving this some thought—"

"But what he said! What I told you I thought he said!"

"Fuck your mother?"

He winced again, and I knew I'd been deliberately cruel, repeating the phrase, enunciating it clearly, perhaps because he'd interrupted me, which pissed me off.

"Yes . . . that."

I said, "I think it's significant that you're always distressed about these bums you come across. They get under your skin. You always take them so personally."

He looked at me coldly, without expression.

"I mean, for some reason, you choose to notice them, and often it's when you find something that's broken or torn or thrown away or ruined."

He stood up and walked into the kitchen.

"I think it has something to do with your father," I said as he stood there with his back to me. The father he hardly remembered and had told me about during one of our long college walks, who died when he was a child.

"You don't know what you're talking about," he said scornfully.

"Just listen—"

"I've heard enough," he said, still not turning around. "I'm through listening to you." And he flicked a hand behind him, swatting a fly away.

Infuriated, I bolted from my chair and rushed at him. I don't know what I had in mind, maybe to punch the back of his head, or barrel into him and kick him when he was down. Whatever I'd intended, at the last moment I veered aside, rushed past him and out of the apartment.

I hit the street seething, that I'd been brushed aside so arrogantly. And after reading nearly a whole book because of him! I walked for a while, without paying attention to where I was going, eventually found myself at the Odessa, went in and ordered meat and potatoes, and the comfort of that old habit helped restore me. It was dark when I finished, and I headed to one of the coffeehouses, thinking about Michael.

What did I owe him anyway? I'd done what I could. If he didn't want to listen, why should I put up with him?

I resolved to kick him out. After all, I'd never actually invited him to move in. And how could I hold myself responsible for the direction in which he'd gone? The drug had done that. I didn't owe him a thing.

But when I returned that night, he was curled up on the couch, looking harmless, as everyone does while asleep. I didn't wake him. And the next day I was in a different frame of mind altogether.

. . . and Seeps into My Psyche

I woke up, as it's said, and lay flat on my back, staring up at the ceiling. If not for the sticky humidity, I might have laid there longer. I pulled on the tattered pants that were now several sizes too large, tied the clothesline belt that held them up, shrugged into a faded cotton shirt. Feet flapping inside loose sandals, I walked to the front room and flopped into the throne chair by the open window, unrefreshed by sleep and fatigued by the strenuousness of getting dressed, and gazed out at the panoramic scene, the quilt of tenement rooftops, the bigger buildings beyond, the river and bridges, the pollution haloing the horizon.

Eventually losing interest, I picked up the yellowing *New York Times* on the floor. It had been there since Martha left; the same issue she'd plunked down next to my place setting the last time I ate in the apartment. The lines came in and out of focus as I made my way down the columns, but for some reason I kept at it, perhaps in the belief that reading had intrinsic value, proved that I wasn't merely wasting time. Or it might have been the reputation of the *Times* itself, the so-called newspaper of record; a grown-up perspective on life, impeccably formulated by implicit grown-up priorities, which accounted for its unquestioned, mature approach to domestic and foreign affairs, the arts, and even leisure, tourism and travel, education, fashion, finance, sport, food— in fact everything we think and do. And I bought into the con as I labored to read the simple sentences, skimming the wavering lines, thus belonging to a respectable club, one that would obscure the more potent exigencies of existence, with its unrelieved tedium, the effort producing a dull, throbbing ache behind my eyes.

When Michael walked in, I looked up, over the edge of the open pages. He'd brought someone with him, which had become his habit. Loath to meet another of the strays he found in the park, I ducked down behind the paper. Ben, the Holocaust survivor with whom Michael seemed to have an affinity, had unnerved me, with his haunted look. And more recently, the French diplomat to the United Nations who spoke at length about Pascal and a spiritual epiphany he'd had while playing Palestrina's *Missa Brevis* on a church organ, but upon looking around, found the dishabille setting of my pad too much for him and left before I'd have had to flee myself. This time it was a woman, who lingered in the kitchen as Michael entered the front room and sat down on the couch.

Stubbornly, I continued to skim the lines of print, none of it adhering, until, abruptly tiring of the fiction that I was actually reading, I lowered the paper and looked at him.

At once, he leaned forward and began telling me about his latest guest, as if she weren't there, a few feet away. Her name, he said, was Lulu, and the reason he'd brought her . . . well, it was a long story . . .

He'd seen her in the park. She'd just that morning gotten in from California, though she was actually from Kansas City and had for a while lived not far from Culver City—that miserable place where he'd done time—before she went to Haight-Ashbury . . .

The paper lay on my lap, and I glanced at it as he rambled on, a feeble escape that only diverted my attention enough to blur his words.

"An act of generosity," I heard him say, tuning in again, "that would be a mitzvah." A good deed to erase a multitude of sins, a gift of his mitzvah to me, or something to that effect.

I nodded and made sounds in my throat so he would more quickly finish his stream of consciousness and I could get back to the news. And in fact he finally did shut up and leave me alone. Except, when he left the apartment, Lulu remained behind, in the kitchen, checking her appearance in the angled, distorting mirror over the bathtub and poking at her short, frizzy hair. He'd dumped her there, with me.

I raised the *Times* and went at it again, hiding behind the massive pages, hoping that when I looked up again, she'd be gone. My eyes grazed down the column, as if the meaning of the words might reveal themselves without effort, and though the going was tough enough without additional obstacles, I surreptitiously eyed Lulu over the edge, watched her finger her hair and tug the short ends toward her ears. When she stopped fidgeting and entered the room, I dove back down, pretended not to notice as she sat on the couch, or to hear her soft, choking sounds moments later. But they only got louder, and I finally put the paper down and looked squarely at her.

She had pouty lips and big brown eyes. They glistened, and as I watched, a tear slid down her cheek and she made another strangled sound.

It was a sob. You read so much about them, but I couldn't recall actually hearing one before. Then tears were sliding down both cheeks, and she covered her face with her hands and sobbed into them.

I didn't know what to do. Something, of course, was expected. We're trained to respond; it's a part of upbringing. And out of that I heard myself say, "C'mon, now. Don't cry. What could be so terrible?" in a soothing tone that sounded, to my surprise, sincere.

She stopped crying then and looked up at me, hopeful, waiting for me to say more, which encouraged me to continue.

"Maybe you'd like a cup of tea . . . ?" Michael was big on tea, and I'd gotten into it too, because it seemed so civilized.

"Yes," she said. "That would be good."

So I put the paper aside, went into the kitchen, put a pot of water on to boil, returned to my chair and, to keep her mind off her troubles, whatever they were—I didn't want to know—asked her about Haight-Ashbury.

The question cheered her up. It was great, she said. There was no place like it. I'd heard that before, and already believed it: a perfect place out there, in San Francisco; a hippie heaven on earth.

The water was boiling, so I got up, poured it into cups, dunked the teabags, added honey, and brought the result back with me, solicitously handing Lulu a cup. She took a sip, said, "It's too hot," and put it down on the trunk.

"Listen," I said, thinking strategically, "you must be tired, after all that traveling. Why don't you take a nap? When you wake up, you'll feel better."

Her head was tilted up at me, her big eyes trusting. "Okay," she said.

I took her hand and led her to the bedroom. It was drippingly humid in the small cell behind the curtain, but when she lay down, I covered her with a sheet anyway—a comforting gesture—and returned to the front room and my newspaper.

Yet I'd hardly resumed wrestling with a story I'd either read already or hadn't when Lulu pushed the curtain aside and reappeared. She couldn't sleep, she said, because it was too hot. Sitting back down on the couch, she sipped her tea and said it was cold, as if that was my fault. I turned to the open window and looked out. It wasn't this hot in San Francisco, she said. She'd heard that New York was awful in the summer but hadn't believed it until now. It was cooler in San Francisco. In fact, sometimes it was actually chilly, what with the fog and the breezes. She got up and went into the kitchen. Her hair was frizzy from the humidity, she said, gazing up at the distorting mirror. And it was too short. She'd gotten it cut because she was looking for a job, but the stylist had been a butcher. The short cut accentuated her cheeks, didn't it? Made them appear too full.

I didn't respond.

"*Well*, what do you think?" she demanded, looking at me.

"It looks okay to me."

"It doesn't make me look like a chipmunk?"

"Don't worry about it," I said. "It'll grow back."

"But what do you *think*?"

"What difference does it make what I think?" I snapped. "You don't even know me!"

Her mouth dropped open and her lips quivered. My fault. I was a bad person.

"I'll warm up your tea," I said, and got up to boil more water.

Morning was a rash of people heading to work on the street below with a briskness that belied their sorry predicament. Then the banging and hacking began, repairs to dilapidated apartments, faulty plumbing, rutted streets; putting a smoother face on the rotting edifice. Then noon, with its whistles and bells, and another lull, shattered by radios blasting out of open windows, an especially annoying human stupidity, blotting rumination. Then more blessed quiet, to be surreptitiously undercut by the imbecilic restlessness of twilight, which slid into nighttime darkness and the hoodwink bait and lure of expectation.

There seemed no point to leaving the pad, except to avoid whoever else might be there. In my own rooms, at least I could alleviate boredom with grass or hashish, or the latest something Emery had synthesized. Sitting by the open window, I took in the guignol from my superior perch as Michael and Lulu came and went. I took distant notice of them, might well have emitted a churlish vibe that kept them away.

I was sitting there one evening, in my usual spot, when Lulu entered and went about her business as if I were invisible. I'd by then attained that enviable state. She wore her waitress uniform, sat down a few feet away on the couch and peeled off her stockings. The sight of her bare, creamy flesh caught my notice, engaged me as nothing else had in a while, and when she leaned over the steamer trunk to roll a joint, her cleavage, nearly falling out of a halter top, further stirred me. She licked the paper, sealing the deal; I was at full attention. Looking up, she saw me gawking and grinned.

"Michael won't be back tonight," she said. "He's visiting his mother."

Her confidential tone was an invitation, and I said the first thing that came to mind: "You want to take acid?" It was what I did best, after all.

"Sure," she replied.

So we swallowed the pills, and, while awaiting the rush, finding myself in a script I hadn't composed and didn't control, I moved to the couch to share the joint she'd rolled. My head was spinning when she rested her head on my shoulder.

Who was she? All I knew were the legs and breasts that had brought me to that spot.

Then the drug hit, and losing my mind in the paisley swirl, trembling in her proximity, took her hand and led her to the curtained room, because it seemed that's what she expected, or what I expected of myself; it wasn't clear. In confusion, I watched her slip out of her clothes. Like a magic trick, they fell to the floor, and there she was, luminescent in the dark, her skin astonishing alabaster. A goddess, lifting her arms toward me as she lay on the mattress, beckoning, as I stood rooted, earthbound, at a loss. Her clothes had somehow fallen off, and mine were plastered to my body, permanently there, impossible to remove.

Then her hands were at the rope holding up my pants, deftly untying the knot, and as she fell back on the bed again and my clothes fell away, I stood there, naked, perplexed. How to get from where I stood to where she lay? I couldn't just jump; I might hurt her.

Taking my hand, she pulled me forward, to tumble down as her thighs parted, blossoming, a welcoming flower as I slipped into her, liquid sensation shooting to my brain, warm and encompassing. And then she was moving beneath me, calling forth my own reflexive response.

But thought wasn't through with me yet. It rarely ever is.

The room was soon a cauldron of swirling energy, inflections of color, a gale to which I refused to surrender, struggling to locate myself in the hurricane. But I could hardly keep up with my thoughts. They billowed into clouds and evaporated just as quickly, yet somehow added to the smoky fog while, down below, miles away, my shaft hardened—to solid rock, it seemed—eliciting a quickening excitement, heavy breathing, moaning . . . *Lulu,* I thought, but the name meant nothing. Who was Lulu? It was a puzzle, softening me, delaying satisfaction, as her spasms came and went and I hardened and softened, moving in and out, in and out, a piston pumping in a cylinder . . .

It went on and on, my mind spewing half thoughts as I pumped. Who was I? Who was she? What was I doing here? And always, when it seemed I'd finally find release, the moans beneath me louder, her insides and my numb cock welded together, liquid suction burbling with each stroke, thighs lathered, sheets soaked, I'd soften again, lose the promise. The numbness had now spread from my prick to the rest of my body, consuming everything but the brain and its ragged thoughts, which prohibited release from this interminable fuck . . .

After a while I noticed that the room was brighter. Could it be? We'd gone all night? Yes, light filtered in, suffused the room. And then, abruptly, I stopped, gave up on still another teasing possibility.

It was hard to pull out, I was glued in so tight. My cock emerged with a sucking sound, a flat champagne pop for a false celebration, and I rolled off her and onto my back, to stare at the cracked ceiling, tingling all over, thoughts still raging, fighting each other, one moment declaring me a failure, the next a great lover.

She'd never been fucked like this before.

But Lulu appeared neither overwhelmed nor disappointed. Composed, she sat up and swiveled from the bed to the open window, which faced an air shaft, to gaze out at the walls of the adjacent building, a clothesline, other windows. I lit a cigarette, hands trembling with pent-up frustration, as she leaned out, her breasts resting on the ledge, her profile voluptuously soft at the edges. A Renoir, I thought, and captioned it *Morning scene*, simulating a lyric, contented mood I didn't feel.

She began to hum softly then, which touched me, as nothing else had to that point, then turned to me and said, "I want you to meet someone."

"What? Now?"

"Yes," she said.

We didn't go far; up the block and around the corner, to the third or fourth floor of a building on Avenue C. Lulu knocked, and seconds later a young guy opened the door. He was a few years older than me, and to my surprise, wore a suit and tie.

"What brings you here this early, Lulu?" he said, smiling at her, nodding at me, opening the door wider, inviting us in. "Another minute and you'd have missed me."

Clearly, he was dressed for work, and I smelled coffee, which wafted me back to another time and place, not at all unpleasant. Waking up in the morning, coffee brewing, the measured possibilities of a new day. And in my impressionable state, the affable character who led us inside personified that reality, wore his clothes not like a uniform but lightly, a fact of circumstance, conveyed a sense of self-containment that trumped my usual disdain for those who wore a suit.

"Frank," he said when we were in the kitchen, offering his hand.

"Peter," I replied, shaking, studying his face, seeking an answer there, though I hadn't formulated a question, seeing wide-open eyes and a genuine smile.

"Play us a tune, Frank," Lulu said.

He pulled up his suit-coat sleeve and checked his wristwatch. "I've got a minute, if I play fast," he said, grinning, and brought his coffee cup to the upright piano in the adjoining room, which contained little else. He set it on top, sat down on the circular stool and began to play. It was a honky-tonk tune, his suit coat flaring out and back as he pounded the keys, enjoying himself.

Out the window, as he played, the tenement facades took on a ragtime appearance, implied rooms with similar scenes, coffee brewing and pianos rollicking as the day moved from one perfect moment to the next. It wasn't eye-popping, like the miracle of waves and particles seen simultaneously, but equally glorious in its own way, and unlike the psychedelic mysteries, had the beguiling quality of being ordinary while turning that concept on its head.

But all good things must end.

Frank stopped playing, the sound track ending, bringing me back to another earth. He pushed off the stool, took a final sip from his cup, and said he had to run.

Lulu and I followed him out, but he moved too quickly down the stairs for us to keep up and was out of sight by the time we reached the street. I asked Lulu what kind of job he had, and she said he'd come to New York to work in an advertising agency, that he made more money in a month than he could make doing anything else; enough to buy a house in Haight-Ashbury. I despised nothing more than advertising, but even so, couldn't dismiss the piano player. I'd met him, after all; he was more than a representative, he was a particular person, sane, grounded, admirable. Who was I to pass judgment?

The cliché was true: It's not what we do that matters, it's who we are.

Lulu linked her arm through mine and we walked back through the tenement streets in a dream, the perambulating couple on Grande Jette Isle, as she talked about Frank and his aspirations and the inkling of another type of life entranced me. I recalled that past when getting up was a staple complaint, and it didn't seem bad at all. Then, back in the apartment, she unknowingly took up the theme, describing her part-time job as a waitress: the camaraderie of the workers, the bastardliness of the boss, the coffee break, the little things that make a day tolerable. I tried to hang on to that good feeling, but my attention flagged, and eventually her voice became a drone, to which I absently nodded. Finally, she lay down and went to sleep and I returned to my usual chair, to stare out the window.

I'd just dozed off when Lulu woke me. She hadn't slept well, she said. It was too hot. Wasn't there a fan in the apartment?

"It would interfere with experiencing things as they are," I said.

She stared at me a moment, at a loss, and choosing to ignore my explanation, went on: "The air doesn't circulate at all in here. It just sits, hot and heavy. You really need a fan to at least stir it around." And then: "San Francisco never gets this hot. You even have to wear a jacket, because of the fog, and the breezes." And then, plaintively: "Isn't there someplace we can go to cool off?"

I had a few bills in my pocket, and gave her most of them while walking her to the door, urging her to go to the Charles, the air-conditioned movie house around the corner.

"But what about you?" she asked.

"I've got a few things to do," I replied, ushering her into the hallway. "Sit in the second or third row. I'll join you in a while."

She must have passed Michael on the way downstairs. He walked in just as I sat down in my chair. He was agitated, as usual, strenuously rubbing his palms together. Before he could say a word, I told him that our mutual college buddy, Mark Greenbaum, had decided to put out another of his mimeographed poetry magazines and needed material:

"The poem about despair you started would be perfect!"

"You think so?" he said.

"Yeah, absolutely," I replied, out of the chair again, turning him around, guiding him out to the hallway. "Maybe knowing it'll be published will inspire you to finish it."

Then he was gone too, and I propped my feet on the sill and smoked Emery's latest concoction; Pythagoric paraffin, he called it, because it eliminated depth perception, reducing the world to two dimensions. Down below, cartoon teenagers who appeared inches away pried open a fire hydrant, flooding the street, spraying passersby. After a lot of squawking and posturing, the cops chugged into the frame and shut the hydrant. They'd barely left when the teenagers leaped out of hallways and opened it again.

Then Lulu returned.

The theater wasn't air-conditioned, she said. And the film had subtitles: she didn't go to the movies to *read*. Why didn't we go to a real movie? If we were in San Francisco, where there were breezes and movies were movies, that's what we'd do!

Then Michael showed up again, declared, "Mark Greenbaum is a flea!" and flicked the air with the cavalier swatting gesture I'd come to know.

In an instant I was past them, downstairs, on the street. I didn't know where I was heading until I turned onto Mark's block. Perhaps, having brought him up, if only to get rid of Michael, I'd put the idea in my own head—of a time when Mark and I had been buddies, when politics was as much my religion as his, when we demonstrated together and met every afternoon to deride columns and editorials in the *Post*. I was looking forward to that—as if the past would be there for me whenever I wanted—and was disappointed when he wasn't in. But sticking to our old routine, I walked up to Saint Mark's Place and ate at the B&H. And afterward, I moved on to Astor Place to buy a hand-rolled cigar from the Cubans who labored behind the smudged plateglass window.

The apartment was empty when I returned. I sat down in my chair, propped my feet on the sill, smoked a pipeful of paraffin, then lit the cigar and blew smoke out the open window.

Street sounds filtered up from below. Cars in the distance honked with goofy urgency. This is the life, I thought, closing my eyes—to find Donald Duck throwing a tantrum on my lids.

Day at the Beach

It was a bright, sunny day when I saw Tom again. I spotted him on the avenue, looking gaunt and leathery, and even older than usual amidst the teenagers congregating on the Avenue A near the head shop. He was zigzagging through the throng, his eyes on the ground, dodging bodies as if they were inanimate obstacles. It was amusing, and in that spirit, I stationed myself in his head-down path and was waiting for him when he stopped short, staring at my feet.

"Tom," I said.

He looked up, recognized me, appeared relieved.

"How've you been?" I said.

Before he could answer, his attention was diverted by a bus moving toward the curb up the block, where people were waiting to get on. "Maybe I should get on it," he muttered, still gazing, rubbing his chin in what seemed a parody of thoughtfulness. But I could see he was serious when he turned back to me with a questioningly look.

"You going someplace?" I asked.

He grabbed my arm, startling me. "I gotta get away!" he said urgently. "There's a guy looking for me!"

"You're in trouble?"

"But I can't!" he said, his eyes darting back to the idling bus as people filed on. "I don't have any bread!"

"I think I can help you," I told him, and dug into my pocket for change, meanwhile asking, "Who's after you?"

"A guy Leo knows needs a place to crash. He's meeting me here and I don't know what to tell him!"

"Why don't you just tell him the truth?" I asked, handing him a quarter.

He turned and took a step toward the bus, then turned back. "The truth," he repeated, marveling at the meaning of the word.

"Yeah. Just tell him—"

"The truth!" he said again. "I'll tell him the truth!" He seemed delighted, then frowned. "Why didn't I think of that?" he said to himself.

I was wondering that too when the bus, pulling away from the curb, backfired. At the sharp sound, Tom bolted and took off.

"Hey!" I shouted, watching him run to the corner and disappear down Tenth Street.

A moment later he peered around the edge of the building, just his head showing. "C'mon, let's get outta here!" he said, beckoning with an arm, and then frowned, puzzled. No one else was fleeing, just him. Nothing untoward was happening on the sun-splashed street.

I'd deduced what had sent him running, said, "It was just the bus, backfiring," walking toward him, gesturing as it the bus pulled away. "No one's shooting at us."

Reassured, he eased out of his hiding place behind the building. "Oh," he said, abashed.

I'd seen all I needed to realize he was out of his mind.

"Listen," I said. "Are you hungry?"

He gave it a second of thought. "I'm starved."

"Well, why don't we go get something to eat?"

"Okay," he said, nodding at our momentous decision. "Let's do that." Then he turned doubtful again. "But I don't have any bread."

"That's all right," I told him. "I have enough for both of us."

At this solution to another apparent calamity, he fell into step beside me.

We crossed the street and I led him down the block to one of the Polish restaurants facing the park. Through the plate glass I could see that the counter stools were occupied but the tables in back were vacant. Tom, meanwhile, strode to the door, turned the knob and pushed, and when it didn't open, looked at me and said, "It's closed."

Reaching past him, I pulled instead of pushing, and led him inside, past the occupied counter and to the vacant tables in back.

We sat down at one of them, and a cook from up front brought menus. Tom opened his, stared at it for several seconds, quickly made up his mind, then closed it and looked around. There wasn't much to see: a calendar on the wall, empty tables and chairs, salt and pepper shakers and napkin holders; the utilitarian ambience of a typical Eastern European restaurant. But it kept him busy until the cook, acting as waiter, returned. Then, as I gave him my order, Tom flipped the menu open again and studied it, perhaps trying to find whatever he'd settled on before, or maybe changing his mind and looking for something else.

The waiter stood over him, waiting, and then said, "I'll come back."

"I'll have this!" Tom blurted, and the waiter turned back and bent over to read the entry. "This!" he said, pointing. And then, moving his finger: "No, this!"

"Okay," the stolid waiter said, reaching for the menu as Tom extended it with a flick of his wrist that sent it flying out of his hand and halfway across the room, where it landed on the floor. The waiter retrieved it without a word, turned back to look at Tom as he continued up front. Tom didn't notice. He was now studying the salt shaker, apparently unaware of the farcical scene he'd created. Out of sight, out of mind, I thought, watching him peer at the rice nodules inside, open the lid, sprinkle salt onto his palm and lick it.

I said to him, "So where've you been?"

He looked at me with surprise, perhaps having forgotten I was there.

"I haven't seen you since you were staying at Mark's pad."

A moment passed before he said, "Yes," nodding, recalling that distant time and place.

"So where've you been since then?" I asked again.

"Upstate," he replied. "Woodstock."

I nodded. "I know that area. I used to go to camp up there when I was a kid."

"I had a room," he said, looking off into the distance. "There was a mountain, with trees on the slopes . . . a forest descending to the back of the house . . ."

"Sounds great," I said.

A casual remark; but there was nothing casual about Tom's state of mind. He seized on it as if it were of grave significance, said, "Maybe I should've stayed," gripped his lips with two fingers, then plaintively asked himself, or me, or both of us, "Why did I come back?"

Then the food arrived and I went at it.

Tom, however, as gaunt as he was and as hungry as he must have been, looked at his sandwich warily, removed the top slice of bread and stared down at a slab of meat. He pursed his lips in disgust, slapped the bread back on top and pushed the plate away. Was he a vegetarian? Had he forgotten?

It left me wondering how he could even take care of himself. "You want to order something else instead?" I asked.

He looked at the sandwich, grimaced and shook his head.

"Listen," I said. "If you need a place to crash, you can stay at my pad."

He leaned back and rubbed his chin, pondering the offer.

"You've been there. There's a couch, mattresses . . . There were a few people crashing there, but usually only Michael's around. You met him, I think—"

"I'll do it!" he abruptly declared, and with the exuberance of having reached another difficult decision, slapped the tabletop with his palm, making me jump.

But as were leaving, he recalled that he was staying at Eighth Street, so he didn't need a place to crash. By now his forgetfulness was no surprise, though no less alarming, so I walked through the park with him, down the promenade to Avenue B, then down Eighth Street, so he wouldn't lose his way, and led him into the building and up to the second floor, where I knocked on the right door.

Several seconds passed before I heard Carl say, "Who is it?" through the door.

Tom shouted back, "It's me! Tommy!"

Then the door opened and he scooted past me, a child glad to be home, relieved to escape an overbearing parent.

Eighth Street had changed again, and again it was Leo's impetus that brought it about, after he visited and passed out samples of a new drug. As always, he left before the results were in: jar lids filled with cigarette butts and an open pizza box with congealed slices on the telephone spool table. Dishes moldering in the sink, the garbage pail overflowing, the toilet clogged and unusable. Nor had anyone thought to open a window to air out the lingering odor of old smoke. Or if they thought about it, they lacked the energy, and the will, to get up from where they sat in the front room, staring at the walls. The acclaimed new drug, dubbed STP, had established the absolute primacy of static existence, rendering all ambition futile.

Like Patrick, Carl came upon the ruins of high times and transformed the place. He began working on a loft bed in the walk-in closet where he'd pitched his sleeping bag. Busting up the spool table and using hammer and nails to build something engaged Leo's usual docile teenagers. And Rose put aside her psychedelic notebook to help Emily decorate the new interior, a meditation chamber beneath the loft. Then the construction crew moved on to the rest of the pad, and Gary emerged from his small back room, with its Rosicrucian texts scavenged from trash bins, to work on the mural Carl envisioned covering the walls.

As the meandering mountain streams, pagodas, and stupas took shape, brown rice, soy sauce, and green tea became the staple in the commune, and the curtain that had once been a divider, in an era when privacy seemed important, was taken down, the main room once more stretching from front to back.

The place now had the look of an ashram, with mattresses end-to-end, dormitory style, and plank tables with a candle and incense burner next to each. All that remained of the old configuration was a battered armchair, an artifact of history that sat at the end of the long room. It was an anomaly Patrick had rescued, and on which he most often sat, an anachronistic king on his throne, facing the wide aisle between two rows of mattresses.

And now Tom was there, claiming a portion of vacant wall, drawing and then painting his own version of reality. It was unlike anything else in the pad. Where the mural was a dreamscape of what-could-be, with its wandering mendicants and cross-legged gurus resembling hobbits, his piece consisted of globes in a geometric design: a molecule or an atom; or his retinal projections, rods and cones, emerald rays, bright yellow spheres; or perhaps celestial orbs out there in the universe somewhere, if one were only high enough to see them.

From his throne chair, Patrick monitored Tom's presence. The two had never gotten along, but to explain his animus, Patrick complained about paints and brushes Tom left behind when he was through them, to harden, lose their pliancy, become unusable. And he didn't like the way Tom wordlessly grubbed cigarettes with an imperious scissoring gesture, perversion of the peace sign, and then forgot about them, leaving one burning in one place while he scissor-cadged another smoke elsewhere. Patrick had been a cop, after all, found logic in the essence of law and order, brooded over transgressions. But aware that his viewpoint was at odds with the commune's new sensibility, and its tolerant version of acceptance, he said nothing, and bristled with anger. To him, Tom's lack of discipline was a spiritual failing, and Tom himself the personification of entropy—the karmic punishment for a lack of vigilance.

Patrick's dossier of grievances simmered, until he opened the bathroom door one day, flicked the light on, and saw Tom on the toilet seat, pants collapsed around his ankles.

"What are you doing in here?" he demanded.

"Taking a shit," Tom replied gruffly.

"In the dark?" Patrick said. "How can anyone know you're in here?"

"They'll turn on the light, like you did."

Patrick had standards of consideration that no amount of drugged experiences had yet obliterated. "That's ridiculous!" he shouted. "I won't stand for it!"

"Close the door," Tom replied, "and leave me alone."

Patrick backed out and slammed the door. He couldn't very well attack someone sitting on a toilet seat, for the same reason he wouldn't have taken a shit with the light off and the bathroom door open. But he waited there, in the hallway, and hearing the toilet flush, gripped the doorknob with a fist. When Tom tried to open the door, Patrick held on so it didn't budge, and when Tom struggled to open it, thinking it was merely stuck, Patrick abruptly let go and pushed, smacking Tom in the face and knocking him on his ass.

Later, he characterized it as a Zen act, a calculated awakening, carefully considered and coolly applied to stun Tom into awareness. And in fact Tom's bloody nose did make him aware—of Patrick, as he fled the spoiled sanctuary, leaving a spattered trail of blood on the floor.

Sitting by the open window, I lit a joint and drifted out beyond the tarpaper rooftops, the Con Ed smokestacks, the sluggish East River, the squat factories on the other side, the ochre haze rimming the scene, to a childhood memory of yellow safety barrels bobbing on the ocean surface, wooden jetties marking blocks where people roomed in houses during the summer, canvas-backed chairs and umbrellas camped in the sand where hamlets of adults conversed, babies and toddlers crawled and waddled, children played.

The beach . . .

The cluttered scene out the window as I dripped sweat conjured sweltering millions, summer upon summer, suffering the heat and humidity, all of us together, jamming into trolleys, subways, cars and buses, in utopian exodus.

It choked me up.

When Michael walked in and saw my long-lost look, he asked me what was wrong.

"Nothing," I said. "It's beautiful, actually," and I told him about the beach, that ennobling, collective escape.

"Let's go!" he said when I was through.

His enthusiasm sobered me. I'd promised a place where age and sorrow did not exist, a Holy Land where we would find nostalgia alive and well, in all its recollected fullness.

"Let's go now!" he said, and paraphrased me, in his own poetic way: "All of us, moved by the heat of a hazy summer day, repairing to the ocean, to the beach . . ."

"Well, all right!" I declared, reinfected with my own virus. "We'll do it!"

Or maybe I was looking for an excuse to use my parents' car, which on impulse I'd borrowed when they went on vacation. Except I hadn't used it since, except to move it occasionally from its parking spot ten blocks away in Gramercy Park, a safer neighborhood where it was less likely to be stolen.

Even leaving it downstairs for a few minutes after retrieving it worried me as I raced upstairs to get Michael—and once inside, stopped. Tom Eckhart was in the kitchen, gazing at the room with childlike wonder. I'd heard that since Patrick bloodied his nose at Eighth Street, Tom had been sleeping in the park and on rooftops. And now he'd shown up here.

Michael seemed lost as well; Tom's arrival had thrown him into a dissociated state. But where Tom appeared to have achieved his distraction as a consequence of advanced drug use, Michael was no doubt rent by his usual troublesome thoughts: What would we do now? Could we still go to the beach?

Tom was looking around as though he'd never seen a room before. I took the room in too, following his gaze, saw the gas oven, the box of wooden matches on the stovetop, the blade of a knife protruding from the drainboard next to the sink . . .

"We'll all go to the beach," I announced, and with that led our little family downstairs to the car.

It took a while to get out of the city. In my reverie by the window, the epic crawl of humanity to the sea, the crowded subways and buses, had gotten there without delay, and we were only inching along, across a bridge, then in slow-moving chrome and steel from Brooklyn Heights to the Gowanus Canal. Finally, we picked up speed and rolled past warehouses and factories lining the sporadically seen waterfront to the right, and residential blocks to the left, church steeples rising here and there, marking unseen parish villages in a dense grid of humanity.

I'd almost forgotten the joy of speeding along in the bubble of a car, being in but not of the world. The sky was a soft blue punctuated with feathery cirrus clouds, the sun shimmering off the water of the bay as we swung around the Belt Parkway from Bay Ridge to Coney Island to Canarsie, where I recalled the wooden housing project when I was just a boy, my first school—a three-room Quonset hut—the two-wheeled bike I learned to ride before I knew anything about organized sport . . . That stretch of highway, past the swamp where the row houses had once been, always got to me.

And then we were on newer, wider, faster roads, flanked by trees and bushes, in the country, it seemed, now that we'd left behind the trees that cropped up amidst brick and concrete, an exhibit, a limited tableau of nature. Not that the approach to Jones Beach was any less manhandled, but the sky had dominion here, over a tamed landscape that its spaciousness rendered wild, the scrub brush bordering the road as exotic as the Caribbean. There was open bay on both sides, the campanile to the south a beckoning landmark. This was not the beach of my bobbing barrels, but it didn't matter. That dreamscape had been archetypal, and the ocean is the ocean wherever you go, lapping at all beaches everywhere.

As we got closer, however, concrete made a comeback, in a landscape of parking lots, which were nearly vacant. And after we parked, the great migration I'd envisioned was nowhere to be seen. In fact, there were only a few people on the paved walkway that led from the lot up toward the boardwalk and the sand. Still, with mounting anticipation I peered ahead, beyond the well-mown grass and manicured shrubs, saw a band of ocean beneath the fulsome sky, and then, beyond the wooden boardwalk, the wide stretch of white sand . . .

Which was empty.

How could it be?

I squinted at the dazzling expanse from the foot of the boardwalk, spotted a few human motes on the vast sprawl, with yawning space between.

Where was everyone?

Michael and Tom had taken off their shoes and were headed toward the ocean. I took off my sandals and followed, the three of us walking gingerly on the hot sand.

We'd brought a blanket, which we spread not far from the water, using our sandals to anchor it against the hot wind before sitting down, an oasis of three in a desert of space.

We sat awhile, in the bright daze, then Michael, who couldn't help but fidget, began to play with a handful of sand, and kept at it, transferring the grains from hand to hand, trying not to lose any. Tom, who had no compulsion to do anything, sat with his long legs drawn up, scanning the wide-open emptiness. And I stared at the water, thinking.

When you spend time with the ocean, you come to notice changes, nuances, different aspects from day to day. Turbulent days, and days when it's placid; days when benevolent sandbars fill in the depths and you can walk out farther than usual, and tricky days with an undertow that can suck you under in a moment and vacuum you out to sea. After a storm, the surface might be still as a lake; and for unknown reasons, on certain mornings jellyfish cover the wet sand, or the ocean throws up stinking, bloated fish, or seaweed mucks up the water in a leafy stew, or sharp shells close to shore discourage wading.

I thought about all this, in an effort to connect with that heaving bathtub, and then turned to the imaginable as I stared at the horizon where the water met the sky, envisioning another continent, a shoreline of teeming beaches, blankets spread on the sand, wicker picnic hampers, children playing at the water's edge . . .

We hadn't brought any lotion, and the brutal sun was cooking our pasty skin. Michael brought up his own past, recalled throwing a spaldeen back and forth, mixed it in with memories of the Brooklyn Dodgers, Jackie Robinson, Peewee Reese, Gil Hodges, and all that, but we couldn't play catch because no one had thought to bring a ball. We had cigarettes, but hot gusts of wind blew out all our matches, and no one was willing to cross the hot sand stretching between our blanket encampment and the distant boardwalk to get a light. And hot as it was, we couldn't persuade ourselves to go in the water; with no one else out there in the choppy surf, it seemed dangerous. Or maybe it was just too much trouble. So we just sat, listening to the monotonous breaking waves while the sun beat down like a punishment, baking our brains, hour after hour, or so it seemed, though who knew when we'd gotten there or how long we'd endured since we had.

Eventually we'd had enough, and trudged back across the burning sand to the boardwalk.

"That's me," Tom said as we put our shoes back on.

"What?" I asked.

He pointed to a stenciled drawing on a metal trash can. "Cancer . . . the crab."

It seemed an idiotic remark.

The smell of hot dogs and hamburgers reminded me that I was hungry. The others stood there sniffing too, for none of us had eaten that day, which was not unusual, but the surfeit of fresh air made us ravenous. We pooled out money. Tom found a quarter in his pocket, probably the same coin I'd given him a week or two ago, to get on a bus, and Michael had two dollars, which I'd need for gas. What could we do, starving for food, so far from Manhattan and everyone we knew?

Tom said, "We can get something at my parents' house."

I looked at him in surprise. That Tom Eckhart had parents had never occurred to me. He'd told me about being a teenager, but that was different than picturing him as a child, when a father and mother mean something, imply upbringing. I said, "In Bayside, you mean?"

"Yeah."

It was a long way, but his matter-of-fact voice placed it nearby. "Okay," I said. "We'll go there."

Once we crossed the bay, however, and got on the highway, we hit traffic. Where were all these people coming from and going to? They certainly hadn't been at the beach. It snailed along until I couldn't stand it anymore, got off the highway and headed what seemed to be north on local streets . . . which led to other streets, to cul-de-sacs, to school complexes, hospitals, shopping centers, commuter railroad stations, suburban towns without a center, until I couldn't tell if we were headed east or west, north or south. When I finally emerged from the tangle of streets without sidewalks and onto an actual boulevard, I was way the hell out from where I'd gotten off the highway to beat the traffic. And now the traffic was stop and go, with lights every block or so timed to frustrate me. Out of old habit, I'd turned on the radio, and paid for every few minutes of music with a garble of ads, but finding myself in the old milieu, among the hoi polloi listening in their own cars, it didn't occur to me to turn off.

Michael, who sat next to me, had turned back toward Tom and was asking about his family. Curious, I listened over the radio drivel.

His father kicked him out of the house, Tom said, and he hadn't seen him since.

"Why?" Michael asked.

"Because he doesn't want to see me."

"I mean, why did he kick you out?"

The question had me pushing buttons, looking for music, something to turn up loud, to blot out his father obsession, when Tom replied, "He thinks I'm insane."

That would have shut me up, and it did silence Michael for a while, but then he turned to the backseat again and wanted to know more, which somehow led to Tom's first day at school . . . kindergarten, the singsong voice of the teacher, the tiny containers of milk at snack time, the little chairs and tables.

"As soon as I saw the miniature furniture," he said, "I knew something was wrong. I told my mother I wasn't going back, and she had to drag me there after that."

The little desks and chairs, the cookies and milk . . . Who could forget them? But I'd had a different reaction, and revisited it now, recalling the sense of unknown possibility, and, not for the first time, wondered what it was that made Tom's alienation so thorough.

It was getting dark when we finally broke through from Nassau County to Queens, moving sluggishly from light to light, cars, trucks, and buses coughing exhaust as I waited impatiently for the next lurch forward with the window rolled down, or sweltering with the window rolled up. The utilitarian streets were tired-looking, with their gas stations and used car lots, plateglass storefronts, industrial lots bound by barbed and razor wire. I knew this world. I'd grown up in it. So why did I still believe I might find something different? An aesthetic facade, with buttresses or friezes, a splash of vibrant color, something, anything, to ameliorate the vacuousness. Was that too much to ask? In mocking answer, neon flicked on here and there, adding garishness to a commercial landscape smudged by dusk.

It was full dark when I rolled down another nondescript main street and Tom told me to turn at the next light. And suddenly there it was! A street with hedges and picket fences, tidy houses nestled in shrubbery, a canopy of trees that blocked the flow of streetlights, creating pockets of alluring shadow.

A block or two later he told me to pull to the curb of this wonderland. I cut the ignition, the engine died, and pleasing residential sounds flooded in; crickets, whirring sprinklers watering lawns. Even the air, stultifyingly humid before, was a comforting sitz now that the sun had set, and fragrant with the smells of mown grass and damp soil. Clusters of leaves cloistered the sidewalks and parked cars, obscuring the two-story shingled houses, imbuing them with mystery.

"You lived here?" I said to Tom.

"Yeah," he replied. "I'll be right back," and he was abruptly out the car door. Though there was no movement on the street, he paused to look both ways, with the caution of a child, then loped across and up a driveway, disappearing into darkness.

I lit a cigarette, blew smoke out the window and watched it drift. I took in the cozy homes, listened to the soothing sprinklers, and basked in the contentment of the moment, to which, with the usual sleight of mind, I supplied a legerdemain of supposed cause and effect, recalling a world of conversations overheard, the reverberant words and gestures of adults, the fairy-tale belief that true meaning lay beneath the arcane grown-up surface. It accrued to everything—the chores and routines, the meals cooked and placed on the table, the daily comings and goings. A world of hidden purpose, of great things.

And then, perhaps because he'd been a boy here, Tom's miniature desks came to mind, and with that, everything suddenly had the aspect of a colossal lie. The hiss of sprinklers watering the lawns punctuated a smug complacency, and the lush trees casting streetlight shadows became a black forest tunnel, a grim fairy tale of imprisonment.

I launched the burning cigarette out the window, startling Michael from his own reverie, the orange tip arcing over the sidewalk and a picket fence, landing in a shaded grotto.

A moment later Tom reappeared across the street. He didn't check for traffic now but ran right at us in his loping stride, cradling a bag under an arm.

Yanking the door open, he fell onto the backseat, shouting, "Drive! Drive! Let's get outta here!"

Summer of Love

"Biggest be-in west of the Mississippi! Today! At Golden Gate Park!"

I'd hitchhiked and ridden freight trains, barely slept and hardly ate for almost a week, and now, standing on a downtown street in San Francisco, the kid hawking newspapers on the corner seemed to have been put there by fate, to welcome me. There were no flowers in his hair, as in the popular song, but he had long hair and a disheveled hippie look, and just seeing him put a bounce in my step as I hurried past, flashing him a peace sign. Around me, the commuters on Market Street heading for work occupied a separate universe as I walked among them, loose sandals flapping, my feet burnt and burnished by the sun over three thousand miles, as befit a pilgrim journeying to his mecca.

From a map I'd studied on the road, in gas stations and diners and while sitting on boulders and in pavement lots, I thought I knew the way, and confidently hiked up Market, away from the business district, past derricks and bulldozers growling on construction sites behind plywood fences plastered with posters done in the unreadable, emblematic pyschedeco style that thrilled me now, and seemed a signature for the cubist landscape of buildings seemingly piled atop one another on the hills; a world that was ours, it seemed to me, in defiance of logic and its actual provenance.

Coming to the foot of Haight Street, I veered onto it with quickening step and mounting excitement, cresting a small hill then heading down the long incline that I knew would lead to my destination.

Hippies began to appear at Fillmore, and a few blocks later, at Divisadero, they were everywhere. And then I was swallowed by the sidewalk crowd, borne along in a contact high in a stately procession of headbands, beads, and necklaces, wreaths of flowers, colorful robes and motley fabrics. I floated more than walked, enveloped in a bubble of well-being, anointed by the liquid sun, dazzled by the spectacle.

This is the high point of my life!

I was too besotted, and uneducated, to see the warning in that giddy thought. Things are never as good (or as bad) as they seem.

Basking in the too good to be true, the hippie stream brought me to the intersection of Haight and Ashbury, where I separated myself from the throng, moved aside and stared at those street signs on the corner. It brought tears to my eyes, and I imagined a plaque affixed to the building there, in some distant year, THE FUTURE BEGAN HERE, to which I'd point with pride and tell my unborn children: "I was there, at that moment!"

Stepping back into the constant flow, I was carried again, expecting more of the same, a heady elevation, a delirium of happiness at belonging to something greater than myself. But a few blocks later the crowd began to thin, the collective high dissipating, and then it was gone and I stood alone, deflated, among three-story buildings and prosaic neighborhood stores.

Up ahead, the street abruptly ended and the park began. I considered returning to the mythic intersection, to reimmerse myself in the mass, to recapture the buoyancy. Then I recalled the hippie on Market Street touting the biggest be-in west of the Mississippi, and hurrying up the block, plunged into the park, looking for it.

I expected to find it easily, and after walking awhile, was perplexed. There was no sight or sound of the glorious event as I followed the road through groves of trees, over rolling hills, past pocket meadows and a children's playground. An event of such magnitude! It was bizarre.

Spotting a group of people, and certain they were heading to the be-in—though they did not look anything like hippies—I followed, saw others heading the same way and walked faster, eventually entering a concrete clearing, where I stopped and frowned at the facade of a museum, falling behind my would-be fellow pilgrims, watching them mount the broad steps and move inside.

With renewed purpose, I struck off in another direction, left the parked cars and a line of slow-moving traffic behind until there was no one but me, hiking beneath the shaded canopy of high trees that eventually gave way to an open, airy landscape of stunted growths resembling giant bonsai, where I spotted the ocean and abruptly stopped.

The Pacific.

I'd crossed from one coast to another.

An impressive, one might say mythic, journey.

But the power of expectation trumped the moment: It wasn't what I'd been seeking. Disappointed, I turned around and headed back, still looking . . .

At some point I heard the strains of music and hurried toward the sounds, saw flashes of color through the trees and broke into a run.

Bursting through undergrowth, I emerged on a hillside and looked down upon an immense gathering. It filled a long meadow shouldered by low hills, stretched from a sound stage at one end to distant suburbs at the other, where the crowd dwindled into discrete groups, picnic blankets, children playing.

I panned this assemblage and gazed back down at the dense pack below, where the air shimmered with vibration and color . . . and then, before I knew it, I was plunging down, to embrace and be embraced by the horde, sliding, stumbling, taken by gravity down the hillside and onto the field, where I bounded over and around bodies until momentum released me and I stood in the center of everything, lost in a crowd . . . where, suddenly claustrophobic, I scrambled as desperately to get out as I had to get in, stumbling through to the other side, gasping for air, relieved at escaping.

But I was torn. The crowd, an immense presence, held me there, in thrall. I wanted to be in it, and of it, but was repelled by it as well. Walking again, I kept to the fringe, close but apart, circling the gathering, two, three, four times, truly in a dream, emotions pulling me this way and that. I traipsed behind the massive sound stage in front and then up to the hillside where I'd begun—thinking, briefly, that this was where I belonged, among the observers—as I kept moving, back down the hill, along the side and to the rear, where smaller sound stages had been set up, and then along the far length of it, a circling sleepwalker.

I might have continued walking in mindless circles if not for the smell of cooked food, which drew me into a cove I'd somehow overlooked before. This too was a dream, appearing out of nowhere, a crush of people behind a rope barrier, inclining toward racks of chicken grilling over pits. Only now did I realize how hungry I was, and stood there staring at the food along with the others, salivating from the smell of it, cooking. Someone told me the Diggers were barbecuing the meat. I'd heard about them, that they distributed free food and clothes, and as I stood there, starving, I took pride in that: that we, all of us, were not ordinary people. We were hippies. We cared about and took care of each other.

But as the wafting smoke from the pits made me faint with hunger, the supplicants around me lost their noble aspect, and in their tattered clothes were merely destitute; emaciated teenagers in baggy pants, young women with gaunt faces and sunken eyes, all of us fixated on the racks of grilling meat, which now seemed a less generous offering. The chicken tenders beyond the rope barrier laughed among themselves as we awaited the next round of handouts, nibbled pieces from the racks, gestured with drumsticks as if enjoying a joke, which was on us. And when they finally approached the barrier to dole out a few pieces, they held the food high, like animal trainers. The crowd would then surge forward, shouting and stretching, a few managing to latch onto a bone, then squirreling out of the crush as the rest of us pressed forward, jostling for position before the next feeding. It seemed we were being taught a lesson: that those who want what others have deserve whatever they get.

Eventually, I staggered away, aware of my ravenous hunger now, feeling weak and dizzy. I might have been limping before, but only noticed it now, and the feeble decrepitude it implied, as I wandered in a daze toward the rear of the field . . .

"Help yourself."

I'd come to a standstill, and the containers of food I'd been staring at came into focus. An older man reclined on a blanket, watching me.

"Go on," he said, gesturing at the food.

I fell to my knees and began digging coleslaw and macaroni salad out of the containers with a plastic spoon, cramming the food into my mouth, hardly chewing before swallowing.

The old man watched me, and when I'd finally had my fill and stopped eating, said, "You must've been hungry."

I looked at him more carefully now, as he regarded me with mild curiosity. I could see he didn't expect gratefulness, and some lucid part of me appreciated his indifferent generosity. But seeing the liver spots on his bald head, the crow's-feet at his eyes, the ordinary clothes he wore, I all but dismissed him, because he clearly wasn't one of us.

"Yeah," I said, and getting up, limped away, back toward the hippies.

The solid mass I'd seen from a distance was thinner up close. Maybe half the crowd had left. There were patches of grass now, openings between clustered groups, gaps in the rows facing the main stage, where still another band was playing. I breathed easier, moved through the seated bodies, looking for a space to sit. And now that I was satiated, a cool detachment had come over me, and taking in the scene, I wondered what I'd been so euphoric about earlier. It didn't look like much, just a lot of people, listening to a band play.

I thought I heard someone call my name, but kept walking, looking for a spot. Hearing it again, I stopped and saw him waving, coming toward me. The curly hair, the scar on his cheek, the chipped-tooth smile. Tony from

Sunnyside. Earlier, I might have been relieved to see someone I knew, but now I didn't care.

"Pete!" he shouted again, and then he was next to me, slapping my shoulder. "I thought it was you!"

"Tony," I replied without enthusiasm. He was a good guy, and I'd always liked him. But I was in California now, a brave new world, and didn't want to think about the old world back East.

He said, "Chris told me she saw you near the stage earlier, and I told her no, it just looked like you, but then I remembered you saying how you wanted to come out here . . ."

"I got here this morning," I said, and realized it was true.

He gripped my shoulders with two hands, smiled into my face. "C'mon back to the blanket. We got a spot on the other side, near the stage, me and Chris and Ernie."

It was an unappealing prospect, but I followed him across the field.

"We been here all day," he said over his shoulder. "Sal was here too, but he went back to the pad . . . How's Martha, by the way?"

Martha . . .

It took me a moment to remember. "I don't know," I said. "She left . . . a while ago."

"I liked her," Tony said. "She was down to earth, y'know?" He laughed. "A real farm girl . . . Over here, Pete. This way."

Christine jumped up from the blanket and hugged me as Ernie watched, grinning. Then Tony all but yanked me down to the blanket and pushed fruit and cheese at me, treating me with the same deference as when I'd delivered drugs to their pad. Christine asked about my cross-country trip as I dutifully nibbled at the food.

And suddenly I was recalling torrential rain in Nebraska; a sheriff who grilled me in Idaho for sitting on the grass, shoved his missing thumb in my face, a souvenir of the Korean War, and accused me of being a draft dodger; desert where I baked in the sun outside of Salt Lake and had hallucinations. But I was talking to myself more than them, and at some point it became fodder to kill enough time before extricating myself without seeming abrupt. And having reached what seemed an acceptable interval, I dutifully took their address, repeating it aloud, forgetting it as I did, and got away.

The ocean breeze was at my back as I headed up to Haight Street, and hours later a damp chill in the air had burrowed into my skin. It was dark then, and I hewed to the sidewalk crowd for warmth, down one side of the street, until the crowd thinned, then crossing and joining the cloak of bodies moving the other way. By then I'd long since given up reading the flyers stapled to telephone poles, hoping to find somewhere to stay, an unlikely message addressed to me among the ads for concerts and lectures, the pleas for lost dogs and cats. Yet I still clung to the belief that a place would somehow find me as I shuffled along in the crowd.

When it happened, I was numb, in my flimsy shirt and nearly bare feet—Tony, shouting my name, beckoning on a corner. I stumbled out of the procession, this time glad to see him, and abashed at having felt put-upon in the park hours ago.

"Where you been, Pete?" he said, throwing an arm around my shoulders, steadying me. "We been expecting you back at the pad."

I said, "I forgot the address."

"That's what Chris figured, when you didn't show up. You seemed spaced out, preoccupied . . ."

We climbed Ashbury, leaving the crowd behind, and I wanted to say more, as a way of apologizing for my earlier indifference, but I'd been alone for nearly a week and had trouble speaking. Nothing that came to mind seemed worth saying, which wasn't like me. Perhaps Tony noticed, because he jumped in, told me about the weather, how chilly it was there, in the summer. Fingering my cotton shirt, he asked, "Is this all you have, Pete?"

"Yeah . . . just what I'm wearing."

Maybe they could find me something for me, he said, a poncho, or a flannel shirt for the evenings; the Diggers had a free store where anyone could get clothes.

"Yeah, I heard . . ."

Near the top of the hill we turned onto another street and he said, "I should tell you, Pete—I might've given you the wrong impression. It's not really *our* pad. We just share it."

I wondered about that as we entered a stucco courtyard and I followed him upstairs into one of the garden-type apartments.

Just inside, in a small kitchen, people were gathered around a pot in the kitchen. And through an arch a few feet away, blankets on clotheslines partitioned a large room into separate spaces, the transparent attempt at ensuring privacy belied by the bustle of people. The sense of them crammed into that place was discombobulating as Tony introduced me to this person and that and I nodded and shook hands, forgetting names as I heard them.

The place was too crowded. It overwhelmed the niceties, only a few people genuinely friendly; space, I'd come to understand, was too valuable for anyone to be pleased about newcomers.

Then Tony led me down a hallway lined with teenagers who sat against the walls, passing a joint as music blaring from the main room coated the place, *Sergeant Pepper,* which ameliorated the saturated scene, bestowing a loopy, goofy, jolly feel to it.

Christine and Ernie were waiting in a small back room. Tony led me in and gestured us toward a closet door, and when we were all gathered there, he yanked it open and shouted, "Sal! Wake up! Look who I found!"

Sal Ianotta was lying on a pile of clothes. He might have been sleeping, or maybe not. But he was playacting when he opened an eye, looked at me and said, "'S'bout time you showed up."

I laughed, because it was expected of me, and it left me dizzy, my knees buckling, Tony helped me to a cot, the only thing in the otherwise bare room, and I flounced down, next to a girl who was curled up, facing the wall.

She turned when I hit the mattress and shouted in my face: "What the fuck do you want?"

And as I recoiled, Tony was hovering over me, telling her, "It's all right. It's cool. He's a friend . . ."

Instantly, I fell asleep, and was dead to the world a long time or maybe only a few minutes before emerging with eyes closed, or not, to a blur of movement, voices and footsteps, a door opening—

In a dream merging with wakefulness, I blinked at the harsh light. Tony was standing over me, saying, "We gotta go, Pete. We gotta leave."

I heard the words, the shuffling sounds outside the room, and looked up questioningly,

"We gotta go, Pete. Now. Right away. The landlord called the cops."

In a daze, I got up and followed him out.

The idealistic couple in the doughnut shop wanted to start a commune. They wrote down the address so we'd be sure to find their pad.

We showed up early that afternoon, but already more than a dozen people were there, scrambling to claim floor space in what had once been the living room. The following evening there were twice as many, jostling with those who'd staked out spots in the main room, claiming spots in the kitchen and hallways, everywhere but the bathroom and the bedroom, to which our benefactors had now retreated, closing the French doors against the deluge.

Through chintz curtains, their mattress floated in an ocean of space, while on our side of the doors, there was hardly room to turn around. One room for just two people: it smacked of injustice as I lay amidst the wall-to-wall bodies.

Not long ago I'd also had a mattress to myself, in a room I thought of as my own, a curtain separating me from those who slept on mattresses, a sofa, and in the chair by the window. I'd struggled with the meaning of generosity then, pitting comfort and presumed selfishness against sacrifice and sharing, and eventually, unable to tell anyone to leave, I'd left instead, for Haight-Ashbury, and the same moral conundrum, seen from a different point of view.

Tony called the five of us a family. If we didn't take care of each other, he said, who would? Without discussion, he became the father, deciding who would return to the pad before the others to secure our floor space, loosely marked by blankets; who would wait on the food line to the kitchen, and bring plates of rice and beans to those who held our spots in the main room; and which of us would sprawl over a vacated space, preventing encroachment by the human pool whose nature it was to fill any hollow, nudging us awake when the room slept restlessly and one of our group went to the bathroom.

Emerging fitfully from sleep in the morning, the odor of unwashed bodies, the wheezing and snoring, brought me back to the coarse present. It took a while to remember where I was, which was disturbing.

The sensory world usually situates me in what appears the most objective of worlds. But now my senses had run amok. I was mainly confused, and though it's my nature to be voluble, I hardly spoke anymore. With imagination, but lacking clarifying expression, the details that came to mind were untethered, fluid, rendering situations and circumstances less distinct than I knew they should have been.

Often, I'd think about my pad on Eleventh Street—not as I'd left it, with Michael and the others always there—but in quieter times, when I sat at my perch by the front window, gazing out at the city in pleasant solitude.

One afternoon, returning early to the apartment on Ashbury and finding it empty, I sat by the bay window, gazing down the steep hill to the city beyond; a sweet moment akin to those when I viewed the panorama of another city over tenement rooftops.

I was momentarily distracted by the blankets strewn on the floor, the bulges here and there a pitiful attempt to hide meager possessions after someone's clothes had disappeared when people returned to the pad one afternoon.

I turned away, looked out the window again, at houses across the street stepping down the steep, slanting pavement; fragile, insubstantial; plywood facades on a movie set that a slight breeze might topple. Below, on Haight Street, the usual procession was a slow-moving undulation of bodies across the intersection with Ashbury.

Why are we here?

The question came to mind, and an answer arose; not the usual, everyday chatter, but a voice emerging from the question, which had come from some deep core within me:

To be together.

It was the simple truth, an answer from a void, the reshith of nothingness . . . which I quickly embellished with the notion of a collective vibration, a generation coming of age, drawn to this place. The embellishment was hollow sentiment, no more than artifice, really, in the wake of the unadorned truth: that we were a gathering herd, a migration of lemmings, a mere phenomenon, nothing more.

I put the epiphany aside—the truth, which resides in its hidden place and can't be traduced—and took false solace from the embellishment, the pleasing notion, which explains, alters, justifies, and never shuts up.

Another day, looking for meaning, I wandered off, eventually found myself downtown, and took a bus across the bay, to Berkeley, in a reverie of recollected demonstrations and protests, the be-ins of another, different community of people, who thought as I did, or as I once had. In fact, I'd never been comfortable among those as opinionated as me, though we shared the same opinions, but I glossed over that, and getting off on a street with department stores and office buildings, struck off toward the university campus where the great free speech battles had been fought, hoping to find my brethren there.

There were no signs on campus of what had once occurred. Summer school students strolled past as I sat on a bench. They looked young and carefree, with their books and briefcases and knapsacks. A few glanced at me without curiosity, and I felt lost, in my baggy pants and worn-out shirt. Then a man about my age, in a suit and tie, strolled toward me, paused, went to his pocket and pulled out bills. He handed me two dollars, though I hadn't asked for anything. And I felt poor, and resented my own gratitude as I watched him walk away.

Later, I wandered the streets, down Telegraph Avenue and then up into the hills, through residential areas, looking for something, though I didn't know what. It got dark, and I found myself in a grove of trees, looking down. The streets below curved through the hills, and on the flatlands farther down, streetlights marked a vast grid of houses that abruptly ended at the shoreline.

The moon glistened in the vast pool of water, the spires and spans of a bridge outlined against it, with the dark shapes of ships in the bay, and office towers lit up on the other side. This scene, this other community, also seduced me . . .

If only I could have remained there, looking down, content in its generalities. But it was getting chilly, and I was hungry, and I had no place to sleep, so I reluctantly abandoned that perch and came down the mountain, traipsing through streets that up close were ordinary in their particularity, and took the bus back across the bay.

I walked in on a crisis. The place was abuzz, everyone on their feet, agitated, gathered in groups. Tony pulled me aside, into a family huddle, except Ernie wasn't there. Caught rifling through a dresser in the off-limits bedroom, he said, and ordered to leave. I noticed then that we stood apart, the other groups eyeing us suspiciously. First, the clothes in the main room disappeared. Now this . . .

"We're a family," Tony said, "and families stick together."

An ethos of unconditional acceptance, more Italian than Jewish; an assertion of loyalty that confounded me, since I had no sympathy for Ernie. I'd resented the royal couple their separate room, but it was another thing to steal from them. And then there was Tony, who had done so much for me, and whom I'd come to rely upon.

"Then I guess we all have to leave," I said.

Tony looked at me with disbelief. "Why would we do that?" he asked.

Having my own notion of honor, I didn't understand his question, said, "Well, if Ernie can't stay, then we'll have to go too."

"That doesn't make sense," Tony said. "Of course we'll stay. Where else can we go? But while we're here, we'll make sure Ernie's taken care of."

He was up on the roof, where Sal would smuggle him food. He'd sleep there and join us in the morning, when we left the pad.

Then, another day, the couple suddenly opened the bedroom doors—perhaps responding to that same sense of injustice I'd felt—and the tide of bodies flowed inside, filling the once opulent space, until the mattress the couple slept on appeared as spacious for two bodies as the entire room had been before.

And still people kept coming, saturating the place, spilling into the hallway outside and down the stairs to the front door of the building.

It ended abruptly.

The neighbors called the landlord, who called the cops, who arrived one morning to clear out the stairwell and then the apartment itself.

A day or two later we came upon the well-meaning couple, toting sleeping bags and knapsacks, in the doughnut shop where we first met. They'd been evicted, they told us, and I thought about that place—the main room, the bedroom, the kitchen and bathroom and hallways—and pictured it empty, a padlock on the door.

It seemed inconceivable: all that space, gone to waste.

Christine had been happy in the Sunnyside apartment in Manhattan. It was a lark, after the suburbs and a year in one of the prestigious women's colleges; Vassar, or maybe Sarah Lawrence. I'd never asked her where she'd met Tony, but then, young people like ourselves from all over were mixing with each other, leaving social class assumptions behind. Though now, in the Haight, she appeared uncomfortable with Tony's boyhood pals, rarely spoke to them, or to me, just to Tony, to whom she clung.

Sal still had an attitude about him, feigning self-possession; presenting himself as an irrepressible happy-go-lucky character, a joker quick to poke fun at people as our small caravan moved from place to place. But though he always had lumbering Ernie as a sidekick, guaranteed to react with appreciation, it was Tony he looked to for encouragement and support, eyeing him for a laugh or a smile. Without it, it seemed he'd lose his flaunted self-confidence.

Ernie, I didn't know at all; except that he could be a faker. He hardly ever said anything, and because it bothered me that I thought he was stupid, I looked for something about him that would disprove it. Until he was caught stealing. And then I lost respect for him and all but ignored him. He and Sal had become inseparable, a comedy duo, the two of them clowning around in a goofy, inclusive slang that excluded everyone else.

But the change in Tony was the most disturbing. Where he'd once exuded optimism, he now strained for it. And there was something going on between him and Christine, who was often moody and querulous. She'd snap at him, and he'd tell her to lower her voice and draw her aside, where they'd bicker out of earshot. Or he'd veer away from her on the street, to engage me about one thing or another, in order to get away from her, or jump into the back-and-forth gibberish between the two goofballs, leaving Christine to slog along on her own.

And I'd retreated even further into myself, while we hung out in the park or traipsed from place to place, looking for food and shelter. With my mouth sore and my gums bleeding, the others receded into the margins of my pain. Tony urged me to go to the free clinic, where a doctor told me I was depleted of vitamin C. He gave me a shot of penicillin and a bottle of pills, and warned me not to bite into anything hard, like an apple, which could pry the teeth out of my mouth.

We'd split up in the morning, from wherever we slept the night before. Christine with Tony; Sal with Ernie; and I went off by myself. We'd meet up again in the afternoon, in the park panhandle, to wait with a hundred or so others for the stew the Diggers served out of a van. It was a sorry scene of abject need, bringing to mind the thirties, with its breadlines, not the carelessness of hippie poverty. Christine, worn-out, bedraggled, sat on the grass, looking forlorn, as Sal cracked wise and Ernie grinned at his one-liners. Tony, a sometime participant in their routine, was uncharacteristically silent. And then the van would arrive and we'd wait in line with our bowls, and after eating the watery stew, quickly put that sorry scene behind us and head for hippie hill to bask in the sun as if nothing mattered.

And then one day the van we'd come to take for granted didn't show up, and the five of us trudged up toward Haight Street in a somber mood.

Sal broke the silence, made a joke of it, said the stew wasn't much anyway and we'd be better off just stealing our own food instead of standing in line for it. The others quickly agreed, and I was confronted with the same dilemma as when Ernie was caught stealing. I would have begged instead. Perhaps sensing my discomfort, Tony assigned me the role of decoy, an accomplice lingering over candy bars at the front of a store, distracting the grocer while the rest of them snatched food in the aisles and hid them under Christine's poncho. I wouldn't do the actual stealing.

It was a small neighborhood store, and we were the only ones in the place. The grocer, waiting on me behind the counter, saw them dart out and ran after them, down the street. I was gone when he returned.

When I joined the others in the park, Sal was whooping it up, Ernie grinned like an idiot, and for a change even Christine was animated.

"Cheer up, Pete!" Tony said, slapping me on the back. "You did good!"

"It's my gums," I told him, deflecting my shame with my pain as I ate gingerly, softening the food in my mouth before swallowing.

Tony pulled me aside afterward, said, "You never stole anything before, Pete?"

Sure I had. And property was theft, after all. But that was a more convincing argument for department stores than a neighborhood grocery with three aisles watched over by a middle-aged man. And the candy bars and comic books I'd filched as a boy seemed different, less serious, than stealing food because I was hungry.

Twilight came quickly that day, without the usual subtle gradations. Suddenly, it was dark. Tony had met someone who said we could sleep in his kitchen, and the five of us settled in between the refrigerator and the stove and got through another night.

Usually, we'd begin looking for a place to crash in late afternoon, then meet on a corner and head as a group to whatever pad we might have found. We weren't picky. Anyplace with walls and a ceiling was all right. We slept in kitchens and bathrooms, in a church with simple wooden cots, on linoleum or concrete floors, in hallways and basements.

And then, one evening when Tony, Christine, and I waited on the corner, Sal and Ernie didn't show up. It was dark when we gave up on them and went off to find whatever we could for the night. We settled on an alley with an enclosure for garbage cans, which we removed, curling up inside the narrow, roofed shelter. It was a cozy crib. When you have nothing, almost anyplace can be satisfying. Then lights went on in the building overlooking our spot, people talking loudly, silhouettes in a window moving about. It probably had nothing to do with us, but their voices filled the alley, and in our homeless insecurity, we took it personally. Scrambling out of our nook, we ran away.

It was late now, and the usual crowd on Haight had thinned. And it was cold. We went to the park and burrowed into a clump of bushes, to fitfully spend the night.

At daybreak, stiff and aching, we trod back up to Haight through the chill fog. The street was deserted until we spotted two people in the recessed entrance of a boarded-up store; Sal and Ernie, facing one another, their legs splayed. They were laughing, talking gibberish, and didn't notice us until we were close enough to see the food on the ground between them.

Sal, startled, shouted, "Hey, you guys, look what we got," and gestured at the spread of cheese and cold cuts, cans of soda, a jar of mustard, a loaf of bread. "Me and Ern struck the mother lode! C'mon, dig in!"

We moved into the enclosure, hunkered down against the walls and reached for the food as Sal told us how he and Ernie had slipped into a kitchen when everyone was asleep, raided the refrigerator, and snuck out before anyone woke up. Christine built herself a sandwich, Tony ate slices of meat and cheese, and I rolled the bread around in my mouth, gumming it up before swallowing. Sal couldn't stop himself, was on a jag, went on and on, shooting glances at Tony, who wouldn't look at him, and then abruptly interrupted.

"We waited for you last night," he said, and left it at that.

Sal jumped in again, frantic now. By the time they found a place, he explained, it was late, and if they'd left, someone else, of course, would have taken the space, and what good would that have done anyone?

"We slept in the park, Sal," Tony said grimly when he was through.

Sal ducked his head, shattered. And I remembered the day he brought Tony to my pad, how proud he'd been, as if introducing an older brother. Now, with eyes averted, he waited for Tony to say more. Any response would have done. He could at least have been contrite in response to outright anger, or taken a different direction with something else. Anything to heal or paper over the breach. But Tony didn't look at him or say a word as we sat in the chill silence, eating stolen food.

The next night, when Sal and Ernie didn't show up at the corner again, none of us even mentioned them as we set off on our own.

It was just the three of us then, seeking food and shelter.

And now the tension between Christine and Tony was harder for me to avoid. When she complained and he drew her aside, and I tried not to listen, it seemed I was an eavesdropper. When he moved away from her to talk to me, I could sense her resentment.

One afternoon when they began arguing on Haight Street, I fell back in the crowd, purposely losing myself, and slipping down a side street, escaped.

I awoke with a start and peered at the cloud-lit room for several seconds before recalling where I was. I'd gotten the address from the shelter hotline. The place had been empty when I arrived late at night, but now there were two bodies in sleeping bags on the floor. I curled back into a fetal position and pulled the thin blanket over my shoulders. But it was too cold to fall back asleep, and as I lay shivering, I heard footsteps coming down the stairs.

Before I could close my eyes and feign sleep, the man who'd ushered me into the basement room the night before saw that I was awake, or sensed it, and was nearly on top of me when I turned and looked up. How had I slept? he asked in a loud voice, hovering over me as I pushed the blanket aside and sat up. I told him what I knew he wanted to hear, turning away to put on my shirt, tie the rope that held up my pants, and slip into my sandals. But he wouldn't leave me alone, said I'd dropped off as soon as my head hit the mattress, so dead to the world that I hadn't even stirred when the others showed up, marveled at how tired I must have been.

Dressed, I turned back, to thank him and say good-bye, and he spoke faster, said, "Eggs and butter are in the fridge and the frying pan is on the stove, help yourself," and gestured at the far side of the room. Much as I wanted to get away, I couldn't refuse food, so I moved around him and toward the convenience kitchen.

But he still wouldn't leave me be, came up behind me to open the refrigerator and point out the eggs and butter, then lingered by the stove, asking where I was from and how long I'd been in San Francisco. I threw answers at him while turning on the gas and cracking eggs into the pan, in my discomfort hardly paying attention, when, to my relief, he heard noises across the room and hurried away.

He sat down on the cot I'd vacated, looming over the two boys in sleeping bags as they sat up and stretched, and spoke at them as he had at me. Bemused, they nodded in mechanical agreement to the same questions and replied with similar answers while getting dressed. The old man's neediness was painful to witness, and I hummed to myself to blot him out, filling my head with sound, and in my agitated self-distraction poked blindly at the eggs and broke the yolks, only noticing when the pan began to sizzle and I looked down at the smoldering mess.

The boys rolled up their sleeping bags and stood up. As insistent as our host had been before, he now became frantic, darting about the basement room, plucking objects from shelves and counter tops and thrusting them at the boys. A bronze skyscraper he'd bought at the Chicago World's Fair, a petrified rock from the painted dessert in Arizona, a crystal ball Statue of Liberty from New York, where he and his wife had gone on their honeymoon. She'd died of a heart attack seven years ago. He'd owned a gas station then, as his son did now, only his had been in Daly City and his son's was in Barstow, in the San Joaquin Valley, outside of Los Angeles. His son lived there with his wife and their little girl, his granddaughter, of whom he could not have been more proud.

"Wait!" he said. "I have a photo upstairs!"

When he left the room, I bolted out the basement door. Fleeing, afraid he'd pursue me, I ran across the lawn to the sidewalk and up the street, and kept running, block after block, until I saw the park. Slowing, catching my breath, I crossed one more street and went inside, to be enveloped, welcomed, by the surrounding trees and the smoky fog. They seemed to protect me. I passed a children's playground, a shuttered carousel, then came upon the broad meadow I'd often gazed at from hippie hill, on the other side.

A solitary figure sat on the hill, and recognizing Christine's red poncho, I broke into a jog. As I approached, Tony raised his hand in greeting.

He made room for me as I walked up the hill, patting the poncho he'd spread on the wet grass, inviting me to sit. "Long time no see, Pete," he said.

Pete . . .

It startled me. It had been so long since I'd heard my name.

It was chilly, now that I wasn't moving, and I drew my knees up and linked my hands around my calves, which drew me into myself, in search of a different kind of warmth. We sat in silence then, as the fog slowly lifted from the meadow, veiling the houses on a hill in the distance; a fantasy scene of a magic city.

Tony said something, words pouring out of him and rushing past me. I could only grasp the sound of his voice, its familiarity, and it lulled me as the distant city on a hill took form.

My attention came and went, and I heard him say, "I probably should have told you before, when Chris was being so difficult. I don't blame you for splitting like you did, Pete."

Pete . . .

Tears filled my eyes.

"She wants to have it, and maybe things will eventually get better between us, but then again, who knows, maybe they won't . . ."

He stopped and looked at me, waiting.

A bubble rose in my chest and lodged in my throat. I couldn't speak.

"So what'd you think?" he asked. "A baby's a big responsibility, and I don't know if I'm ready for it . . ."

I swallowed, understanding what he was asking, overwhelmed by it, and in a choked voice said, "I'm sorry."

"Sorry?" he said, puzzled. "About what?"

I wanted to explain, but couldn't. I tried to meet his eyes and failed.

"What'd you mean you're sorry?" he said, irritated.

I meant I was grateful that he'd asked, that he thought so highly of me, and that I didn't feel worthy of it. But I couldn't say that; I barely understood it myself.

And as he waited on me, crushing me with expectation, I bolted, ran away, down the hill.

I heard him behind me, shouting, "Pete! What's wrong? Where're you going?"

I didn't turn back, just kept running, up the concrete path to Haight Street, and then up that street. And when I couldn't run anymore, I walked.

Squandered Transition

I raced upstairs, bursting with unreasonable excitement, taking the worn steps two and three at a time, and rapped loudly on the wooden door. The sound reverberated in the sixth-floor hallway, and as it died away and I stood there waiting, I heard a baby cry somewhere and the dull thud of a jackhammer in the distance. The ordinariness of life. It rendered my outsize expectation foolish. But hearing the shuffle of footsteps inside, my irrational exuberance returned, and when the door swung open, I fairly exploded, shouting, "*Michael!*"

He might have been asleep and dragged himself out of bed. Startled, he blinked heavily, and then did a curious thing, widening his eyes as he took me in, improvising, feigning astonishment out of genuine surprise. "What are you doing here?" he said. "I thought you'd be gone longer." But because Michael was a thinker, not an actor, his foray into make-believe ended abruptly and he reverted to character, scratching at the Socratic beard that now bristled on his cheeks, then yanking at the hairs, no doubt painfully, perhaps in retribution for his fakery.

"Can I come in?" I said jokingly, slipping into pretense of my own, pretending not to notice the changes he'd just gone through.

"Of course, of course," he replied, still punishing his face as he backed up.

I followed him in and stood in the darkened kitchen. Window shades, which I'd never pulled down, were drawn over the front room windows, and the place had a dim, disreputable feel to it. Not at all like California, I thought, out of the blue. Until then I hadn't thought about it except as misfortune, and looked forward with anticipation to returning to the city and my pad, recalling the scene out the window, my little room with the mattress on the floor, the old familiarity.

Michael was saying, again, how surprised he was to see me, that he hadn't expected me back so soon, that had he known, he would have cleaned up the place. Then he added, preemptively, before I brought it up, that he was sorry he hadn't sent me the money I'd called about, that he hadn't been able to locate the people I'd mentioned, who owed me money, except for one guy, who said he hadn't gotten the hashish yet, what with the breakout of war in the Middle East, but he was working on it and—

"Where's Lulu?" I asked, interrupting.

He was doing that kneading thing with his hands, and observing him more closely, I noticed he'd lost weight, appeared drawn, haggard. But more than that, where he'd always been neat, whatever the circumstance or situation, he looked sloppy now, his clothes disheveled, as though he'd slept in them, his beard untrimmed and flecked with tobacco, and above the rough growth, the pasty cheeks splotched with a pink rash.

"Lulu?" he said.

"Yeah," I said, losing patience. "Lulu. Where is she?"

"Well . . . that's right, she was here when you left . . . She lost her job, or quit . . . Yes, I think she quit. That was after she received a letter, from her parents, in Oklahoma . . ."

"So she's gone?"

" . . . Yes. She left."

"What about Ray?" He'd been there too, before I left.

My eyes acclimated to the gloom while Michael wrestled with details and fumbled through another explanation. I saw empty soda cans and ashtrays full of butts in the front room; Ray's spoor. And beneath the kitchen sink and its pile of dirty dishes, an open trash can with dried-out pizza slices, candy bar wrappers, grocery brown take-out bags, and the like.

"So he's gone too," I said, cutting him short.

"Yes . . . He left . . . a while ago."

"So you're here alone now."

"Uh, not exactly . . ."

As if on cue, the curtain to my bedroom was parted by a hand, followed by a long face, which peered out. It had thick brows that hooded deep-set eyes, and the tuft of a goatee on a nearly pointed chin. We stared at each other over Michael's shoulder, an extended moment that the stranger broke with a flashing pearl-white smile. He emerged then, tall, gliding into the kitchen, followed by what seemed his opposite, short, wiry, with a ruddy, pugnacious face. A sidekick, I thought. The two of them stood there, behind Michael, the tall one sizing me up, the pug scrutinizing me distrustfully. I looked at Michael for an explanation and he ducked his head.

Looking up, he said, "We were about to shoot some speed," suddenly excited, but then ducking down again, reconsidering his reaction. Because of me, and what I might think.

"I prefer the term 'amphetamine,'" the tall one said, and smiled again, teeth gleaming as he nodded, saying without words that of course he and I agreed and shared the same amusement over Michael's misnomer. "Methamphetamine, to be exact."

"This is Skids," Michael said with admiration, and in an aside, "And this is Freddy."

Freddy squinted at me and without a word slipped away into the front room, disdaining niceties. It annoyed me; it was my apartment, after all. But I could also see his point.

Skids had been observing me, and now stepped forward, nearly elbowing Michael out of the way. "*This,*" he said fulsomely, "is the man!" He spoke as if to Michael, while in fact ignoring him. "And it is indeed a pleasure to finally meet you face-to-face, though our friend here neglected to mention your name . . ."

"It's Peter," Michael said sheepishly, and added, "I told you about him."

"Yes, and only good things too," Skids said, this last to me, reassuringly. And then to Michael, critically, "But I couldn't very well recognize him before seeing him, now could I?"

Michael appeared bewildered. "I didn't know . . ."

To me again, Skids said: "Not that we ever spoke, but I *have* set eyes on you before, and you made an impression. To be truthfully honest, I sensed in you a unique presence, a certain charisma, if you will." He paused, perhaps expecting a response, and getting none, smoothly added: "Give me a moment and I'll recall where we were at . . ."

I waited, impassive.

He rubbed his goateed chin, a thoughtful gesture, then raised a long finger, signifying discovery. "It was at a poetry reading, I believe, in one of the coffeehouses. I don't recall whether you yourself read, but as a listener, it was apparent you weren't buying the usual beat boilerplate. I could see it in your face as you ruminated, exercising your inner judgment."

"You must be confusing me with Michael," I replied. "He's the poetic type. I haven't gone to a reading in months."

"I commiserate," he said quickly. "There's not much out there to listen to, is there? It seems everything is derivative nowadays." And again fingering the tuft on his chin, he went on, "Then it must have been in the park. I believe I saw you there with a lovely chick, and I must admit, though I believe to each man his own, I envied you your good fortune."

He waited on me again, while I peripherally noticed Freddy on the couch, unwrapping a tinfoil packet and preparing the works: syringe, spoon, belt.

"Well, then," Skids said, before too many silent beats passed, "it must have been in one of the watering holes, perhaps the Annex or—"

"Maybe you remember seeing me in front of the Cave," I said. "You used to stand out there, wearing a turban, peddling speed."

It deflated him. His shoulders slumped and his jaw dropped, his airy confidence visibly shaken. But he recovered quickly, snapped his long fingers toward my face, said, "What a memory! What a memory! That was months ago. They say, you know, that those who have their eyes open can remember every little thing, and you prove it true."

I turned away from him and said to Michael, "I've got some things to take care of, but I'll be back tonight, and I want your friends out of here by then."

"Why, of course," Skids put in, not so much working on me now as saving face, and, speaking to my back as I left, announced: "A man's home, after all, *is* his castle."

There's clarity in contrast, enhanced perception in transition. It's a natural high, and easily squandered.

Wallowing in recollected gesture and phrase, in personal accomplishment, I bounded downstairs and into the street: *You used to stand out there, wearing a turban, peddling speed.* That had taken the air out of him! *I want your friends out of here by then.* My place had become a crash pad before I left, or rather, fled, because I lacked the cool, unencumbered state of mind to do what was necessary. But now I was a new man, taking control of my life. Yes, my home *was* my castle! He was right about that at least.

And just as expectation had blinded me to the mess I'd left behind as I bounded upstairs and pounded on the door, my triumphant moments while up there, confronting a hipster speed freak and his elfin sidekick, now overrode the sorry state that had so recently left me tongue-tied, stealing food, wandering streets in search of a place to sleep. If the crux of a balanced existence is to be indifferent to both the highs and the lows, I'd already gone in a different direction, gotten back on the roller coaster in no time flat, unreflectively welcomed it, catapulting from homeless despair, to giddy ebullience at coming home, to clear-eyed assessment at facing down a slick Visigoth, and back up, or down, to ebullience again as I hurried away, reveling in my vainglorious homecoming. The tenements cut a swath of shade across half the street, the scene not at all like the sun-drenched Haight, with its gingerbread houses. Stoops, doorways, fire escapes, and brick facades fell away as I barreled past. How quickly thought undoes us!

Hyped on adrenaline, I was a convincing force, and by mid-afternoon had collected a few debts, and with bills in my pocket—a rags to riches story—sat in a glistening luncheonette of formica and mirrors, pushing the remnants of a BLT around my plate; the first meal I'd bought in weeks. Out the plateglass window, the park across the street, lush with trees, was my sprawling estate. But ordinariness was looking over my shoulder as I restlessly considered my next move.

I considered walking up to Astor Place to buy a hand-rolled cigar and returning to the park to sit on a park bench, smoking, as music from across the street wafted into the soda shop. But that was too tame to suit my grandiose mood, and instead I left the place in a hurry, chasing a different idea.

Leo wasn't at Eighth Street. Why did I think he would be, when he was so rarely there? But hearing my plan, Artie, one of his teenage couriers, directed me to a pad on Tenth Street, a hideout, he called it. In fact, Leo wasn't there either, the door opened by Emery, who'd never liked me much. Uncharacteristically forthcoming, he said I could find Leo in the Albert Hotel, in the West Village; which might have been true or not, as I waited in a run-down lobby a dozen blocks later, hoping I'd spot him when he entered or left. Instead, someone whom I didn't much like latched onto me, and in exchange for a few cigarettes led me to a big shot dealer who lived in an elevator building near Union Square. I recognized him right away: Dewey Egbert, a blowhard I'd met a few times at the Sunnyside pad, who boasted he was the biggest dealer in Baltimore, which there was no way to disprove. I'd never trusted Dewey, and he didn't have anything now anyway, but when he stepped out of his apartment and into the hallway, naked except for the towel around his waist, his flabby everyman look on a lanky frame disarmed me. So I believed him when he vouched for a guy who lived on Avenue C near Houston, and I followed that lead south and east, coincidentally passing the luncheonette where I'd been so briefly content what seemed hours ago.

It was nearly dark by then, and darker still when the kid furtively emerged from a half-boarded-up building, handed me a brown paper bag, pocketed my bread, and fled in the other direction. Nothing about it felt right, but I'd long since lost contact with the alarm bell of my intuition, and once more giddy with anticipation, I rushed to the Forum, where I ordered coffee and tipped the waitress with a capsule from my brown bag, then circulated among the tables, distributing more capsules, and moved on to another coffeehouse to distribute the rest.

I sat in that second place a long while, sipping cups of tea for an hour or so, maybe more, awaiting the rush, before grudgingly acknowledging that the rumble in my stomach was not a harbinger of the glorious high I'd envisioned, only the result of all the tea I'd drunk, on top of the coffee. It meant I'd been burned, and worse, that I'd misled everyone I thought I was turning on. How could I have been so foolish as to trust Dewey Egbert?

Disconsolate, I retraced my steps, apologizing to as many of my victims as I could find. To my surprise, no one was angry, and reveling in my own gratefulness, I careened down Tenth Street, back toward my pad, the streetlights shaded by trees, a row of poor man's stately facades on my left, when a hand reached out and grabbed my arm, stopping me in my tracks.

"Kathy!" I exclaimed, turning, seeing her leaning against a car.

"Peter!" she said, echoing me, throwing me back on myself, which perhaps was her purpose. But she tugged at my arm and smiled, so I'd know she wasn't mocking me.

Kathy Baker had a way of getting under my skin and disarming me. It always bothered me that she could do it so easily, and more than once I'd wondered if she'd achieved that ability though drugs. She had a certain presence, after all, yet none of the accompanying mannerisms or vocabulary. Instead, it seemed she did books, of all things, could usually be found in the Forum in the evening, reading hard covers in old bindings: Gurdjieff, Ouspensky, Rudolf Steiner, Krishnamurti. The names meant nothing to me.

She patted the fender, said, "What's your hurry? Have a seat."

I'd been running around most of the day, thinking big thoughts, and hesitated now, as if movement was my natural condition.

"C'mon, sit awhile," she said, thunking the fender again. "I haven't seen you in weeks . . . Weren't you on your way to California?"

"Yeah, I was in Haight-Ashbury," I said, propping myself next to her. It was pleasant beneath the overhanging trees on a summer night, the air a humid but not uncomfortable envelopment, a salutary fish tank. I wondered why I hadn't noticed it until then.

"So when'd you get back?" she asked.

"This morning," I replied, and having said it, realized it was true. "Wow, this morning. It's amazing . . . how the environment gets to you, I mean. To think that only yesterday I was there, and today . . . I've been running around all day, thinking a mile a minute."

"Where were you running *to*?"

The way she put it, I felt rebuked. "I don't know," I said. "It seems the environment took hold of me and wouldn't let me go." I gestured broadly at the block. "I mean, it's so *dense* here. The buildings, the people, the traffic, the noise . . ."

"Don't they have buildings and people and traffic out there too?"

"Well yeah, of course, but it's not the same."

"How so?"

My mind went blank. I couldn't think of a thing. "Well . . . it's hard to put into words . . ."

"Give it a shot."

Recalling Golden Gate Park, I said, "There were lots of trees—bigger than here, and different. Like eucalyptus, which has a unique smell . . . And there are houses, mostly, instead of buildings, only two and three stories tall, and in some places they climb the hills—or what they call hills out there, which are what we'd call mountains. In the morning, the fog obscures them, and as it lifts, they emerge as if in a dream, and the smell of eucalyptus permeates the park . . ."

"Sounds great," she said when I fell silent. "So why'd you come back?"

Again I went blank, then spoke quickly, overriding memory: "Actually, it wasn't so great. For one thing, it was incredibly crowded—"

"It's not exactly deserted here," Kathy said, gesturing at the facades, as I had before.

"Well, yeah, but it was crowded in a different way. You expect crowds in a city, and it was more like a small town there, with too many people in it. And I grew up here, y'know—not in Manhattan, but in Brooklyn and Queens—and you get used to certain things. I mean, the way people talk and what they talk about . . . and you know what you can expect from them. I don't know if it's culture or mannerisms or what, but when you're accustomed to it, anything else seems foreign, even if it might just be different . . ."

While I was talking, giving vent to whatever popped into my head and then attempting to analyze it, to keep other, more personal things at a distance, Tex, a local bum, familiar in the neighborhood, had been moving unevenly up the block, and now he stopped in front of us and held out a hand, asking for money. I stopped talking, dug into a pocket and pulled out two bills, a five and a one, and stared at them a moment, hardly seeing them, before handing him the five. He looked at it longer than I had, and then, without a word, continued up the block.

"*What did you do?*"

The sharp question startled me, and realizing what I'd in fact done, I said, "What?" as if I didn't know what she was talking about.

Kathy bought my contrived innocence, but didn't excuse me. "For chrissake, Peter, you can't just give a five dollar bill to any stranger who puts out his hand!"

I felt foolish, but replied defiantly: "Why shouldn't I?"

"It's not a matter of 'should' or 'shouldn't,'" she said, as if addressing a child. "He was asking for spare change. He would have been content with a quarter, and if you felt the need to be particularly generous, he would have been more than happy with a dollar . . . But five dollars? That's insane!"

"But I *wanted* to give it away," I said stubbornly, stupidly.

"Well, if you really *wanted* to get rid of it, why didn't you give it to me? At least you know me . . . I mean, you're not making any sense, Peter . . . Or maybe you think you're rich?"

"No, of course not," I said, abashed.

"You don't have to prove you're a hippie by giving away your next meal. Or is that something you picked up out there?"

"No," I said. "I guess I just wasn't thinking."

"You *guess?*"

"I wasn't thinking."

"Well, okay then," she said, relenting. "We all make mistakes. And you *are* my favorite hippie, you know, even if I find you exasperating."

I didn't know how to take that. She was both sincere and mocking.

But she wasn't through with me.

"The beads and headbands, peace and love and all that—it's too much, and it's bogus, or at best, naive. But I'd say it's mostly bogus. You're one of the few hippies around here who actually seems to believe in all that. Like those capsules you passed out tonight—"

"You know about that?"

"*Everybody* knows about it, and I was sitting right there in the Forum. You walked past without noticing—and without offering me a dose too, which is just as well—but then, you were so eager to turn everyone on, it seems you hardly knew what you were doing . . . like when you gave old Tex five bucks. It seems you have Haight-Ashbury on the brain."

"It wasn't all so great there," I said. It slipped out.

I was relieved she didn't pick up on it and question me. Instead she said, acerbically, "If not for your hippie innocence, you'd be persona non grata."

She'd lost me. "What'd you mean?"

"I *mean,*" she said, annoyed, "though people had every right to feel put out, no one held you accountable . . . You didn't suffer for your poor judgment. Instead, they suffered your foolishness."

Warding her off, I said, "I'm not as innocent as you think. I've done things that I felt bad about . . . that I regretted afterward."

"Yes, you have a conscience," she said. "That's not my point. What I'm saying is—"

"But everyone has a conscience."

Kathy looked at me a moment. "It would be nice to think so," she replied. "But in fact a lot of people don't care who they hurt."

"Maybe so, but they have a conscience too," I insisted. "They might lose sight of it now and then, but it's there all the same, because it's part of who we are, whether we know it or not, whether we call it conscience, or character, or soul, or—"

"Oh please!" she said, pushing off the car. "You don't know what you're talking about."

"It's why everyone was so good about the capsules tonight," I went on, worked up. "I mean, they could have gotten angry. You said yourself that they had every right. But they didn't, because people are more generous than we give them credit for. I realized that afterward. It's something I'd overlooked, that I'd forgotten about. It's—"

"You haven't learned a thing!" she said, raising her voice, thrusting a finger at me. "But you'll probably have to fall flat on your face before you wise up." Then, abruptly, in a different, matter-of-fact tone, offering neutral advice, she added, "People aren't always going to make allowances for you, Peter."

And with that she turned away and headed up the block without a backward glance.

Leo's Hexagram

Leo's birthday party took place in the backyard terrace of the coffeehouse on Tenth near Avenue B. There had always been a coffeehouse there, and though it had gone through several different owners and name changes, it was still basically the same place—the Omega now, the Blind Justice one night long ago, where he'd danced on a tabletop.

The lantern-lit terrace was always crowded on a summer evening, but Leo had reserved it for the party, and his friends and acquaintances arrived in a festive mood.

Nearly all of the Eighth Street crowd were there. Rose, done up in rouge and kohl and sparkle makeup. Ray, with a cowboy hat and a fringed shirt. Carl wore a toga, and Annie, with whom he shared a closet, an elegant black satin dress and a faux pearl necklace. Leo's teenage lieutenants, all three of them, sported flashy Hawaiian shirts, and then Emily showed up, in a sari with tiny inset mirrors, and Gary, who'd become religious of late, an acolyte in civilian garb now, ostentatiously nondescript. Richie Klein, who now ran in exclusive speed freak circles, sat fidgeting in a crimson cape and gaucho hat with a peacock feather in the band. And finally Arnie Glick arrived, unfashionably late, and was coolly received, though everyone wanted to pet his dog. He took a seat at a side table with the local dealers, who had been then awhile. They would leave early, after their more expensive, store-bought presents were opened and duly noted by the influential birthday boy.

Beaming, Leo reveled in the attention as people embraced him and set their gifts on the main table. But before he opened them, the specially made cake was brought out from the kitchen, set down and lit, and the gathering sang the traditional song as he looked on with glistening eyes. He was touched, momentarily overwhelmed by sentiment, his usually articulate hands speechless. But his fingers were as nimble as ever as he opened the presents, the guests oohing and aahing like children as the wrapping paper came off and the gifts were unveiled: an intricate, handmade psychedelic drawing; a hand-knit scarf and string of homemade beads; a paperback copy of the *Bhagavad Gita*, and an almost new hardcover *I Ching*, from Rose, whose card was an aura piece like those in her trip book—of Leo, haloed in gold. The more expensive offerings included a brass incense burner, a hookah pipe, and a pair of leather boots with a trick heel where contraband could be hidden, which got a big laugh.

By then tea had been served and the traditional cake mostly eaten, and the dealers and local poobahs began to leave, now that they'd made an appearance. The rest gathered closer around the main table, an intimate group as Leo threw down the yarrow sticks and Rose recorded the yin and yang of his birthday I Ching. When the hexagram was completed, she consulted the table in back, found the pattern, and began to read aloud.

As she spoke of heaven and earth, in the flowery language of ancient translation, and the meaning of it unfolded, the night sky seemed to press down on the terrace, a dark lid over the tenements and adjacent backyards, the clotheslines and clutter an all-too-human reminder of the ground below, as the lines of the hexagram put it, compressed by the heavy lines. The dozen or so people huddled at what now seemed a beggars' banquet seemed to share a common fate, and when Rose was through, the mood subdued, the costumed finery was transparent child's play in an indifferent universe.

The reading hit Leo hard. He believed in omens, after all, lived in accordance with them. To him, they were reflections of the moment, or of underlying conditions that would play out in time. The clicking sound on pay phones throughout the neighborhood, which it was rumored were tapped. The bearded young men in the old and newer coffeehouses, wearing not baggy, but tailored hippie outfits. And what possible interpretation could there be for the cameras in the park during the day, capturing ordinary scenes as if they were tourist sights? It was all of a piece with the crackdown in hospital laboratories, where orderlies were no longer trusted with the keys to cabinets where certain chemicals were kept, which made it hard to supply Emery with the necessary ingredients. And now this I Ching reading with its solemn conclusion:

> *Contemplate the four directions . . .*
> *Keep private counsel . . . Work on inner purification . . .*
> *In a time of upheaval, the superior man refrains . . .*
> *It does not further one to cross the great water.*

*   *   *

As usual, the rent at Eighth Street hadn't been paid, but until the eviction notice came, no one knew how long it had been; three months, the official form said. A half-dozen people and a few transients were living at the pad. Patrick and Rose, who'd been there from the beginning. Ray, Emily, and Gary. Carl, of course, who'd made the place his reclamation project, and was later joined by the self-possessed Annie, who never lost her cool. The teenagers, of course, who also had no idea where Leo was; in hiding somewhere, they said, Vermont, maybe, or upstate New York; Leo and the bread he might have come up with to save the place.

Carl, the first to recognize the new tao, got a job selling candles and incense at the head shop on Avenue A, which was booming. Then Annie joined him behind the counter, and Patrick was hired to make hash pipes in a back room. Rose contributed what she could from her trust fund, and Gary and Emily scavenged thrown-away items to sell on the sidewalk at Astor Place: used clothes, dog-eared books, record albums, odds and ends. But all of it was only a fraction of what one of Leo's drug deals would have produced.

When the second notice came, it was apparent they would never raise enough unless they went uptown and got full-time jobs and, worse, kept them for a while. Then Patrick moved out—no one knew where—Carl and Annie found their own pad, and the remaining crew fell back on their old ways, living in the actual present without regard for an abstract future. And why not? If you don't think about it, who can know the future or even glimpse its outline until it presents itself?

It arrived one day as four neatly dressed young men. Rose let them in and returned to her usual spot, to resume her latest series of drawings, heads outlined in glowing marker colors, auras of green, yellow, indigo, purple, orange. L.A. Ray, stringy thin now, with gray skin and jaundiced eyes from the sketchy drugs he'd been taking, was sprawled on a mattress in the main room, along with Marty and Artie, who had nothing to do now that Leo was incognito, and without any drugs to make boredom more interesting. Farther back, Gary and Emily were working on still another mural, or rather, redoing it, since all the walls were already covered. She was adding a Peter Max rainbow to a Himalayan mountain scene, and he redid the same hovering angel he hadn't gotten quite right the first and second time around.

Ill at ease, the four intruders tired to ignore the occupants as they examined the place, peering into rooms and closets. They checked the floors for splinters and the walls and ceiling for cracks, turned on faucets, flushed the toilet, gathered in a huddle and spoke in hushed voices, out of squeamishness or a sense of danger or both, since the bedraggled tenants they pretended not to see were silently hostile and somehow filled the rooms like alien beings with a curious power. The well-reported neighborhood, cited in the *Times* as New York's answer to Haight-Ashbury, was considered glamorous, and this dissipated scene with its strange people confounded them. But they were there to assess in order to buy, and so they pushed nervousness aside and hewed to that assignment. With their future comfort in mind, they reimagined the place with a stereo here, a leather couch and recliner there; perhaps louver doors to create separate, private bedrooms. And of course (voices lowered even further), the walls had to be painted—the ridiculous murals would definitely have to go.

Arnie Glick had been unwelcome at Eighth Street because he had a merchant's persona. But these intruders were a quantum leap beyond his particular money trip and his meager notion of prosperity, which consisted of eating in a restaurant once a day. Where he had somewhat risen above bare necessity, these guys had a different floor, took for granted an acquisitive culture whose edges Arnie only nibbled at. To the Eighth Street tenants, these assessors were spiritual barbarians, and with the disdain of a superior race, they silently regarded the interlopers with disdain as they poked around and spoke to each other, making plans for the future.

End tables, lamps, a record cabinet . . . Completing their inspection, they bowed out of the place with awkward politeness.

They called the real estate agent to tell him that the tenants were still there and work had to be done before they'd move in, because the place was a wreck. The agent called the landlord, who called the city marshal, and in due course the place was cleared out and a padlock clamped on the door.

Rose had the bread to find her own pad, but she hung around to the end, then moved in with two of her old sorority sisters who'd just found a place in the neighborhood, where it seemed everyone wanted to be. They took turns shopping, cooking, and cleaning up, and Rose discovered that the old pre-psychedelic routines, the schedule of household chores posted in the kitchen—who would take out the garbage on this or that day, clean the bathroom, do the shopping and the dishes—no longer suited her. She found the custom of private rooms as anachronistic as the nightly on-time meals and the girlish group excursions to the supermarket or the movies. And then there was the oddity of having to consider the feelings of others, which were easily bruised, when all she wanted was to sit in silence, drawing, sewing, or examining her thoughts.

Her solution was to make herself scarce, to find places to go, which more often than not was the Omega, where she now did informal, nightly I Ching readings—Leo's hexagram had given her the idea—to which she added tarot and astrology, holding court as a fortune teller of sorts. She looked forward to it, and used the afternoon to prepare for the evening.

With theatrical flair, she'd rouge her cheeks and put kohl around her eyes, put on a long, flowing, peasant dress, a jangle of cheap bracelets, pendulous earrings, and wind a head scarf around her head into a turban, becoming a dress-up Gypsy. It was a contrived role, but she got a kick out of it, and it suited her expressive self. Where before she'd been a haphazard confidante and the repository of local goings-on, she was now a recognized adviser, with skills ranging from tea leaves to Turkish coffee grounds and everything in between.

It happened that one coffeehouse idler paid a lot of attention to her—Big Ed, he called himself—and Rose found him attractive, despite the huge, tacky silver peace symbol that lay flat on his curly-haired chest in the vee of his flamboyant open-neck shirt. He was tall and lean, with a bushy beard, and like Tom, didn't talk much but was a good listener. When he casually invited her to move in with him, without making a big deal about it, she agreed; and by moving in with him, extricated herself from the sorority pad without offending her old friends.

Ed's pad was curiously bare of all but utilitarian necessities, but thinking to make lemonade out of that lemon, she volunteered to decorate the place. Sure, he said, if it made her happy. So she bought fabric to serve as a bedspread and for curtains, did a few colorful sketches to tack to the walls, and shopped in out of the way places for plants, scatter rugs, and throw pillows.

And it intrigued her to crack his nut, to see what he was about. He was enigmatic, mysterious, and most of all, had no aura she could divine. It didn't occur to her, however, that the way he doted on her stories and gossip might be a clue to what made him tick. He couldn't get enough of them, and finding it easy to confide in him, she told him about everything that came her way. The big drug deal in the works that Arnie Glick had boasted about, for instance, and other deals she'd picked up on and revealed more about than she knew she should.

Expressive types can be undone by silence. It all but compels them to spill their guts, out of disquiet at not knowing what the other is thinking.

And then, abruptly, after the vacuum of his silence had sucked up everything she had to offer, Big Ed disappeared, leaving Rose in the apartment she'd decorated, with not a personal thing left anywhere to indicate where he might have gone or who he was.

Like one businessman measuring himself against another, Arnie Glick both envied and resented Leo's success. If there was a brand name among psychedelic drug dealers, it was Leo Makaris, and Arnie gave him his due for that. But Leo had never been particularly friendly toward him, and more often than not he'd had to grovel for Leo's favors. But now, with Leo in hiding and at least temporarily out of the picture, Arnie imagined filling the void he'd left behind. It might also have occurred to him that stepping into those shoes at a time when drugs were scarce might well restore his reputation, which had been in decline ever since the fire next door had chased everyone away.

That basement pad had been a hot spot, where people came to him for blotter acid, sugar cubes, and the like, homemade concoctions, this before Sandoz and Owsley and buffered pills and tablets pushed small-timers and amateur chemists aside. And now, with no pills or tablets of any kind to be had, the old entrepreneurial days seemed relevant again.

Arnie had no trouble finding enterprising characters who could cook with beacon burners and needed cash, and through them, he secured a half-gallon wine jug of liquid LSD; actually, somewhat less than a quart before he diluted it and sold eyedrop doses at an inflated price.

Overnight, after weeks of obscurity, Arnie Glick became a character to be dealt and reckoned with. With his profit, he bought new boots, a silk shirt, and cut a proud figure when he strode out for his nightly meal. There were others who had emerged on the scene, for the same reason, and they all dined together, a guild of sorts, meeting in the coffeehouses they frequented. And during the day, he was greeted in the park while walking his ubiquitous dog, and invited admirers and sycophants back to his pad, where a new, shifting crew now smoked grass and hash and angled for a psychedelic shot from the bottle of spiked wine. Arnie reveled in his new circumstance, and took advantage of the deference with which he was treated to hold forth as a philosopher king of sorts. A debunker, he scoffed at faddist cosmic illusions and health food diets, and derided India and the Orient in favor of the Greeks, declaiming for the meat and potatoes of the mind-body, the good life that had less to do with Mars, Pluto, or Vishnu than a full belly.

The subtext was that he wanted to be taken seriously. And in accordance with his philosophy, and his psychology—which he also dismissed, along with the planets, Buddha, and the Hindu gods—he understood that celebrity could be short-lived, that when the stuff that had so recently made him a magnet was gone, he'd be back where he was before. So Arnie thought a lot about the next big deal.

It would require more cash than what he had on hand, more than he could raise from the small-time coffeehouse crew. Which meant he had to contact people he didn't personally know—not only friends of friends, but their acquaintances; anyone at all, in fact, who had at least a hundred dollars, a nice round number he settled on, his bottom line. It would be the biggest he'd ever put together; a deal to rival those Leo had been known for.

As a result, by the time it was ready to go down, a lot of people knew about it.

On the big day, Arnie was in the kitchen, taking a bath, when he heard the soft but persistent tap on the door and assumed that someone had gotten the time wrong and arrived early. In fact, an hour early. Annoyed, he stepped out of the tub, tucked a towel around his hips, opened the door, and gaped at the business end of a police revolver.

The three plainclothes cops in the hallway pushed their way in, told him to welcome anyone who showed up, and positioned themselves out of sight. Plaintively, Arnie asked if he could at least get dressed. The lead cop said no, they preferred him that way; it looked more natural.

Half an hour later the parade began. They showed up alone or in pairs, and Arnie opened the door and beckoned them inside. Before anyone could even ask why he wasn't dressed, two of the cops appeared, slammed them against a wall, frisked them, then shoved the startled visitors into the small bedroom, where the third cop ensured their silence with his grim-looking gun.

In all, a dozen were arrested; later to be released for lack of evidence, since the shipment never arrived. A lucky break, for them, yet one more indignity for Arnie Glick, who would become the butt of coffeehouse jokes: caught with his pants down.

Patrick Malone had a complicated relationship with cops. He admired them as tough, unsentimental, disciplined, and fair, no doubt because he thought of himself that way. And it was his unusual obsession to meld this inner centurion with that of the truth seeker whose sacrament was psychedelic drugs.

It was a confounding contradiction, and led him to take risks few appreciated. Once, spotting what he was sure were two federal undercover cops one evening, he invited them to Eighth Street, where he promised to turn them on. Perhaps he was reliving his own experience, when he'd been turned on by Timothy Leary; only in this version, he would play Leary's part and the two cops would see the light and become, like him, law enforcement apostates.

The two cops, in hippie guise, were amazed to find themselves in an actual hippie pad, with incense and burning candles and third eye depictions of blue-skinned gnomes in a Lord of the Rings mural. The communards were equally amazed, and the place went silent when they walked in. Leo, making a rare visit, pulled Patrick aside and castigated him for putting everyone in jeopardy, as the cops waited in the entrance hallway, eyeing the real hippies who so brazenly populated the place.

Rejoining them, Patrick explained that he'd made a mistake, that there were no drugs to be had, and since everyone was uptight about outsiders, they'd have to leave. The two guys, seemingly relieved, quickly split.

And then there was Memorial Day, when Patrick found himself in a group of a dozen hippies lounging on the center grass oval in the park when a SWAT team, responding to a noise complaint from one of the neighborhood's older immigrants, marched into the crowded park and surrounded the oval. The precinct captain, a reasonable man without an ax to grind, had the day off, his holiday replacement giving head to the cops' hostility toward hippies.

Hundreds of people from throughout the park gravitated to the cordon and stood five and six deep behind the cops, staring at the dozen trapped in the oval as the squad commander, speaking through a bullhorn, ordered the dozen to give themselves up. In response, the hippies linked arms. Plastic visors clicked down on riot helmets along the police perimeter, billy clubs raised in attack position as a frisson of fear rippled through the park.

And then, in the roaring silence, Patrick, of all people, stood up, disengaging himself from the huddled group, arms held high, palms open. The silence held as he moved into the no-man's-land between the cops and the hippies, the puzzled crowd murmuring, not knowing what to make of it. I watched too, taken by the suspended moment Patrick's actions created, a respite of opportunity, a chance to avert disaster, which I assumed had been his intent. But as the police cordon parted to let him pass and then closed ranks again, Patrick seemed oblivious to the possibility he'd fashioned, walking with grim purpose toward the open paddy wagon, looking neither right nor left.

The crowd found its voice then, forgot about Patrick as he climbed into the wagon, people shouting, protesting, the moment lost, and then, at an invisible signal, the helmeted troopers charged into the oval.

The crowd scattered in the opposite direction, as if propelled by centrifugal force, fleeing the mayhem of clubs hacking and chopping at bodies, of cries and screams as the dozen hippies were dragged out and thrown in the wagon where Patrick sat curled in a corner.

Abruptly, it was over, the paddy wagon slammed shut and driven away, the cops marching off in a phalanx, the park dazed, as in the aftermath of a tornado.

There would be no more police riots that summer, but afterward, the oval remained empty, taboo, no matter how crowded the park.

And now Patrick was again among those held captive, in Arnie Glick's bedroom, glaring at the cop who held the gun as one more customer in the hallway knocked on the door.

"Who is it?" Arnie said, as he'd been told.

"It's me . . . Bernie," came the reply.

And in the crowded room, Patrick shouted, "Run, Bernie! Run!"

Bernie ran downstairs and a cop bolted after him, while in the bedroom prison cell Patrick was slapped across the face and slammed against the wall.

The cop pressed the gun barrel to Patrick's forehead. "One more word outta you," he said, "and I put a bullet in your skull."

Patrick, defiant, looked back at him, said, "Go ahead. Shoot."

Emily was accustomed to feast on the atmosphere of stoned garret settings and basement hovels. With the aid of certain drugs, all manner of ordinary objects could conjure an adventurous life of the mind, populated by poets and artists; accentuated, enhanced, framed and composed in a truer-than-life gallery, an archetypal world of myth.

But now, in crash pads and on the street, she found no elevating beauty, even with the interlocution of drugs. The low-down aspect of the ordinary had no enchanting veneer, it was merely squalid.

At Eighth Street, when she and Carl were working on a wall whose cracks inspired improvisation, the contours of a mural, he'd told her that desire fostered illusion. She suspected he was talking about her, but the intensity of Carl's declarations was intoxicating, and she fell in love, again. Emily fell in love a lot. But not recently, taxed as she was by a succession of dismal hovels that lacked redeeming aesthetic value.

So she went back to the Gramercy Park penthouse of the rich young socialite, where she'd once stolen shirts and vests from a walk-in closet emporium and brought them downtown to one of the men she'd considered a true love.

The penthouse was a fabulous place, with its expensive oil paintings, thick-pile rugs, and a terrazzo bathroom with a massive Jacuzzi in which she and the other girls reclined with their benefactor, smoking hashish from an ornate hookah. The silk kimonos they wore were embossed with dragons and lotus blossoms, and the Turkish pillows were actually from Turkey, not some bargain store in the West Village. Scented candles burned in ceremonial splendor, and she floated in a Belladonna haze, wind chimes tinkling on the gargoyle-guarded balcony that overlooked the charmingly well-heeled twentieth century scene.

It might have occurred to Emily that she'd sold out. Or maybe not. Sold out what, after all? What was there to sell? In a cruel hand-to-mouth universe, things had fallen apart, entropied, as Carl might have put it. You could almost see it happening before your eyes. In the penthouse the cosmic truisms were of course no less true, but at least it wasn't decrepit.

Still, encountering the haughty women in the lobby, on their way in or out with their clothed poodles, it had to occur to Emily that poverty was at least honestly unpretentious. And it would have been difficult for her to laugh silently at these absurd paragons of society when they looked at her condescendingly, like dirt.

Nobody likes feeling cheap.

Stoned, I gazed down at the street from my sixth floor window, ogling the depth and breadth of dimension; the fire escape friezes on tenement facades, the cylindrical garbage cans clustered on the sidewalk like sculptures, the clunky cars parked at the curb, gleaming with garish chrome. A few people peered out of windows and lounged on the stoops, and occasionally a minuscule figure entered the funky tableau, and I'd track that living puppet from my superior perch, wondering about its unconscious internal commands.

One afternoon, grooving on this diorama, I recognized a compact figure down there, walking briskly, a fedora hat pulled low on his forehead. The last time I'd seen him, he'd been in the backyard terrace of the Omega, and now he was back. He'd stayed away as long as he could, it seemed, before his mission to save himself, and all of us, from our worst selves overcame him. It was sad, seeing Leo down there, recalling the hexagram, knowing that the superior man had not been able to refrain, was no more superior than anyone else.

A few days later, while passing a newsstand, a tabloid headline caught my eye: L.I. DRUG FACTORY RAIDED. I looked around furtively, afraid someone might find my more than casual interest suspect, moved closer and peered at the full-page photograph.

I recognized Emery covering his head with a Gestapo raincoat while being led into a police station. And next to him, half a head shorter, Leo, trying to shield his face with cuffed hands, the grainy mind-set of the *Daily News* an everyday distortion I mistook for truth: that he knew what he'd done was wrong.

A Crisis of Meaning

I'd lugged the steamer trunk up to the roof, dragged it across to the adjoining building and down the stairwell to the crash pad door, where no one answered my knock. Jeffrey had said he'd take care of the trunk while I was gone, keep an eye on it until I got back. And now I wondered what to do.

I stood there in the chalky light from the open rooftop door, pondering it. A girl was waiting for me in the park. We had plans to hitchhike to Boston, where I'd gone to college for a year. I hadn't much liked it there, but in retrospect, recalled it fondly. So I told myself that Jeffrey would find it there when he returned and lug it inside, and I split.

Of course, it was gone when I returned, as I'd known it would be. In fact, the building was a junkie lair, and Jeffrey, an ex-junkie himself, had talked about moving out. He'd never laid eyes on it.

"It's my own fault," I said to him, sitting in a new pad, which he shared with his girlfriend, Marlene. "I never should've left it there." He frowned, taking the loss to heart, and I quickly added that it only contained some old clothes and books and the notes I'd made while doing research on my master's thesis.

"Your master's thesis?" he said, alarmed.

"It's not a big deal," I assured him. "It was on the Spanish Civil War, and I lost interest in the subject a long time ago."

The notebooks of handwritten script, quotes I'd copied from old newspapers on microfilm in the stacks at the New York Public Library, months of work . . . All that time spent, squandered. It seemed I should have felt bad, but how can you lose time when it's already gone? It did bother me that my parents had taken out a loan so I could go to graduate school, and now I wouldn't get the degree—even though that money was gone now, like the time I'd spent on the thesis. But then, unlike the time, the money hadn't been mine.

Losing the books that were in the trunk bothered me more, what I'd read and thought about . . . my notebooks, ideas I'd jotted down, doodles even . . .

the things that had moved me, put down on paper, evidence of the person I'd been, defining the world as he saw it.

"It was nothing, really," I told Jeffrey. "Just possessions."

I'd lugged the trunk across the rooftop after getting a second eviction notice, and pictured it locked inside when I returned. But it came as a shock when I climbed the stairs one afternoon and saw the padlock on the door.

I stared at it in disbelief, breathing the mildewed air of the hallway, an incense redolent of chagrin, picturing the main room. My window perch overlooking the city . . . the candle's flame, emitting waves and particles . . . the stillness of a long, perfect night that seemed to go on forever. Unlike the master's thesis, which was a framework of ideas, these were things I'd perceived. A more profound work in progress, an epiphany of who I might possibly be. My supposed career as a journalist was nothing compared to it.

And then I thought about the trunk—not what was stored in it as it sat in the hallway where I'd abandoned it, but as itself, a totem resting in its usual place inside, a porcelain-smooth puddle of melted wax coating the top of it and flowing down one side like a drip-sand castle . . .

It was a sad rush, as I stood there in the hallway, my heart dipping, leaving an empty feeling in my chest.

I stumbled downstairs, knowing I was leaving the building for the last time. On the ground floor the super popped out of her apartment, no doubt having seen me enter earlier, knowing that I'd find the padlock on the door. She regarded me with an uncertain frown; a hefty black woman who in recent weeks had gently reminded me about the rent, as if I might have forgotten to pay it—for three months.

"You have somewheres else to stay?" she asked.

"Yes, yes," I replied, embarrassed by her concern. "I'll be all right."

I moved past, toward the street door, eager to get away, but she followed me outside and called out, "You take care now, y'hear?" as I moved away.

I hurried up the street, didn't pay attention at the corner as the light changed, then dashed across as cars approached. On the next block, I passed the narrow church that never seemed open, then the basement apartments, Arnie's inn and Tom's pad next door, gutted now. Beyond them, a passage led to a courtyard and the newer building where the Sunnyside gang had treated me like a king when I dropped by. Across the street, farther up the block, was Arnie's latest pad, where I'd popped in on him that spring morning long ago, and the building where Roger had weaseled a dose from Leo before going berserk, and the one that contained the timeless chamber where I'd witnessed Mohammed's miracle one night.

Near the end of the block, I veered into a hallway, trudged up five floors, and knocked on a door.

Jeffrey opened it. He was glad to see me. "You can stay as long as you like," he said, in his soft drawl from somewhere in the South.

An emotional sort, he still hadn't gotten over the loss of my trunk. He gripped me by the arm and pulled me to the soft chair by the window. As with my old sixth-floor throne, it was the seat of honor, though instead of a panorama of the city, I saw a sprawl of tenement backyards, discarded appliances, a gingko tree, a jungle of weeds.

Marlene, heavyset, with frizzy hair, served tea, and Jeffrey lit a cone of incense and rolled a joint. And as I sat there in the regal chair, my shattered mood as I'd walked up the block, flashing on the past, flip-flopped, became an impressive résumé, the place of honor by the window a deserved tribute for one who'd been around as long as I had and experienced so much. I was one of the old ones, an Olympian in the company of Tom and Leo, Rose and Patrick, Emily and Arnie Glick and Leo Makaris and the rest. All of them giants. And as I sipped the tea, I took the deference with which I was treated as my due.

Maybe I was grieving. I had no energy, felt lethargic. I lingered at Jeffrey and Marlene's pad most of the day, gazing out the rear window, chewing the fat with Marlene until she tired of my company, found some chore to attend to, and split, leaving me to myself.

That's when I came across a pulp magazine someone had left there: *Astrology Today*. Bored, I picked it up, at first merely perusing it, and then poring through it. Afterward, I went out and bought several more of the same type.

The scheme they described fascinated me—sun, moon, and planets passing through astronomical houses, determining behavior, providing answers, predicting the future. I couldn't get enough of it.

Jeffrey was rarely around during the day. He was out peddling grass. And when he walked in, I'd tell him about my latest discoveries and he'd listen with rapt attention.

"What about me?" he asked, after I'd bent his ear with the pseudo science of it. "What are Cancers like?"

In fact, I wasn't sure; I'd concentrated on planets and houses that pertained to me. But I discoursed on his sign anyway, embellishing my pulp knowledge with what I'd observed of him in the course of ordinary, earthly life. "You're a survivor," I told him. "You zig and zag this way and that, like a crab, but you always find your way and never lose your good nature."

Marlene, a solicitous and protective presence who always seemed to loom over him when he was around, said, "I could have told you that myself, Jeff. And I don't sit around all day thinking about astrology."

It was a rebuke. I was almost always there, after all, reading my magazines, and she was growing tired of my presence. Thinking fast, I said, "I understand your misgivings," and drawing upon Jupiter, allied to my moon in Pisces, told her, "As a Capricorn, you're pragmatic and empirical," though in fact I considered her obtuse and stubborn. And having thus softened her up, because people like nothing better than hearing about themselves, I went on to explain that I was empirical too, and as proof, told her what had won me over to the influence of the planets.

I'd been sitting in the park, watching couples stroll the paths beneath lights emanating haloes, as someone strummed melodious chords on a guitar. An idyllic scene. Then two dogs got into a snarling fight, and a moment later I heard a siren approach, and then everyone was moving, hurrying in all directions.

"As if a switch had been thrown," I said. "Where before there'd been contentment, there was now chaos. Clearly, the unseen force that at first possessed the smaller animals now possessed the larger ones . . . I was affected too, of course. I was nervous and jittery instead of placid and calm. Even the lamp light, so soft and soothing before, was now harsh, illuminating too much—if you know what I mean—and the air itself, formerly gentle and comforting, had become thick and the humidity stifling."

Jeffrey listened intently, and Marlene, whose reaction was more important to me, seemed captivated as well. I paused several seconds, adding suspense to my tale.

"The next day, out of curiosity, I checked the movement of the planets the night before and discovered that not only had the moon been full, but it moved from Taurus to Gemini—the astrological houses—each characterized by the moods I'd witnessed . . . It blew my mind!"

Jeffrey, impressed, shook his head in wonderment. "Amazing."

But to my disappointment, Marlene merely shrugged and said, "It might have been a coincidence."

Her skepticism gnawed at me, and it became my challenge to turn her around, to win her over.

I told her about Cancer, for instance, when we were alone in the pad, as we usually were. I'd since boned up on it, in order to dissect Jeffrey, transposing him to an amalgam of inclinations and tendencies. I told Marlene everything I could recall, and a few things I again drew from personal observation. Why

Jeffrey worked so hard, dealing nickels and dimes all day, as if it were a nine-to-five job, and above and beyond that, the source of his good nature. It was his most significant quality, which I knew Marlene valued, having taken it upon herself to defend him against anyone who might take advantage of his innate generosity.

"You're right," she said when I finished. "Jeff is like that."

Emboldened by her agreement, I went on to expostulate on Capricorn, her own sign, a salesman eager to seal the deal, telling her: "You're pessimistic, but that's good, because it's rooted in a realistic take on the world . . . and you seek security in authority, or provide it as an authority over others, which is no doubt why Jeffrey relies on you."

Pleased, she brewed another pot of tea, freshened our cups, and sat back down to hear more. When I left the pad to take a walk, I knew I'd done well.

But Marlene's good nature was more capricious, less unconditional, than Jeffrey's. I sensed as much, and the specter of her possible disagreement kept me on edge. I knew I had to be careful, and what's more, my natal chart objectively confirmed it: my planets were currently in distress, my moods swinging from house to house. A discordant word or phrase could undo me at any moment. Leaning on Jupiter, which had become my doppelganger, it was clear my task was to anticipate problems in advance; though less clear that my planetary configuration consigned me to explain or talk them away, rather than confront them.

One afternoon when I was running off at the mouth, ascribing my financial difficulties to Saturn and predicting that next month would be better for me, Marlene cuttingly recited my words back at me. "Next month?" she said with a raised eyebrow.

Realizing I'd made a serious mistake, that I'd brought my constant presence to the fore, I scrambled out of there.

I spent the day wandering the park and side streets, then moved on to the coffeehouses in the evening, and then, at night, to the Avenue.

The Avenue . . .

The strip of sidewalk on one side of the block, on Avenue A between Tenth and Eleventh, had once stirred my imagination, appearing larger than life, mythical. Barcelona, controlled briefly by the anarchists—a chapter in my lost thesis—a vision of a utopian, egalitarian society. But after hanging out there, it was clear there was no more equality on that street than anyplace else. In fact it was brutal, a testing ground of weakness and strength, where perceived indifference or vulnerability rendered people deserving of respect or not. And though I wouldn't admit it to myself, I was among those to be taken advantage of or ignored. With my astrological shield to protect me, my pulp interpretations, I'd linger amidst the sidewalk throng, drawing conclusions, ascribing qualities, situating myself among the invulnerable.

Everyone might have had long hair and worn beads and bandannas, but it meant nothing, really, seemed to mock what I would have them believe. On the strip, the big-time dealers were surrounded by admirers and sycophants, in a tribe of the more or less slick or bumbling, with its grapevine in which a drop of truth or fact quickly became rumor, like the childhood game telephone. The narcs among us, drug deals gone bad, government surveillance, threats of vengeance, even ethnic resentment toward the Puerto Ricans with whom we shared the neighborhood . . .

It was an ugly marketplace, yet I stuck around, even gravitated to it, because I had nowhere else to go, except the pad where Marlene had me in her sights. I thought about that, a lot, put off going back as the night wore on and the talk got nastier, hoping she'd be in a good mood when I finally returned, or that Jeffrey, who for some reason still looked up to me—perhaps because we saw so little of each other—would be there to shield me with his admiration.

Spotting me on the Avenue one evening, Arnie Glick offered to buy me dinner, and I of course agreed.

The Forum served food until eight o'clock, and he ordered his usual meat and potatoes. Taking my cue from him, I did too. Since the bust, Arnie had regained his reputation among small-time merchants, and they approached our table as we ate, some to exchange greetings, others to sit down and talk about upcoming possibilities. They nodded vaguely in my direction, and I made myself invisible; concentrating on my plate or staring into the room, pretending not to listen.

It was not the first time I'd retreated into anonymity. In the basement apartments, I'd been a pinhead in a dream; and in Haight-Ashbury, lost in the crowd. Now, diminished by the breezy self-assurance of the dealers, I was a cipher. But I had another eye too, which took in the inconsequential talk and left me unimpressed, disdainful, even, of the shallow characters who seemed to know nothing but buying and selling.

When we finished eating and the dealers moved on, Arnie suggested we go someplace else, maybe to a club to listen to music. I suggested Slugs, on First Street. I knew the place from my college years, when a few of us who were into jazz would come into the city on a Friday or Saturday night. He'd heard of it and liked the idea, and we walked down there and settled into a corner table in that smoky den.

The music put Arnie in a good mood, and he bought a round of beer and then another. I felt good too, in that vibrating hovel, reexperienced what it felt like to enjoy myself without scrutinizing my reactions, rediscovered the forgetfulness of that familiar immersion. And then I lost that head and noticed how awkward Arnie appeared, tapping on the tabletop, trying to lose himself in the flow of sound and not quite succeeding.

As long as I'd known him, Arnie Glick never had friends, only acquaintances, and when we left the club and he invited me back to his pad, I concluded that he'd sought out my company that night because no one else he knew would hang out with him unless they wanted something.

He still lived there with his dog, who nudged me, then licked my hands beneath the table. And the place was still gloomy and dank. Arnie had flicked on the overhead light, and when I shielded my eyes, lit a candle and turned it off. "You never did like electricity," he said. "Why is that, do you think?"

I lit a cigarette from the pack on the table. "Because it's artificial," I replied.

"Artificial?" he repeated, lighting his own cigarette, drawing in the candle flame. "What does that mean? How can anything be artificial? Everything that is, *is.*"

I had to think about that, which surprised me. Arnie's remarks usually didn't require reflection.

And then he continued to surprise me, speaking with gravity, in a way he hadn't with the dealers or while we were in the noisy club. He'd been in a funk, he told me. Recently, it seemed he had to convince himself that things were important, when in fact he didn't care.

"I don't even like getting high anymore," he confided. "Even on acid."

"Really?" I replied, as if the notion were inconceivable, though the last few trips I'd taken had been difficult.

"I mean, I've heard of people having bad trips," he went on, "but I couldn't imagine it . . . wanting, you know, to jump out of a window. Not that I ever would. It's just that when I'm on acid now, I feel a sense of . . . I don't know, dread, I guess you'd call it, and I can't seem to make it go away."

I said, "Maybe there's something particular bothering you."

"You mean, like, psychological?"

"Yeah . . . maybe."

"I don't know," he replied. "I never paid much attention to that kind of thing. But Patrick once said something interesting—that after a while, when you get high, you set up a whole new set of defenses, different than those you set up before, though they protect the same things."

"What things?" I asked, thinking about his relationship with women; that he'd never been with any I knew about.

"I don't know. Whatever it is that people fear . . ."

Fear.

The word produced a frisson in me. It was not an unusual reaction. On the Avenue, when some vague something got to me, it set off a throb in my plexus, and I'd start trembling. My hand was quivering now, as I took a long drag on the cigarette.

"I never thought I'd say this about Patrick," Arnie said, "but he might've been right. Sometimes I get a glimpse of myself setting up a defense . . . It's like I'm looking sideways at it, watching myself deflect what I don't want to see . . . detaching myself, to avoid what might be painful."

I said, "Maybe you've just been living alone too long."

He shrugged. "Maybe . . . I don't know. To tell you the truth, it would be easier if it *were* a particular thing, y'know? Then maybe I could do something about it. But it's vaguer than that . . . more of an overall feeling. And then I find myself . . . *scoffing* . . . like, y'know, thinking, 'What's the difference. What does it matter?'

"Remember how liberating it once was, to realize that nothing matters? That the past doesn't have to inhibit us? That only the moment exists, and everything seems possible? But now, that thought, which pops into my head all the time—that nothing matters—it leaves me deflated, wherever I am, whatever I'm doing . . . It tells me there's no reason to care, about anything."

I knew what he meant, and plaintively said, "C'mon, man. Lots of things matter."

"Like what?"

"Well . . . like people."

"What people?"

"I don't know . . . people in general."

He tamped out his cigarette in the metal ashtray, his brusque movements roiling the candle flame. "People, 'in general,' are only out for themselves. No one cares about anyone else. *That's* reality, not all this hippie peace and love crap we're supposed to believe."

"You're wrong," I said, sitting up. "I mean, look, I lost my pad, and Jeffrey didn't hesitate to take me in—for as long as I needed, he said. And then tonight, you saw me on the street and bought me dinner and then beer—why was that? Because you knew I had no bread." It struck me then that he might have bought my company, because he was feeling lonely, and I overrode the thought, saying, with conviction, "So I can tell you from experience that everyone isn't just out for themselves."

"All right," he said grudgingly. "Maybe not everyone."

I sat back, feeling triumphant, or almost so, since he was still down; or maybe it was his persistent seriousness, which I wasn't used to, and which for some reason had unnerved me. "Look," I said, "maybe your problem is just astrological."

"You're kidding."

"No, no, I'm serious."

"I don't believe that stuff," he said.

"But it's all very logical. Take the moon, for example. We know it controls the tides, and if it can do that, it obviously must have an effect on the chemicals in the brain."

"Why is that obvious?" he asked.

But my thoughts had already moved on: "I mean, look, the sun just left Leo, and you're a fire sign—like me. We thrive on a higher energy level, and now the sun is in Virgo, a low energy sign, which can be a letdown for types like us. But in a few weeks it'll enter Libra, an air sign, higher energy, and then reality is bound to feel more amenable to us. I mean, I'm looking forward to the change."

"But I've felt this way for a while," Arnie said, "more like months than weeks."

"Yes, but there are also more prolonged periods, the influence of planets that are farther from the sun," and I began to go into their characteristics, beginning with Jupiter, which was my favorite, and then on to Saturn, toward which I'd taken an intense dislike. And then, seeing he was losing interest, I concluded, "So you see, there're lots of reasons that explain why our moods can last awhile, what with the larger, slower planets moving from one house to the next."

"How long is 'awhile'?" he asked.

"Sometimes years."

"I don't want to wait years," he replied, and standing up, stretched exaggeratedly, indicating that he wanted me to leave. "And I don't believe any of that stuff anyway."

Finally, the other shoe dropped. I'd entered the fifth-floor pad one afternoon, rattled about something or other, and without being asked, began to sum up my day, as I was now in the habit of doing, when Marlene interrupted, saying,

"Why does everything always have to be good or bad with you, Peter? Whenever you walk in, you announce that it's a good day, or a bad day. What's good? What's bad? Why do you have to label everything?"

It was the kind of thing Patrick might have said, and it jolted me. I always took Patrick seriously. Marlene, on the other hand, was just someone to deflect.

"You make these pronouncements as if what seems true to you is true for everyone," she went on. "You say, 'It's weird out there,' or 'It's ragged'—whatever that means. You're like Chicken Little, and the sky is always falling down. I have to tell you, Peter, I look at the sky and I don't see it. To me, one day is pretty much like any other, with its ups and downs."

She held up a hand, to forestall interruption, though I was at a loss as to what I might say, her remarks too pointed, too accurate, to deflect.

"And don't tell me about the planets, how they explain this or that. Oh, I'll admit that at first I found it interesting, and I'll even go so far as to say there might be something to it, but when you say that this happened because of that, and next week or next month something else will happen because of Mars or Venus or whatever, I ask myself, 'What's the difference?' You know what I'm saying? What's it matter if a dog barks because the sun goes down or the moon comes up? The fact is: the dog *barks*. Everything else is bullshit."

Clearly, I'd underestimated Marlene. There was more to her than I'd imagined. And even more than that, as I would eventually realize.

But I didn't see it when she ushered a girl into the kitchen the very next day and beckoned me out of the bedroom, where I'd retreated to stay out of her way. "This is Gloria," she said, gesturing to the girl who sat at the table, fidgeting with her hair, which fell in a curtain down one side of her face. "Glo is from my old neighborhood, out on Long Island, so you can imagine my surprise when I saw her in the park . . ." She went on to say that Gloria had run away from home and needed a place to stay, confiding all this as if the girl weren't there and I was still an honored guest whose status hadn't eroded. Then she brewed tea, solicitously served the two of us, even set out a tin of English biscuits I hadn't seen before and urged us to help ourselves. In short, she swept us off our feet, and as Gloria and I sat there eyeing each other, abruptly excused herself and left.

Gloria wore a flimsy T-shirt and had drawn I-love-you hearts on the thigh of her ragged jeans. She was attractive and coltish, like the teenyboppers who hung out in the park and in front of the corner sub shop, and as she played with her hair, she regarded me with wide-eyed interest. I tried not to stare at her nipples, which poked at the fabric of her cotton shirt, and she smiled, inviting my attention. My flesh went liquid within my oversized clothes, and my cock went hard, an erection poking into my pants.

I said something, the words bumping into each other, and she nodded and smiled, as if my babble had been profound, which turned me on all the more. And the next thing I knew, we were in the bottom bunk in the other room, tearing our clothes off, humping for all we worth.

Humping. It was Gloria's word, when we lay satiated afterward. I liked the animal sound of it, and when she touched me again, I respond like a stag in rut.

Afterward, she stroked my prick as she nibbled at my ear and said, "I love you."

And I replied, "I love you too," and meant it.

Tough Dharma

One night, about to enter the Forum, I spotted Patrick Malone. I stood rooted in the entranceway, unsure whether to approach him or duck back out. The last time I'd seen him, or rather, tried to see him, it hadn't gone well. And now he sat alone at a table in the crowded room, his hair cropped short, hacked actually, as if he'd cut it himself. Was he making another statement, like the time he wore a Franciscan robe and sat cross-legged on the sidewalk in front of this same coffeehouse, an alms bowl cradled in his hands, to indicate that the people he knew were too greedy to help him? Or was he doing penance for his recent behavior: his surrender in the park; his bravado in Arnie's pad, when he'd dared a cop to shoot him; the fool he'd made of himself over a woman?

After seemingly offering himself in the park as a sacrifice, Patrick had sat alone in the jail cell, away from the others, and afterward refused to talk about it. But following the bust at Arnie's, he went the other way, basking in his celebrity in the coffeehouses he suddenly frequented. He pretended indifference, but couldn't help but inject details about the lawyers who gathered at the courthouse and got all of them released because of insufficient evidence. And he took part in the conspiratorial speculation about who the informer might have been.

At some point people glommed to his false modesty, or merely lost interest and moved on to other things. But Patrick continued to hang out with the crowd, which was unusual for him. He had a girlfriend then, which was also unusual, an attractive woman who drew much comment. He took pride in her, as if she were an acquisition redounding to his credit. And once, he notably announced, "Because of Suzanne, I'm a new man!"

Ray had been amused by this declaration. Don Juan Goldberg, who had still not fled to Canada, frowned. And the others tittered and said nothing.

Not long afterward he came striding up Eleventh Street to the Avenue, where the usual group of idlers hung out, killing time with rumor. Patrick barged right into the corner huddle and declared, "She told me she was having her period, but I discovered she's been sleeping with everyone in the neighborhood!"

It was a stunning announcement, not the kind of thing a man would say aloud in a group, and certainly not to those he barely knew. Did he expect commiseration? The corner characters looked at one another. Some shrugged. Others grinned. No one said anything.

"She's a slut!" Patrick shouted, pushing it. "And a liar!" It was almost funny—the hierarchy of her transgressions, as he saw it. But then, Patrick always strove for truth, even in his exaggerations; to him, there was nothing worse than outright deceit.

Then someone laughed.

It brought him to his senses. He turned toward the stifled sound, looking dangerous, ready for a fight. The ordinariness of a tinny tune from a radio playing in the corner bodega undercut his grand accusation, rendering it farce. No one cared, when it came down to it, or would have, had he not made an issue of her betrayal. Patrick scanned the group, and everyone averted their eyes; no one wanted to mess with him. Then, abruptly, he turned away and strode back down the side street, ending his flirtation with public life.

Which was the last I'd seen of him. He disappeared, went into hiding. I asked around, because I'd fallen on hard times of my own and seeking company had become my compulsion; to reconnect to a time when I'd functioned as a social being with a sense of myself I could no longer locate.

It brought me to a hallway in an unfamiliar building, with iron latticework crisscrossing the door, a fortress barring the pad inside. I knocked, and waited. After a while I heard footsteps, then Patrick's voice: "Who is it?"

"It's me," I replied to the closed door. "Peter."

"Move away from the peephole," he said, "so I can see you."

I backed up to the hallway wall.

"What do you want?" he asked.

"Nothing," I replied, feeling foolish addressing the door. "I just came by to visit."

After a moment, when I expected he would open up, he said, accusingly, "Who told you I was here?"

"Rose," I replied.

"Go away," he said. "I can't see you now."

Which in other circumstances would have been a joke; it was *I* who couldn't see *him*. Then the peephole clicked shut and I heard him walk away inside.

And now here he was, with butchered hair, sitting alone at a table in the crowded room. I watched him pick up his mug in his deliberate way, sip from it, and set it down on the tabletop with care, his steadfast movements and spartan appearance at odds with the noise and gesticulation around him. Wary, I stood there, lost in sensation, the jukebox pumping a dreamy ether of sound into the red-walled room:

> *Let me take you down, 'cause I'm going to strawberry fields,*
> *Nothing is real, and nothing to get hung about . . .*

"Patrick," I said, and only then realized I was standing by his table, looking down at him.

He looked up slowly, and after a moment nodded, once.

I was abashed, felt foolish.

What a drag, what a drag . . .

How could I have forgotten what a drag Patrick could be?

Finally, he plucked me from my purgatory of uncertainty, tilting his head toward one of the vacant chairs, inviting me to sit. And as quickly as I'd been hapless, I was now grateful.

But then he consigned me to oblivion again, saying nothing, not even looking at me, gazing instead into the room.

Tentatively, I said, "I haven't seen you around."

He looked at me and seemed to be considering his reply. Several seconds passed before he said: "That's because I haven't *been* around."

What a drag, what a drag . . .

How could I have forgotten what a drag he could be?

Recalling the fortress door, I said, "You still in the same place?"

Again he looked at me awhile before responding. "What place is that?" he asked, as if I'd posed a profound philosophical question.

What a drag, what a drag . . .

"The apartment with the peephole," I said.

After a moment he replied, "No, I'm not staying there anymore," and picking up his mug, took a sip.

I waited for him to say more, and when he didn't, crossed my legs and shifted position, turning away, gathering my shattered sense of worth into a compact package, where I could nurse it. My mind wandered then, away from Patrick and into the coffeehouse with its distracting sensations. The room cooperated, enveloping me in indistinct talk, in movement and pulsating music.

Time had slowed, or someone had put enough coins in the jukebox so it continued to play the same song again and again.

> *Living is easy with eyes closed,*
> *Misunderstanding all you see . . .*

Patrick's voice brought me back. I looked at him, said, "What?"

He frowned. "What's wrong with your hearing?"

"Nothing . . . I was just distracted."

"Distraction isn't 'nothing,'" he said. "It indicates something."

Annoyed at being lectured, I said, "I didn't hear you."

He looked at me for a long moment, perhaps deciding whether to repeat himself. "I asked if you were still in the same pad . . . on the top floor."

"Uh . . . no," I replied. It was not something I cared to think about. "I was evicted."

"Evicted?"

For some reason, the word embarrassed me. "Well, yeah, but it's not like someone showed up and kicked me out. I hadn't paid the rent, so . . ." It seemed he'd lost interest. " . . . I was evicted," I finished dully.

"I liked that pad," he said thoughtfully. "The big front room, the view of the city out the window . . ."

My perch. His description brought it back, and I saw myself there, and missed it. But I said, "It's just as well, I guess."

"Why 'just as well'?"

"Well, you know . . . I'd gotten too attached to it." Buddha, possessiveness . . . Surely he'd understand, if anyone would.

But Patrick merely said, "So where are you staying now?"

"With Jeffrey and Marlene. But it's not the same as having my own place, of course. I've been looking for one . . . for me and Gloria actually." I said her name with more pride than I'd intended, and recalling his debacle with Suzanne, quickly added, in a conversational tone, "Do you know her?"

"I know *of* her," he replied.

"Arnie said he'd help me out," I said, changing the subject, "so we can get our own pad."

"Arnie Glick?" He was incredulous.

"Yeah . . ." What other Arnie did either of us know?

"What do you mean, he'll 'help you out'?"

"You know, help . . . front me some grass, so I can make some bread."

"Oh." He sat back. "Of course."

"What'd you mean, 'of course'?"

Patrick leaned forward, his elbows on the table. "I mean, he never does anything for anyone unless he gets something in return. Arnie Glick has the soul of a capitalist."

"The *soul* of a capitalist?"

"I'd have thought that you—of all people—would see that."

"Why me?"

"Because of your background, your politics."

"I'm not into politics anymore," I said.

"Is that what you think?"

"I'm not," I said, adamant, daring him to disagree.

He returned my stare, then shrugged, leaned back and let his gaze drift into the room. I sat back too, and also tried to drift away. Everything I said to him elicited disagreement. I wondered again why I'd sat down, and about his butchered hair—why he'd cut it—and considered getting up and leaving.

He said something then, and I looked at him and asked, "What?" though I'd heard.

"I *said,* you might not be political anymore, but you're an idealist, which comes to the same thing. You want the world to be a certain way."

It jolted me, and my heart began to thump. It seemed he'd found me out. I knew what would happen next if I didn't pull myself together. Paranoia slashing through me, an object of universal ridicule in my own eyes. I pressed my arms tightly to my sides, to quell the spasms that had come over me.

Patrick didn't appear to notice, or pretended not to. He leaned forward, his arms on the table again. "Remember our pact?" he said. "To be absolutely, brutally honest with each another, no matter what?"

"Yeah . . ."

"You've been blunt with me at times, and I can't claim I took it well. But sometimes the truth can be hard to take."

I said, "I'm not afraid of the truth," as my heart thudded in my ears, my hands clasped tightly beneath the tabletop.

"We're all afraid of the truth at times."

I said nothing.

He leaned back, folded his arms on his chest, and after a moment said, "It seems to me, Peter, that you're not growing anymore . . . that you've slipped into easy answers, that you're playing avoidance games . . ."

I could not have imagined him saying anything worse. Panic exploded inside me, and I lashed out, saying, "Of course I'm growing! I'm learning things all the time!"

"Like what?"

He said it calmly, but my mind shut down, went blank. I couldn't even remember what we were talking about.

"What have you learned?" he asked.

He might have said it gently. I couldn't tell. I groped for an answer as he waited on me, tried to come up with something, and out of a dizzying blur blurted, "I know what enlightenment is!"

Enlightenment?

I was astonished.

Like the Buddha?

How could I have claimed such a thing?

Patrick's eyes widened, but again he spoke calmly; maddeningly so. "Then enlighten me. What does it mean . . . to be enlightened?"

"It means . . . to know what life's about!"

He pursed his lips in consideration. "Okay . . . and what is life about?"

Again my mind shut down.

Noises swelled around me and the bright red walls pressed in as I tried to think. Thoughts, half formed, came and went, as I sat in confusion, repeating the question, *What is life about?* as if repetition would produce the answer. At the same time, I was aware of Patrick across the table, waiting on me, and the music, enveloping me:

> *Let me take you down, 'cause I'm going to strawberry fields,*
> *Nothing is real . . .*

What is life about? What is life about? What is life about?

It seemed I was on one of the quiz shows I'd watched as a boy. At any second my time would be up and the room would fall silent, awaiting my answer. But the people around me were in their own world, going about their business, and only Patrick was waiting.

"Change!" I shouted. "It's about change!"

"Change . . ."

"Everything's always changing!" I said. "Nothing remains the same!" And at his thoughtful silence, I was encouraged to continue, adding, "That's why attachment brings suffering. The secret is to accept it! To accept everything!"

Patrick's attention shifted into the room. I followed his gaze, saw the same tall man in red flannel whom I'd noticed at the back earlier, circulating among the tables. A panhandler perhaps, bending down, speaking to the people at each table, then straightening up, moving on, slowly making his way up front. He was now only a few tables away.

Turning back to me, Patrick said, "Okay. Nothing remains the same. Accept everything. So then, what is acceptance?"

"Acceptance?"

He nodded.

"It is what it is. It's . . . basic."

He frowned.

In fact, though I parroted the word all time, telling myself to accept this, to accept that, I'd never actually thought about it. It had become my internal demand in recent weeks, to calm myself down, to still my trembling. Now, in the face of his dissatisfaction with my answer, I said, "Acceptance is . . . letting things happen without interference."

"Yes," he replied immediately, "but first you have to be free of all encumbrances, of all attachments . . . otherwise acceptance is a fraud."

I hadn't heard that before. It was something I had to consider, and I wasn't used to that. It required concentration, holding an idea in mind and looking at it. As it slipped away I thrashed after it, and managed to latch onto a phrase. "Acceptance is a fraud?" I said.

"No," he replied, "*acceptance* isn't a fraud. The *attitude* of acceptance is a fraud, because then it's not acceptance, it's just toleration."

I leaned back, reeling from the truth of it. I'd never thought of toleration that way—as a negative—but yes, of course, it made sense. In that moment, I understood the difference between the two concepts, and in the next felt a newfound respect for Patrick, which echoed back to that morning, so long ago, when he gave me a record player and took it away before I could use it, leaving me with nothing but the notion of possessing it. And now, all the time between then and now seemed no more than a brief interlude, a pause in my education, and he'd picked up where he left off, expanding on that lesson. Suddenly, his butchered head and severe self-containment made sense. Patrick had purposely separated himself from the crowd, sat alone amidst the chaos, apart from the mindless reverie, immune to it.

The big guy in the red flannel shirt was at the adjacent table now, towering over it. He spoke in a slurred voice, sounded drunk. He told them his watch had been stolen and insisted that each of them roll up their sleeves, to show him they didn't have it. One at a time everyone bared their arms, then he swerved toward us, steadying himself on the back of a vacant chair.

"My watch was stolen," he said, blinking heavily. "Show me you don't have it. Roll up your sleeves."

I pulled back my sleeves and held up my hands.

He grunted and looked at Patrick, who had folded his arms tight on his chest. "I don't have your watch," he said.

The big guy stood there, bewildered, then shouted, "Show me!"

"No," Patrick replied. "You'll have to take my word for it."

It took a moment before this answer registered on the interrogator, then he lurched across the table, grabbing for Patrick's sleeve, and Patrick jumped back and to his feet, his chair clattering against the wall. Conversation in the coffeehouse abruptly stopped. The music, I noticed, was gone too, as the two of them stood staring at each other.

Then Patrick calmly said, "Let's take this outside," and tilted his head toward the door.

The big man, baffled, looked at the door and back at Patrick before nodding.

With sudden movement, I was among half a dozen people who filed outside behind them, to see the fight. We formed a rough semicircle on the sidewalk, around the big guy, who stood a head taller, and Patrick, in a half crouch, balanced on the balls of his feet, eyeing his opponent, waiting with fists clenched. The big man lumbered in, and Patrick punched up at him, shooting short jabs into his stomach, one after another. The big guy grunted with each blow, meanwhile pounding down at Patrick's shoulders and back, bludgeoning him, the two of them locked in that embrace for a long while, taking each other's punishment. Suddenly, the big guy backed up into the street, unhurt but winded, gasping for air, and raised his hands in surrender.

"Enough," he said. "I believe you."

Toleration is a fraud, I thought. Patrick had gotten into the fight to make that point.

And maybe he had, but as people moved in to congratulate him and he waved them off, I knew it hadn't been about me. It was about him.

I could see as much as he headed up the block, striding in that methodical way he had while holding things together, one foot planted after another, as if the sidewalk was paved with eggshells.

Lost Tao

People lounged against parked cars and congregated at the curb, discrete groupings that would lose definition as night came on, dissolving into the throng that spilled from the sidewalk into the gutter, yet continued to cleave to one side of the block, never turning the corner onto ill-lit Eleventh Street, but instead clinging to its own mass, the illuminated sidewalk strip, a life raft in a hostile universe.

Carl seemed out of place the night I spotted him on that desultory strip of pavement where rumor, gossip, and innuendo flourished.

Seeing him there, I remembered bursting into Eighth Street, agitated, on a bad trip. He drew me aside when I entered, away from the others and into the tiny closet room with its meditation chamber beneath a loft bed. Beads and crystal balls were suspended from the wooden beams, jars of dry flowers, a brazier of incense, and scented candles; the ambience enveloped me as I sat cross-legged on the bamboo mats. My eyes jumped among the titles of the spiritual titles of books on a grapevine of built-in shelves, to the icons of Krishna, Buddha, and Jesus, to the William Blake sketches, and came to rest on the ornate mandala that filled the wall before me.

Carl climbed up to the loft and returned with a sketch pad, colored inks, and drawing pens, and set them before me. Then he left me alone, in the peace and quiet of that cloister. Had he heard about my pen-and-ink drawings from Patrick, who'd been in my pad when I drew my way out of another overwrought state? Or had he merely followed what he would have called his tao, the source of his certainty, which belied his fragile appearance?

I sat in that chamber squiggling ink, changing colors now and then, an unexpected picture taking shape. Concentration routed scattered fragments of thought, and when he looked in on me a while later, I was a different person.

Carl leaned over me and peered at the intricate web with tiny figures doing various human things within each spider cell. He asked if he could look at it more closely, and I handed him the pad. Could he take it into the other room and show it to the others? he asked, and I nodded, wondering if he meant to bolster my morale, though by then I felt fine. But no, Carl wasn't patronizing or condescending. He was sincerely taken by the drawing. Bringing it back, he handed it to me without comment, leaving me to my therapeutic obsession.

With that night in mind, I watched him move around the corner huddle, trying to catch someone's attention in the tight-knit group. He stretched up on tiptoe and raised a hand. He might have called out a name, but softly, and amidst the talking and gesticulating, wasn't heard. Unnoticed, he moved to another spot, rising up, beckoning with a hand, with the same result.

It bothered me to see that, and when Carl happened to move within a few feet of where I stood, I said, "There seems too much tension now for anyone to handle."

He turned, startled, and stared at me for several seconds, his dark eyes immobile, his long hair pulled back and tied in a bun, accentuating his pale face, with its finely chiseled features. Finally, coolly, he said, "What do you mean?"

I'd meant to be helpful, to commiserate, and his challenge took me by surprise. "You know," I said, and gestured at the tenement facades, the crowd, the tumultuous life raft. "The tension, coming out of the sky, bouncing off walls, bringing out our problems . . ."

He continued to stare at me, thin lips pressed together, and for a moment I thought he'd seen through my remark to its astrological influence, which suddenly seemed insubstantial, shallow. But then he said "Yes," thoughtfully, as if I'd said something worthwhile, "I see what you mean." And turning away, he walked quickly past the corner huddle, gliding with his usual grace around the corner, away from the desperate scene and back down Eleventh Street.

When it was clear the commune couldn't be saved, Carl and Anne had found a pad in Arnie Glick's building. Thin and lithe, like Carl, Anne seemed his natural counterpart. Before moving into his closet room at Eighth Street, I'd heard of her. I'd been at the commune the day Carl wrote to her in a Mexican jail. He took pride in the valentine card fashioned with pen and colored ink; elaborate, elegant, with flowers and vines intertwined around a blotter heart soaked with lysergic acid.

"Annie will understand," he said, and everyone was amused, though I wondered why anyone would want to trip in a jail cell. But then, I hadn't met

Anne yet. And then she came to Eighth Street, gliding through its rooms like a spirit, in full possession of her thoughts and emotions.

She was with Carl the night I showed up at their Eleventh Street pad, and stood behind me, next to him, as I gazed into a room that contained the reassembled meditation chamber. From the doorway I could see the dry flowers in small vases, the beads and baubles, icons and sketches, and the familiar mandala. But it wasn't the same in that setting, and I didn't know what to say. No longer part of a loft bed, it occupied the center of the otherwise empty room. Illuminated by track lights, it seemed a dazzling museum exhibit, a precious artifact, a rococo shrine, and left me feeling sad rather than uplifted.

I followed them to another room, where Carl settled himself on a large mattress. Anne sat down cross-legged on a rug off to one side as he leaned back on the pillows arrayed against a wall that served as a headboard, his legs crossed at the ankles. He gestured me to sit down on the mattress, and I perched awkwardly on a corner, wondering why he wanted to see me. Until I'd spotted him on the Avenue, I hadn't seen or spoken to Carl in weeks.

He and Anne had decided to move upstate, he began, and he'd heard from Arnie Glick that I was looking for a pad. If I'd agree to take care of their things until they reclaimed them, I could have the place.

It was an unexpected stroke of luck, and now that he'd made the offer, I forgot about how false the meditation chamber seemed in its new setting and instead felt honored to be entrusted with its safekeeping.

He went on to explain that they were moving into Lila's pad, and with the money the two of them saved while working at the head shop, they'd be able to rent a house in the country, tend a garden, create their own Eden. It was a nice dream, but a sense of unreality gnawed at me as he confided it, and in my discomfort, I hardly heard the knock at the front door or noticed when Anne got up to answer it. When she returned to her spot, Carl stopped talking and stared beyond me, toward the doorway. I followed his gaze.

It was Gary, familiar to me from Eighth Street. He stood with his arms crossed on his chest, nodded at me, then said to Carl, "I hear you're planning to let Peter have your pad when you leave."

I didn't know Gary, hadn't paid much attention to him before, but I was now struck by his resemblance to Carl. They were both short and thin, with fine features. And despite the tension in the room, the two of them seemed light, airy, almost weightless.

"That's right," Carl replied, in the same challenging tone he'd used with me on the Avenue, and folded his arms on his chest, mirroring Gary.

It startled Gary, and they stared at each other a moment before he blurted, "Well c'mon, Carl! You promised this pad to me! You said I could have it if you decided to move!"

"I never told you that," Carl said tightly.

Why had Carl had offered his place to me? Why *not* Gary? I'd often seen them together.

Plaintively, Gary said, "Why are you doing this, Carl? We used to be friends . . . then all of a sudden . . ." He shook his head. "I still don't know what happened . . . I saw you in the head shop, and you didn't even say hello . . ."

His distress infuriated Carl, but he kept a tight-lipped silence.

"It's not that I have anything against Peter," Gary went on, pulling himself together, finding a reasonable tone. "If you changed your mind and you want him to have your pad, that's your prerogative. But when I give someone your word, I think you owe them an explanation."

"I never gave you my word," Carl said.

"Annie!" Gary said, turning to her.

She'd been rocking softly on her spot, her eyes closed. They snapped open and she stared at Gary in alarm.

"You were there," he said. "We were in the Omega, remember? Rose was there too . . ."

Eyes brimming with sudden tears, she looked up at him pleadingly, the room taking on the quality of her sorrow. Or maybe it was just me, choked up, my eyes watery and my vision blurred. I understood then why some people considered Anne a saint. But I could also see it was a mixed blessing, that emotion rendered her unable to speak, helpless to affect the situation. Closing her eyes, she resumed rocking back and forth, back and forth, returning to her own meditative world.

Gary turned back to Carl, angry. "If you changed your mind, why did I have to hear about it from Arnie Glick? Doesn't our friendship—" He faltered at Carl's fierce glare. "—or even our past friendship, matter at all? You should at least have told me to my face."

"I *didn't* change my mind," Carl replied. "I never promised you this pad, and I don't owe you an explanation. I'm not responsible for your expectations, Gary."

This had nothing to do with me. I didn't belong there. I said, "I think I should go, Carl."

"No." He held up a hand. "That won't be necessary. This will be over in a minute."

Gary took a step into the room. "You can't just dismiss me like that, Carl!"

Then Carl did something I never would have expected. He rolled his eyes at me, sharing his exasperation and scorn.

"I have to go," I said, and stood up. "You can reach me through Arnie when you make up your mind."

"Okay," he replied. "But I've already made up my mind. This apartment will be yours."

But Carl never did get back to me, though he might have tried. I wouldn't have known, since I rarely saw Arnie Glick anymore, or anyone else from Eighth Street or the basement apartments. When I wasn't among strangers on the Avenue, I was in the gloomy pad I'd rented, in a nearly deserted building on a bad block; Ninth Street, between B and C. I'd raised the rent money, but not enough to turn on the electricity, and the pad was always dark and foreboding. For months I'd avoided what I thought of as artificial light, and even developed an aversion to it. But now, when I had no alternative to candles, and the wavering shadows the flame cast in one room left the others nearly dark, I would have welcomed a blazing bulb.

Gloria moved her sparse belongings in, and for a while we played house like an actual couple. But after a week or so, she began leaving before nightfall—to stay with a friend, she said—and I couldn't blame her. The candlelit pad had an ominous feel when it got dark, and I avoided it myself, leaving for the Avenue at twilight and hanging out there till late at night, when I'd finally, reluctantly, return.

I liked to think the situation was temporary, that I'd eventually hustle up enough bread to turn the electricity on, and then Gloria and I would settle into the protective comfort of a longed-for normalcy of sorts. I imbued my scramble for cash with that noble purpose, thinking of myself as a hardworking everyman striving to put his world in order, progressing toward a better life . . . even as peddling nickels and dimes to people I barely knew debilitated me. I flitted from place to place, a phantom following leads, when I wasn't clinging to the life raft, where, if someone deigned to notice me, or went so far as to speak a few words in my direction, I was both grateful and agitated, as if receiving an undeserved gift.

During the day, I often sought out old acquaintances, people whom I'd once been able to look in the eye—if only to prove to myself that I was still someone who could meet and exchange words with others, part of a society where people might talk to each other and take each other's presence as a simple fact of life. So when I ran into Patrick and he told me that Tom was staying with Lila, in a pad she'd rented after returning from Europe, I went off to find him.

It was on the top floor of a building in an unfamiliar Italian neighborhood, south of Houston. Though I hadn't seen her in months, Lila greeted me with a frown, as if my presence itself was enough reason to dislike me. It was the last thing I needed, and I almost turned around and left. But instead I swallowed what was left of my pride and said, "I heard you lived here."

In a toneless voice she replied, "Did you come to see Tom?"

"Uh, yeah," I said. "Is he in?"

She didn't answer, but moved aside, revealing Tom sitting at the kitchen table, eating. He looked up as I entered, grunted, as if he too had no use for me, and went back to his bowl of food, spooning it into his mouth.

I stood there looking at him, gaunt, severe, eating as if alone, as Lila closed the door and moved to the stove. The room was bright, and flashes of light, tiny explosions, popped in my eyes as an excruciating sense of isolation enveloped me. I was frozen in a particular purgatory, enduring a detachment that seemed to deaden the air itself, making it hard to breathe. It was the nightmare that was always in the back of my head: a meaningless universe, a world devoid of feeling. Standing amidst it now, anxiety quivered through me.

Lila said, "Sit down, if you want," and I seized on the equivocal offer as she flicked a hand at the table, making it clear that she didn't care whether I sat down or not. "You want coffee or tea?" she asked when I was seated opposite Tom.

"Uh . . . tea, thanks," I replied.

I knew she'd gone to Europe to paint, but the canvases I saw on the walls had been in the back room in the old basement flat; a mix of the primitive and civilized done in the lush style of Gauguin in Tahiti, orchids, vines, and vibrant greens in a jungle seen through a drawing room window that was no less opulent, with flower fabric on chairs and cushions. And then on a far wall I saw other pieces, devoid of color, abstractions in black on white gesso. I thought to ask about them, but was afraid she'd reply scornfully.

Lila had changed too. She was no longer laid-back, but instead bristled. Her once luxurious mane of blond hair was stringy and disheveled now, and she'd lost weight, and with it, her voluptuousness. But more than anything else, she was no longer an empress, a consort, but instead seemed to occupy the margins of Tom's detachment. Perhaps, out of her desire to be with him, she'd always been under his sway, and in this setting stripped of nonessentials, that dependence was now apparent. It added to the strangeness of the bleak scene in which he sat eating as she busied herself at the stove. It seemed I'd walked into the future, only it wasn't the future, but the true state of things, in which survival was all and everything, rendering my longing for connection a childish anachronism as I sat trembling in the screaming silence.

Then I noticed the plaid shirt Tom wore—it had once been mine, packed away in the steamer trunk that disappeared—and I seized on that connection with the known world, speaking into the emptiness, saying to him, "Where'd you get the shirt?"

He looked up from his porridge, or whatever it was, and replied in a monotone, "The closet," and I knew it wasn't a joke; it was the limit of his interest.

It occurred to me to explain why I'd asked, but it had taken all my courage to speak, and the sound I'd emitted, and his terse response, was too great an obstacle to further effort, to utterance suspended in air, mocking meaning, words collapsing upon themselves and an attendant feeling of futility.

Tom had always been detached, but now he was also incurious. He pushed the bowl away, leaned back and probed his mouth with a finger. He could have been in a cave a million years ago. How could you talk to a caveman, whose life was so basic and severe? What could you say? The accepted social norms meant nothing. Once, months ago, recalling himself as a teenager, he'd rumbled with an imaginary chain, briefly played a role, smiting his enemies, laughing. It was impossible to imagine anything like that now. He inhabited a psychological plateau of absolute indifference, beyond all sentiment.

With a sharp click that startled me, Lila set a steaming mug of tea on the tabletop in front of me. "Sugar?" she said.

"Uh . . . yeah," I replied.

She went to a counter and returned with a dispenser, plunking it solidly down.

Tom looked toward the stove. "Coffee?" he said.

"It's on the burner," she replied, and turning to me, said accusingly, "Who told you Tom was here?" protecting him; as if, impenetrable as he was, he needed protection.

"Patrick," I said.

"Some undercover agent," she replied sarcastically. "Can't even keep his mouth shut."

"He slammed a door in my face," Tom said with sudden resentment. "For no reason."

I knew the story, or at least heard Patrick's version of it; how Tom had wandered through the rooms at Eighth Street, self-absorbed, bumming cigarettes.

Coincidentally, he now asked me, "Got any smokes?"

"Uh, no . . . sorry."

He looked at Lila.

"In the studio," she said.

Abruptly, he got up and left the room.

I blew on my tea, tried to sip it and burned the roof of my mouth. It was an existential rebuke. I'd lost my wits; despite the steam rising from the cup, I ignored the reality of heat. I sat back, waiting for Tom to return, nursing my mouth with a tongue, thinking he might be different when he walked back in. The room was no less suffocating without him there; his deadening emanation still filled the place.

My skin was crawling, my body didn't seem to be mine, and I thought to escape, to flee, when Lila sat down at the table.

"Why are you here?" she asked bluntly.

"No reason," I said. "I just came by to visit." It seemed a ridiculous answer.

"Just to visit," she repeated, also struck by the absurdity of it.

I stared at the cup of tea and the rising steam.

"You came to see Tom, so go see him," she said dismissively, nodding at the hallway he'd gone down.

In that alien dream, I obeyed, got up and moved toward an open door at the other end, where I stopped and peered inside.

The room was as bright as the kitchen, but the resemblance ended there, the floor covered with looseleaf pages and splayed bindings. Tom knelt amidst the ransack. I watched him snatch up a handful of pages, look at them briefly, and toss them aside. Then he picked up another loose sheaf, glanced at it, crumpled the pages in a hand like worthless refuse, and flung it aside in disgust.

I flashed, then, on a dimly lit apartment where I moved around shapes, a table and chairs, and toward light spilling from an open doorway on the other side. I'd paused at that threshold too, stared into a tiny room dazzlingly lit by a solitary candle. It took my breath away, the emerald hue to that cell, from the nimbus that outlined the figure who sat at a desk, head bowed over manuscript pages covered with his scrawl.

Merlin!

It popped into my head; a child's explanation of the unknown.

I'd gone there to buy grass, and when I said as much and he got up and glided into the other room, turning on the overhead light, it seemed the most mundane of errands, hardly worth bothering him about. When I paid him for the ounce, the price seemed impossibly insufficient. And leaving, heading downstairs, it seemed that my life till then had been pointless.

Now, shaken, I backed away from this latest doorway.

When I reentered the kitchen, Lila was waiting. "He calls it his 'memoirs,'" she said. "Everything he's ever thought about and written down. He says he'll burn it all . . ."

I couldn't tell if it was an observation or an endorsement. And as I stood speechless, she frowned, as at a dullard, yanked the door open and said, "He's got the right idea," ushering me out with disdain.

One night when Carl and Anne were in Lila's pad, the women took mescaline. They were in Lila's studio room at one end of the apartment, while Tom idly strummed a guitar and Carl worked on a necklace of beads in a room at the other end. When Leo burst in with samples of still another new drug he'd come across, his sister pointed him toward the men.

Excited, Leo couldn't say enough about his latest score, and urged them to take it.

Tom accepted one of the pills and waited on Carl, who hesitated.

In fact, Carl rarely used drugs anymore, and even then confined himself to low doses; not to get high, he'd explained one night at Eighth Street, but just enough to alter his perspective before he began a project of some sort.

Patrick, in one of his argumentative moods, derided his moderation, dismissed it as recreational. A new world order was in the making, he declared, and they all had a duty to transform themselves totally, to lead the way.

"It isn't necessary to take drugs to become aware," Carl had replied simply.

"Theoretically," Patrick retorted, "but the truth is, we've all become what we are now because of them. Face facts, Carl, without drugs we'd still be programmed by our upbringing, unaware that we're more than that, more than we were taught and trained to believe . . . Without LSD, we would never have transcended our conditioning. We would still be struggling to be something, rather than just *be*."

"It was our fate to be altered by drugs," Carl replied, "but the history of saints and arhats, of bodhisattvas and holy men, testifies to the truth that people have always transcended their lesser selves, with or without drugs . . . and always will."

"A handful of people," Patrick countered, "not a revolution in consciousness where all of us transcend belief and realize that—"

"We die."

Patrick blinked in surprise. "That . . . and other things too."

"But the realization that we die comes first," Carl said.

"Well, yes, but—"

"Death comes first . . . and anyone can have that epiphany, Patrick, with or without LSD. And then the possibility of transformation follows."

Death comes first.

It was the first thing that popped into my head when I heard about what happened at Lila's that night.

Leo was gone when the rush came on . . . a whirlwind of energy that swept away the gentler mescaline vibes in the pad. Anne, following her intuition, left the apartment, and Lila, working on a painting, closed her door against the storm beyond the kitchen, at the other end of the pad.

Without thinking, the two men stripped off their confining clothes and sat naked in the molecular surf, the paisley gale swirling into the room through the open window on that unseasonably warm night, the rays of a streetlight filtering in from six floors below, alive on the ceiling.

Everything emanates energy. The unseen universe is a sublime field of shifting motion and color . . . expanding, filling all supposedly empty space, connecting all things. Or, presenting its other facet, contracting into solid shapes and surfaces, volume separated by space, which we're inclined to call reality, the facts of all matter hard and undeniable.

The apartment turned cold then, with a lack of connectedness.

Carl approached Tom, lying on the couch, staring at the ceiling. Perhaps he felt cut off, isolated, and sought contact, the warmth of another body. Tom, familiar with detachment, didn't want to be bothered. He pressed a forearm to Carl's chest and pushed up, relieving the weight from his body; a utilitarian gesture.

Lila had left her room, moved down the hallway to the open door, and seeing Carl in that moment, suspended above Tom, freaked out, shouted, *"Carl! What are you doing?"*?

Was she jealous and lashing out at a rival? Or, seeing their nakedness, giving vent to a notion of propriety that exploded out of upbringing?

The shout startled Carl as the pressure of Tom's arm brought him upright, and as he dismounted, he looked at her.

"Put your clothes on!" she yelled.

What went through his mind as he took the strand of beads from his neck? Was it an offering, which he calmly placed on the floor as she glared at him? Or did it have nothing to do with her, an adornment he removed before going out as he'd come in?

Then, striding across the room, he leaped out of the open window.

Beelzebub and His Sidekick

I leaned back on the car hood and stared at the sky, a carefree pose to convince an invisible observer that I didn't mind being the only one on the sidewalk strip, that I was self-sufficient just hanging out. But as self-conscious as I was, it was hard to inhabit a particular self for any length of time, and when this one's pretense mocked me and then crumbled, I sat up and adopted another—rubbing my chin with forefinger and thumb, gesturing absorption in profound thought.

But instead of pondering an idea, my pad on Ninth Street came to mind, which explained why I was on Avenue before anyone else: I'd fled the pad long before daylight leaked from its rooms and fear set in.

When I was there, to stave off imagination I'd taken up reading, of all things; Henry Miller's *Cosmological Eye,* not because I knew the author—I didn't then—but because the title flattered me, informed the observer who watched me sitting in the kitchen, reading by candlelight, that I was not frightened, but one in a long line of serious beings, contemplating the cosmos.

But there was no fooling the observer. It knew what I was about. Now, as I sat posing on the car hood, it debunked my latest fiction—the philosopher—and I shifted position again, out of the scholarly pose and into something more prayerful, hands clasped as I stared meditatively across the sidewalk at a brick wall.

On the far side of the block, by the sandwich shop on the corner, a group of teenagers had gathered. They distracted me, and I looked for Gloria among them. She wasn't there. I hadn't seen her for several days.

When we'd moved into the ill-chosen pad, excited about possibilities, we went scavenging in the abandoned apartment across the hall, dragged a mattress off an iron bedstead, a table for the kitchen, a dresser and a cast-iron stove, which became a prominent piece in the main room—an old-fashioned curiosity that would serve as an end table for a candle, an ashtray, odds and ends. But soon enough the semidarkness dampened our enthusiasm, and Gloria found reason to leave before the sun set.

I told her it would get better, and went back next door alone for a bolt of faded flowery material, to use as a bedspread, plates and silverware, pots and pans—as if either of us might actually cook and eat there someday, enacting a domestic life. But the homey stuff didn't make a difference. Night still came on, and with it a sense of uncertainty lingered in the rooms.

The problem was the dark, and scrambling for money to have the electricity turned on became my goal. With single-minded purpose I dealt nickels and dimes to strangers on the Avenue and in the park, and managed to finally scrounge up the thirty bucks security deposit.

Ebullient, I went looking for Gloria, to share the good news. She was among the teenagers lingering outside the sandwich shop, and in my elation, I swept her up with uncharacteristic forcefulness, winning her over, again, like when we'd met and I'd been a tyro of optimism. Hip to hip, we jounced through the park, heading back to our place.

It was a darker block than most, ground-floor hall light spilling out to the stoop as we approached the building, where three figures lingered by the entrance; teenagers, local kids, Puerto Ricans. Seeing them, I hesitated at the foot of the stoop, but with my woman at my side—she, who looked to me for courage—I brushed my wariness aside and led her boldly up the stairs. The teenagers moved aside, then fell in behind us. Sensing them there, I shielded Gloria from possible danger, pushing her forward when we reached the stairwell, urging her to head up. Before I could follow, however, the biggest one moved in front of me, blocking the stairs, and the other two flanked me on either side.

The big one flicked open a thin-bladed knife. "Your money or your life," he said, and pressed the tip of the switchblade to my chest.

It's odd, what we fear. It's not always rational. For weeks I'd been afraid, without any clear idea about what, exactly, threatened me. But now, encountering something solid, I seemed to float free of my body, calmly noticing that the other two were nervous, uncomfortable. It left me almost optimistic, as though true intent, or the lack of it, would inevitably determine the course of events. But the guy with the knife was different, with a desperate look that would trump any second thoughts he might have had. Still, I was more sad than anything else as I dug into my pocket for the hard-earned money and the lost electricity.

One of the others snatched the bills from my hand.

"Now go on upstairs," the kid with the knife said, gesturing brusquely with the blade.

And suddenly I *was* scared, of the unbridled emotion that threatened to possess him, compelling him to obliterate the act he'd just committed by lashing out at its victim. Quickly, I climbed the stairs, and in the half-dark of the first floor landing, partially lit from below, left him behind.

In the full darkness of the next landing I stopped and heard them below, scurrying out of the building; like rats, I thought. And then, reaching my door, I became possessed as well.

My money! My light!

I burst into the pad, where Gloria had lit a candle, and as she watched, rattled through the dirty dishes in the sink until I found the wide-bladed knife I'd taken from next door. It was too dull to even cut bread, and smeared with butter, but in my wild-eyed fury it looked formidable. Gripping it in a fist, I turned to leave.

"Where are you going?" Gloria asked, frightened.

"I'll be back," I replied.

"Don't leave me alone," she said, but I was already out the door.

I rushed downstairs, out to the stoop, and looked left and right at the nighttime street. Why was I surprised that they were gone, when I'd heard them scuttle away? Why would they have waited for me? Not thinking straight, gripping the knife in the pocket of my peacoat, where it pressed against my leg through a hole, I ran up the block to the corner. There was no one in sight there either, except a cop in uniform across the street, speaking into a police phone outside the park entrance. I ran toward him, and he looked up, the phone still pressed to his ear.

I stopped a few feet away and blurted, "Where can I get a gun?"

He looked at me for a long moment, said into the phone, "Hold on a sec," and looked at me again, more carefully. "A gun, you say?"

"Yeah, a gun, a gun!" How could a cop, of all people, be so stupid? They dealt with guns all the time!

"I'll call you back," he said into the phone, hung up and gave me his full attention. "Why do you want a gun?" he asked.

His inquisitive tone, lacking genuine curiosity, sobered me. It was a flat utterance, a cop question, and abruptly made me aware of the silver badge on his cap and the knife in my pocket, gripped tightly in a fist. "Never mind," I said, taking a step back.

He took a step toward me. "Wait a minute . . ."

"Never mind," I said again, backing across the street. "It doesn't matter." My heel hit the opposite curb, and before he could take another step or say another word, I was on the sidewalk, hurrying back down the block.

Now, at the first hint of twilight, with people beginning to congregate and the Avenue stirring to life, I realized I hadn't seen Gloria since the robbery, and wondered where she was.

Music swelled out of the sandwich shop when the door opened, was muffled when it closed. "All You Need Is Love." How could that be true? It would play all evening, now louder, now softer, as the door opened and closed, yet was always there, mocking the lowdown scene. A few kids were in the head shop, moving spastically with the pulsing of a blue strobe light. In the leather boutique next door, which had recently replaced the Forum, two women in suede halter tops and leather pants who'd been slumped in chairs, looking bored, were now posturing for customers who might be watching beyond the plateglass. Behind me, I heard the indecipherable strains of music from another jukebox, in a bar that had just opened across the street with the awful name the Hippie Drome, the tune garbled, the throbbing beat audible, as traffic picked up on the street and a few neon lights flicked on.

"My friend."

Startled, I looked up, at Gazi. His bald head and broad brow gave him a smooth, almost ageless appearance. He was inches from my face, as Roger, the lunatic, lingered a few feet away. The two of them, together, gave me the creeps. Adrenaline began to pulse in my plexus with a familiar dull throb as I sat there on the car hood, pinned to the spot, hands clasped tightly between my legs to quell the shivers that now ran down my arms.

"Gazi!" I said into the growing silence, with an enthusiasm that belied my discomfort; as if we were old friends, a fake smile frozen on my face while he continued to regard me without expression. Roger moved in closer, his thin-lipped sneer giving way to a mocking grin that creased his face. Gazi responded with a grin of his own, the two of them in cryptic communication. At a loss, I willfully misread their amusement and tried another smile, the three of us buddies, having a good time.

"What are you grinning about?" Gazi asked pointedly.

My smile crumpled as my clasped hands fought for control over another bout of the shakes. "I don't know," I replied, trying to keep my voice steady. "I guess because you were."

After a moment he said, "I see," and nodded, Roger snickering. "Tell me," he went on, his tone pleasant, his slight accent not without charm, "what do you know of this latest batch of acid everyone is talking about? The good stuff, which I hear is expected any day now?"

The ordinariness of his question was a relief, and eager to reward him for asking it, I lost control of my tongue, spewed out whatever came to mind.

"I'm expecting it too," I said. "In fact, I'm looking forward to it. I've been all over, trying to raise front money. But people are wary, y'know? It seems no one trusts anyone anymore unless they know them or can vouch for them. And it didn't help that a week ago, when the deal was supposed to happen, the buffering machine broke, so they couldn't make the pills—or so I heard. I had to put people off, and some of them wanted their bread back, no matter what I said. It's tough. You can only hold onto front money so long before people become antsy, impatient. I tried to find some other stuff, other deals, but no one wants the local shit anymore. They won't trust anything that looks homemade, on sugar cubes or blotting paper. They want what looks like—"

"Yes," Gazi said, interrupting. "I know all that . . ."

I felt rebuked, regretted my logorrhea, leaned forward and waited for him to continue. But he just looked back at me without expression. Unnerved, I started up again, said, "I mean, if it gets you high, why should you care what it looks like? And you'd think that with so little around—"

"What are you babbling about?" he asked.

I recoiled from the pointed question, fell back on my arms, propped against the hood. Short of breath, I gulped air, and attempting to hide my lack of composure, looked away, toward the distant corner, as if the teenagers gathered there suddenly fascinated me. But I knew I wasn't fooling anyone. Roger, with his keen sense of attraction for weakness, moved in again as I sat there, pretending. I heard him laugh as Gazi spoke softly a few feet away, words not meant for me and which I both wanted and didn't want to hear.

He said: "It's not what a man says, Roger, that is the key to understanding him, but how he expresses it. Always listen to the voice, to the sound and inflections, to the tone of it, while observing the gestures . . ."

Peripherally, as I gazed toward the distant corner, I saw Roger listening with respect.

"The wise man, having nothing of consequence to say, remains silent. The fool, who speaks without thinking, reveals himself in tone and gesture for what he is . . ."

Was he talking about me? It had to be. But how could he, with me right there?

And as I continued to avert my eyes while eavesdropping, Roger moved forward and, almost in my ear, said harshly, "You don't know where you're at, man."

I'd taken it from Gazi, who knew when to throw me a bone, but Roger was something else, and his obtrusive proximity sparked a defiant reaction. His face was inches from mine; clean shaven, with long sideburns, slicked back hair, and beady pinpoint pupils, his lips a garish smirk. A sense of violation elevating me, I looked directly at him, down into his face, with a righteous glare.

But before I might have said anything, and changed the mood, Gazi lashed out at his companion, apparently having also seen his repellent ugliness, telling him, "You forget what you are, Roger. You know nothing. You *are* nothing."

The condemnation appeared to crush Roger, who took a backward step and hung his head, chastened, as I welled up with gratitude toward Gazi, who turned back to me with a half smile, annoyed at having been interrupted, picking up where he'd left off.

"I have a proposition for you, my friend," he said. "When this deal you spoke of comes about, I propose that you put aside a dozen doses for me—in whatever form they take—and in return I'll give you half what I can sell them for."

I waited for him to say more, but he merely clasped his hands on his chest and waited on me. I wondered if I'd missed something. The expression *a fool's proposition* came to mind, and with it, the impulse to reject his offer—if it could even be called that. But after he'd so resoundingly put Roger in his place, I felt grateful, and heard myself say "Okay."

"Good, good," Gazi replied, pleased. "Did you hear that, Roger?" he asked, and looked toward his sidekick, who had drifted over to the boutique window and was leering at the shop girls preening and posing inside.

Roger turned. "What'd you say?"

"My friend and I have made a deal," Gazi told him.

Grinning, Roger sauntered back. "If you made a deal with Peter," he said, "I'm sure you won't regret it."

Abruptly, I was filled with revulsion.

"We should celebrate," Gazi said, looking at me.

"Yeah, let's celebrate," Roger said.

I didn't say anything.

Roger said, "Why don't we get stoned?"

Gazi looked at me. "What do you say, my friend?"

I thought, *No*. But I was accustomed to avoiding, not confronting. And as they watched me, waited on me, I heard myself say, "Sure . . . why not?"

"Yes, why not?" Gazi said. "Unfortunately, however, I have nothing with me . . . Roger, do you have any dope?"

Roger, looking forlorn, shook his head.

Gazi turned back to me. "And you, my friend? Do you have any dope?"

I thought about the chunk of hashish in my pad, but said, "No."

"Then perhaps you know someplace where the three of us can get some?" He looked at me, head tilted, waiting.

"You're asking the wrong guy," I said. "I've been kind of hard up recently."

"I didn't ask about your state of mind," Gazi snapped, and I reeled back. "I asked if you had any dope we could share."

"Yeah, man, no one gives a shit about you," Roger said.

"Roger!" Gazi snapped. "Shut up!"

And as Roger wilted again, ducking his head, my voice went off without me again, saying, "I know where we can get some grass."

Abruptly, Gazi turned away from Roger, seemingly forgetting him. "Let's go there, then," he said crisply.

In Thought's Caboose

I walked quickly, as if by doing so I might lose them. But I was only going around the corner and across the street, and when I darted into Jeffrey and Marlene's building, they weren't far behind. They fell farther back when I rushed up the five flights, and as I knocked on the door, I heard them on the landing below, climbing up.

Marlene answered, said, "How're you doing, stranger?" more acceptant now that I wasn't always underfoot.

"Good, good," I replied as she frowned, looking past me at Gazi, who now stood at the top of the stairs, then back at me for an explanation.

But before I could say anything, Gazi was beside me, and then past, moving toward Marlene, who stepped back, surprised. And then Jeffrey was in front of her, barring the way. Gazi did a double take, looked at Jeffrey with surprise, and forgiving his misunderstanding with a smile, tried to slip past him and into the apartment. Jeffrey was even shorter and thinner than Gazi, but wiry, and deceptively strong, and he reached out, gripped Gazi's shoulder with two hands and shoved him back into the hallway. Gazi stumbled backward, regaining his balance near the stairwell, next to Roger, who was watching.

Eyes wide in protest, Gazi said to Jeffrey, "What is the matter with you?" fingers splayed, palms open, in an aggrieved pose.

"You can't come in here," Jeffrey replied bluntly.

Gazi continued to stand there with outstretched arms, feigning bewilderment.

Ignoring him, and Roger, Jeffrey said to me, "Why'd you bring *them* here?"

Confounded, I replied, "I don't understand . . ."

Jeffrey pointed past me, at Gazi. "Don't you know what he is?"

What he is.

What did that mean?

"They're my friends," I replied, though it didn't sound right, wasn't true. But having said it, it was mine, and I somewhat believed it.

Behind me, Roger snickered. In the doorway, Jeffrey stared at me with disbelief, Marlene looking over his shoulder, perplexed.

"We'll see you later," Gazi said, and I turned and watched him push Roger toward the stairs and follow him down.

I kept my back to Jeffrey, avoiding him, not knowing what to say, finally turning back as Gazi and Roger shuffled away on the landing below.

"Jesus, Peter!" Jeffrey said. "Now they know where I live!"

That wasn't good. I understood that much. But I didn't quite grasp why. "So what?"

"So what?" he said, "Don't you know what Gazi is?"

"What'd you mean?"

"He's a thief."

A thief.

Gazi rolling joints in Arnie's basement pad from a bag someone had handed him, his fingers moving deftly, producing four, five, six thin joints, leaning forward to set them down on a crate, where I saw only three. And Tom accusing Gazi of stealing his drugs . . .

It all came back to me. But that had been so long ago, it hardly seemed real. A lot of things had happened once, in the past, which no longer existed, was an illusion that misled us. With sudden righteousness I declared, "If you won't let my friends in, then I'm not coming in either!"

Dumbfounded, Jeffrey stared at me from the doorway, he and Marlene watching as I strode to the stairs and headed down.

I was outraged, furious. But as I descended, I thought about them inviting me into their pad, sharing what they had with me, and my anger flickered.

All the more reason! I told myself, arguing against the notion that I owed them something because they'd once helped me out. Toleration was a fraud! I wasn't about to grovel for anyone, no matter what they'd done for me!

Outside on the street, I spotted Gazi and Roger up the block, turning the corner, and was about to shout, but for some reason didn't, instead heading in the other direction.

I didn't know where I was going, but walked quickly, movement churning up feelings and thoughts, fragments, shards, the scenery a blur of buildings, shop windows, traffic . . . When my feet stopped moving, I was standing before a recessed doorway without a door. On one side there was an empty storefront, the plateglass covered with newspaper behind a lattice of iron bars, and on the other, a statue of Saint Sebastian behind smudged glass, crucified with arrows, splashes of red paint oozing from the wounds.

I plunged into the building and up the worn marble stairs, taking them two and three at a time to the top floor, and knocked on the battered wooden door whose flaking paint was covered with handwritten messages.

This is exactly right! This is exactly where I should be!

But there was no answer and no sound within, and I remembered that Mark Greenbaum didn't live there anymore, that he'd moved away weeks ago.

Disappointed, I walked slowly back downstairs and into the street, where I stood on the sidewalk, in a quandary. I took a few steps toward Avenue A, stopped, and following another thought, headed the other way.

My feet took over again, brought me down one block and up another as the street began to lose light. I ducked into a narrow alley between two buildings, came to a concrete terrace beneath a crumbling overhang. The terrace was nearly covered with loose chunks of concrete that crackled beneath my feet as I moved to a door. I knocked and stepped back, to be seen through a peephole, though it was so gloomy beneath the overhang I wondered if I'd be recognized.

From the door came a woman's uncertain voice: "Who are you?"

"It's Peter," I replied. "I was here once before."

Locks were unfastened and the door opened a few inches, the length of a chain. I glimpsed a face, peering out. "What do you want?" she asked.

"I'm a friend of Arnie's," I said. "I'm here to see Curt."

She closed the door, disengaged the chain lock, then pulled the door open and impatiently beckoned me inside. Rona, I remembered. As she locked up, I gazed at the murky room, vaguely illuminated by light filtering through a window high on one wall. Then she turned abruptly, looked frightened, with bulging eyes and wild, tangled hair falling to her waist. The two of us stood there a moment, staring at each other.

One side of her mouth shifted in a secret smile. "I know something," she said softly, leaning toward me. "Want to know what it is?"

"All right," I replied, just as softly.

She cupped her hands around her mouth. "I can't tell you now. Curt's in the other room."

"Can I see him?" I asked.

"Well . . . I don't know," she said, doubtful. "Curt's very busy. He's a very important person, you know."

"Who is it?"

The voice from beyond the curtain on the other side of the room startled her. "It's someone here to see you about something!" she shouted back. "I'll send him right in!" And then she was gesturing frantically at me, and as I moved toward the curtain, shoved me from behind.

I entered a narrow room, dark except for the light from a table lamp on a crate at the other end, fabric draped over the shade. After a moment I made out two men on either side of the lamp, sitting on cushions, conversing in low tones. One had a stubble beard and the other wore sunglasses, despite the darkness. As I approached they fell silent, watching me. I recognized the bearded one as Curt, and said to him, "I'm Peter . . . a friend of Arnie's."

"Oh, yeah," he replied. "Didn't we meet before?"

"Yeah, but you didn't have a beard then."

He grunted at that, crossed his arms on his chest, leaned back and scrutinized me for several seconds. "You here about the deal?"

"Yeah," I said, and added, unnecessarily, "Arnie told me about it."

He nodded, fingered his stubble. "What're you in for?"

"Fifty dollars," I replied, and was immediately ashamed of the paltry number. He was an important person, after all. "Or maybe more," I added quickly. "Maybe a hundred."

"Can you make it two hundred?"

"Sure," I said, though I had no idea where I could get such an enormous sum.

"Far out," he said, leaning forward. "It goes without saying, the bigger the quantity, the better the deal I can make."

Of course that wasn't true. Leo charged the same for a dose whether you bought one pill or a hundred. It was a point of pride with him. For a moment, having descended from a superior race, I looked down at Curt with scorn, which I hid.

"Sit down, sit down," he said, feeling better about me now.

I sat awkwardly on a pile of cushions.

"It's going down tonight," he said, "and then it's over. You dig? It's a onetime thing, so you'd be smart to get that two hundred up to three or four, or more if you can, because it'll only happen once, and then who knows when the next opportunity will come along?"

"Sounds good," I said.

"Of course, I don't want to meet any of your customers. I don't want to see anyone at all except you, because the less people I see, the less people will see me . . . dig?"

I nodded.

"Far out. Now about the merchandise . . . It's been sitting in a refrigerated vault, so it's in mint condition. The only hang-up was waiting for it to be buffered, because the pill machine broke. But now it's operating and everything's ready to go. So come back here at midnight—"

The other guy, assessing me from behind his dark glasses, leaned over and whispered something to Curt, who nodded, then looked back at me. "Actually, it would be better if you don't come yourself. Give the bread to Arnie. Nothing personal, but I'm sure you know what can happen. We don't want too many people in the same place at the same time, do we?"

"Okay," I said, though I hadn't seen Arnie Glick in a while, and didn't know if he was still involved in the deal.

"Far out," Curt said, and turned back to his companion, the two resuming their conversation in low tones, no longer interested in me.

I'd been dismissed. I stood up and left the room.

In the kitchen, Rona drew me aside, away from the curtain, and in a subdued voice said, "Did you hear about Rex?"

"Rex?"

She pursed her lips, exasperated by my ignorance. "You know! Curt's little brother, Rex! It's awful! I don't even want to think about it! They took him up to a rooftop and carved an X on his belly!"

"Oh, yeah, I heard something . . ."

"They carved it right into the flesh, just like this," and she traced an X on her chest, between her breasts, and giggled. "Curt's talking about revenge! He says we can't let the P.R.'s get away with it!"

I said, "Is he all right? Rex, I mean . . ."

She shushed me, a finger to her lips, her head tilted to one side, listening to something, or for something.

I'd heard the rumors, that Rona had taken a swig from a bottle she found in a refrigerator, not realizing it was a liquefied drug Curt was storing there, thousands of micrograms; that she flipped out and hadn't been the same since. On the Avenue they called her Crazy Rona.

I was at the door now, waiting for her to unlatch the locks. She opened them and turned back to me, again holding a finger to her lips. "I'm Curt's woman, y'know," she whispered. "I wouldn't cheat on him, not for anything! You wouldn't believe what he'd do to me if I did . . . and not only me! You too!"

Abruptly, she yanked the door open. "You'd better go now!" she said, and when I walked out, slammed the door behind me.

It was almost full dark now. I hurried down the alley and up the block, heading for the lights of the Avenue. But for some reason I changed my mind, or forgot where I was going, and was almost at Fourteenth Street when I thought I heard someone call my name, and then again. Turning, I watched the approaching figure warily before recognizing Marty, one of Leo's teenage lieutenants. He held up a hand in greeting, but before he could say anything I began apologizing. I owed Marty twenty dollars.

"Forget it," he said, cutting me off. "I know you'll pay me when you can."

"Gee, thanks, Marty . . ."

"I spotted you a few blocks ago and I've been following you ever since. You were really moving . . . So how're you doing, anyway? I haven't seen you in a while."

Marty was four or five years younger than me, just out of high school, yet he seemed relaxed, self-assured. It left me feeling displaced, as if I were the younger one. "I'm doing fine," I said, trying to sound more confident that I felt; to act my age.

"Good, good," he said. "Hey listen, I got something for you," and he took a tinfoil packet from a jacket pocket and opened it, revealing a dozen or so white pills. He held it toward me. "From Leo's stash . . . Go on, take one."

I did, held it up and stared at it, a rare pearl.

"Take another," he said, thrusting the open packet at me. "I heard you have a girlfriend."

I took another, said, "Gee, Marty, I don't know what to say . . ."

"No need to say anything. I know Leo would want you to have it . . . Listen, have you seen Tom around, or Patrick, or Carl, or any of the old gang?"

"I haven't seen anyone in a while," I replied.

He nodded. "It seems everyone's scattered," and I nodded too, and for a moment we shared a common loss. "Well," he said, gripping my shoulder, "things change, right?"

"Yeah, things change . . ."

He backed away, held up a hand. "Good seeing you again, Pete," he said. "Take care of yourself."

I watched him head up the block, and when he was gone, opened my fist and stared at the two pills. Thrusting them into a pocket, I hurried toward the Avenue, ebullient.

My luck had turned! I'd sell one of them and take the other, and in the morning, coming down, I'd have enough bread to eat a real breakfast, bacon and eggs, in the restaurant facing the park where the sanitation men gathered at seven o'clock, to joke and clown around when they were through for the day. And then, with what was left, I'd buy a hand-rolled Cuban cigar on Astor

Place. And bring it back to the park, sit on a bench and smoke it, like the good old days!

I could hardly wait, took out one of the pills and swallowed it, figuring I had time to sell the other one to a customer I had in mind and get back to my pad before the rush came on.

I veered down Eleventh Street, entered a building in the middle of the block, rushed upstairs and knocked on the guy's door, imagining his gratified reaction. Then knocked again, louder, believing willfulness would conjure him. He had to be home! It was inconceivable that he wouldn't be, now that everything was arranged! But he didn't answer, and turning away, I walked slowly downstairs, disappointed, wondering who else might buy the pill, absently moving aside to let someone pass, glimpsing a flowing skirt, a girl I'd met before.

Abruptly, I turned and headed back up. "Wait!" I shouted.

I caught her between floors, where she stood with her back to the wall, her hands poised in front of her to ward me off.

"Don't be afraid," I said gently, gazing up into green eyes. "We met at Jeffrey and Marlene's, remember?"

Curiosity replacing fear, her hands dropped, and she clasped them at her waist. "Yes, I remember," she said. "I thought you looked familiar . . . You wore a red headband."

"That's right," I replied, touching my forehead where it had been. "Listen, I've got a dose of acid . . . There's hardly any around, but this is good stuff. I know because of the source . . . Anyway, what I mean is, do you want it?"

"That's amazing!" she said, color flushing her pale cheeks. "I've been all over trying to find some. That's where I was just going." Her brow creased; she was so lovely, I could hardly bear to look at her. "But I don't have much. What do you charge?"

"No, no," I said, taking it from my pocket. "I want you to have it."

She was incredulous. "For nothing?"

"Yeah, just take it," and I held it out.

She took the pill, looked down at it in her palm, and I did too, our heads nearly touching as we communed over the shell-white gem.

"And if you want," I said, looking up, "maybe we can get together later . . . I mean, I have a dose too . . ."

We stared at each other, my eyes turning watery with swelling affection. She smiled shyly. "I live on the third floor of Marlene's building, 3B . . . I'm breaking up with my boyfriend—"

"Oh . . ."

"No, no, I already told him. It's over and he's moving out. I mean, could you, like, come about ten?"

"Yes."

"Apartment 3B, around ten . . . You'll remember?"

"Yes, of course."

"Because I know how easy it is to forget . . ."

"I won't forget."

Our eyes locked again, then she turned and raced downstairs, clutching the pill in a fist. I watched until she was out of sight, then gleefully bounded down myself, marveling as I hurried toward the Avenue at how things could turn around so fast.

It was nighttime now, the strip crowded as I moved through the sidewalk throng and found a car bumper to sit on, kicking my feet, a boy in love.

"You look triumphant."

I looked up, snapped out of my reverie. Gazi stood a few feet away, grinning at me.

"What did you say?" I asked, though I'd heard him clearly.

"I said you look triumphant.'"

Triumphant?

It was an odd word, and for a moment I had trouble grasping it. "Well, yeah," I replied. "I guess so."

"And why is that?"

I thought of her green eyes and shy smile, and blurted, "My life has changed!"

"How so?" Gazi asked, then Roger was there too, grinning, the two of them flanking me.

I fell into confusion, reluctant to reveal my thoughts, but at the same time felt compelled to say something. Finally, I told him, "I'm on acid," and only then did it occur to me that I had indeed swallowed a pill.

Gazi pulled back, genuinely surprised. "Then what are you doing here?" he said, gesturing with a hand at the crowded strip. "This is no place to get high. You should be somewhere peaceful, quiet . . . your apartment, for instance."

Yes, he was right. I pushed off the car, suddenly anxious to get back to my pad. Already I felt a nibble at the edges of my mind, prefacing the rush. And then, out of a notion of repayment, because he'd given me advice, I turned back and said, "Do you want to come with me?" and as the words emerged, regretted them, wanted to lunge after them, take them back.

"You have some dope we can smoke?" Gazi asked flatly.

The question repelled me; that he would bargain for my company. What kind of person would say such a thing? I looked at him with disbelief, as less than human, and thinking that, shocked by it, heard myself say, to undo the harsh thought, "I've got some hash."

"Well then, we'll join you," Gazi replied. "Won't we, Roger?"

"Nothing wrong with hashish," Roger said, grinning.

Dark Night of the Soul

Glowing globes of lamplight hovered throughout the park, the railings separating bushes and trees from pavement a stark black outline. To the right, in the distance, the hollow band shell brooded over the empty landscape, a trepanned skull, as I hurried down the wide promenade. I hadn't worn a coat, and hunched my shoulders against the nighttime chill.

Again I outpaced the unwelcome two I'd foolishly invited to accompany me. They scurried behind me, laboring to keep up. Only now I wasn't hurrying to get away from them, but to get to my pad before the impending rush broke over me. In my panic, the gloomy rooms had become a beckoning sanctuary.

The promenade ended at the park gates, and I continued without pause onto Ninth Street, making a beeline for my building, Gazi and Roger muttering to each other in my wake. At mid-block I mounted the stoop, then abruptly stopped and peered up toward the open door and the illuminated hallway, arrested by the memory of being mugged.

Gazi, coming up behind me, said with annoyance, "What're you waiting for?"

"Uh, nothing," I replied, and hurried up and inside.

But as I preceded them upstairs, where it grew dimmer, the stairwell indirectly lit from the working hall light below and another one two floors above, I paused again, on the first landing, glancing at the half-dark cul-de-sacs at either end. The drug was coming on now, and with it a flow of adrenaline, which made me jumpy and played light-flash tricks on my eyes. The walls were wavering when I reaching my landing and reeled down the hallway, bouncing off walls, ricocheting drunkenly to my door. I fumbled with the keys, finally got a grip on them, slipped one into the lock and pushed the door open with my shoulder, stumbling inside. Lurching to the candle and box of matches on the kitchen sink, I managed to ignite the wick with trembling fingers as the door closed behind me and the hall light disappeared.

With one hand holding the other, to steady the flame, I entered the main room. There wasn't much there: one mattress on top of another, covered with the faded floral bedspread; a few crates; the wrought-iron stove; a chest of drawers; all scavenged from the abandoned apartment next door. By the time I'd carefully set the candle in its dish on the stovetop, Gazi and Roger were seated on the crates, their coats still on. Turning toward them, I lost my balance and fell backward. It was a giddy moment, and I gave in to it, flouncing onto the mattress with a sense of relief after a long ordeal.

In fact, my ordeal had just begun.

I sat up, my head spinning with vertigo, the walls heaving as my breath moved in and out.

"The dope," Gazi said.

I looked at him without comprehension, then remembered, said, "Oh . . . yeah," tottered to my feet again and moved unevenly back to the kitchen. Feeling beleaguered, I fumbled in a drawer for the hashish and pipe, found them, and returned with relief to my spot on the mattress. But there was no respite there either, for now I was fiddling with the tinfoil, trying to unwrap the hash with trembling fingers, and finally accomplishing that chore, unsuccessfully groped at the small chunk, to break off a piece.

"Allow me," Gazi said, leaning forward on his create, holding out a hand.

He sat above me, looking down, and from my disadvantageous position, I hesitated, reluctant to surrender the hash and the role of host that went with it. But his palm was demanding, and my fumbling fingers were useless . . .

"You're in no shape to do it," he said, echoing my thought, and telling myself he merely wanted to help, I thrust the pipe and hashish at his outstretched palm . . . and ceded control of what seemed much more than that.

Senses suddenly screaming in alarm, I fell back onto the mattress, reflexively linking my hands behind my head in an incongruous, leisurely posture, and gazing up at the ceiling as if I didn't have a care in the world. Completing the picture, I feigned a contented smile, lips frozen on brittle skin in a rictus grin.

I couldn't see Gazi now, only glimpse his hands, working on the hashish, loading the pipe. Then Roger, who I couldn't see at all, laughed, a guffaw that made me sit up just as Gazi extended the pipe, pushing the stem at me.

I took it in my mouth and bit down hard. He lit a match with a nail, the tip exploding into flame, spouting from his thumb, and held it to the bowl. I took a long, slow drag, filling my lungs until the air backed up my windpipe, into my throat, and rose to my head, clouding it. Feeling faint, I fell away from the pipe, onto the mattress, and closed my eyes, energy flaring on my lids.

And as I lay there with my eyes closed, dizzy, I heard Gazi say, "Check the kitchen, Roger."

I understood the words, and yet they were gibberish, made no sense. Which goaded that part of me that can never resist a puzzle, drew me into a mystery. In response, it seemed fitting to keep my eyes shut, to better observe without being discovered.

I heard Roger leave the room, and a short while later come back and sit down again.

"What'd you do for a living, Gazi?" he asked, and laughed softly.

"You're a clever boy," Gazi replied. "Maybe too clever."

I was ruminating on that when Gazi tapped my knee, startling me. I bolted upright and opened my eyes. The two of them were grinning at me, their expressions exaggerated, their faces grotesque masks.

"Good hash?" Gazi asked.

I'd forgotten all about it, recalled my dizziness, blurted, "Terrific!"

The two of them laughed, then Gazi slapped his thighs and stood up. "Our business here is finished," he said to Roger. "It's time we left."

It pleased me to hear that, and I got up too and followed them into the kitchen, to usher them out. But my relief that they were leaving clashed with the false atmosphere. Nothing was what it seemed. And then a mechanical impulse within me took over, the reflex of please and thank you, and I heard myself say, "Thanks for coming over," as the three of us stood in the murky room.

Gazi grinned, Roger laughed, and I forced a smile, though I didn't get the joke.

My hand was on the doorknob when a low growl from beneath the table against the far wall startled Gazi. He jumped away from it and flattened himself against the refrigerator, eyes wide. It fascinated me. I'd never seen him frightened before.

Then the good host reappeared, said, "Don't be afraid," and pointed at the curled-up form in the table's shadow, explaining, "It's Gloria's. She left it here . . . It's only a puppy."

"He's not dangerous?" Gazi asked, doubtful.

"Not at all," I replied. "Pet him. You'll see."

He inched toward the table, crouched down, gingerly reached out and petted the dog.

"That's the way," I said, sounding inane; a parent giving advice to a child.

Gazi looked up, grinning, a gnome with a smooth face that extended from his chin to his bare skull, and said to Roger, "You see? The dog knows me now."

Roger grinned back.

And suddenly I'd had enough, didn't want them there a second longer, and yanked the door open, hall light flooding in. In one fluid movement Gazi stood up and left, Roger sauntering after him. From the door, I watched them, Gazi heading down the hall, disappearing, Roger pausing at the stairwell, turning back.

"Thanks for your generous hospitality," he said. "We'll be in touch."

"Roger!" Gazi shouted from below, and Roger turned away and disappeared too.

I closed the door, locked it, and returned to the candlelit room, to stare at the flame. The liquid flow of it, particles rippling out on waves in perfect symmetry; I always found it soothing. But I couldn't focus, was restless, got up and moved about. I was at the chest of drawers, rummaging through clothes, when I realized I was looking for something, though I didn't know what. And then, on my hands and knees, examining the floor, I realized what it was: the hashish. Not that I wanted any. But where had it gone?

With the object of my search now revealed, I began anew, looking in the same drawers, rechecking the floor, the bedspread, the stovetop table. I moved on to the kitchen, but without the candle, which I only remembered as I stood there, in the half-dark. I considered going back for it, but the search itself was now too important to interrupt, so I kept at it in the gloom, peered at countertops, ran my hands over them, opened the drawer in the kitchen table—

When it occurred to me that I hadn't been in that room after bringing the hashish to the mattress and giving it to Gazi . . .

Glancing in that direction, a pinpoint of light high on the door caught my attention, no more than a dot in that unlit room. Curious, I went over and examined it, saw a tiny hole in the metal, realized it was the light from the hallway—when the dog began squealing and I turned around.

I'd forgotten about it. What did it want? My first thought was that it had to defecate, which was followed by an image of it shitting on the floor. I didn't want that, so I attached the leash, opened the door, and before I could grab my coat, was yanked by the dog's straining body down the hallway, down the stairs, and out to the open doorway to the building, where it lunged down the stoop, tearing the leash out of my hand and bounding to the sidewalk.

I stood there at the top of the stoop, looking down at the dog rooting at the garbage cans by the curb. There was no one on the street, which was only somewhat illuminated by the few working streetlights up the block. The smoky gray nighttime twilight paralyzed me, the street dimmer each time I blinked.

Finding courage, I moved down a step, and then another, calling the dog, softly at first, then louder.

It ignored me.

I moved halfway down the stoop, tried to reason with it, and when it still took no notice of me, adopted an authoritative tone, then scolded it. I took another step toward the sidewalk, and then another, pleading now as the dog continued to sniff at the cans. Finally, I reached the lowest step. It was as far as I would go; the street was too ominous.

Silent, I crouched there on the bottom step, eyeing the leash trailing behind the dog on the sidewalk. Holding onto the banister, I stretched for it when the dog moved closer, and when it was only a few feet away, I lunged for the leash and fell off the step and onto the sidewalk. Jumping up in panic, I scurried back up to the top of the stoop, turned back and, in my frustration, let out a string of curses at the dog.

It didn't look up. Didn't even look my way.

It had no respect for me at all.

I sat down on the top step, cradling my head in my hands.

Woe is me.

The pose brought on the thought, and the thought brought Gloria to mind, my girlfriend, who was never around. I pictured her with the older guy she'd once introduced me to, the two of them in bed together, laughing at me, witnessing my sorry predicament as I sat there. I was a cuckold, of no use whatever except to take care of her dog. It made me angry, and I stood up and called the dog again, sharply.

It looked up at me quizzically, then away, casually returning to the garbage cans.

"Hey, mister. You want your dog?"

In my self-absorption, I hadn't noticed the two black teenagers moving up the block. Seeing them now, in the middle of the street, watching me, my heart jumped in my chest.

"Yeah," I replied, trying to sound calm, crossing my arms on my chest to convey control of the situation, despite appearances. "He got away from me and I can't seem to catch him."

The taller kid grinned, walked right up to the dog, bent down and picked up the leash. "Here y'go," he said, approaching the stoop as I moved down to the bottom step and stretched for the leather strap, which he placed in my hand.

I gripped it in a tight fist as they continued up the block, talking and laughing, turning back to look at me. "Thanks!" I shouted, putting the fillip on my humiliation.

I turned on the dog then, yanked it upstairs and into the kitchen. Its legs slipped on the floor in its panic to get away from me, and it slid under the table, cowering in shadow. Suddenly contrite, I crouched down, petted the shivering animal's body, uttered soothing words. I noticed then that its metal food bowl was empty, and realized it had been hungry. Eager to make up for my bullying behavior, I poured dry food into the bowl, and in my haste lost my grip on the bag, pellets filling the bowl and spilling over the lip onto the floor.

Glancing toward the door, I saw the pinpoint of light, crunched over to it, touched the minuscule hole with a finger, felt the rough edges. It had been punched in the metal, by a can opener, it seemed . . .

And it struck me that Roger had done it when he left the room and I lay on the mattress with my eyes closed. It was why Gazi had sent him into the kitchen! So they could see inside from the hallway . . . to know whether I was inside.

They meant to rob me!

Alarmed, I pressed up the door and peered through the tiny hole, expecting to see them out there . . . and realized that Gazi had stolen the hashish, that they'd already robbed me!

The scene came back to me, Gazi's hands moving over the pipe with a flourish, as if loading it. Me sitting up, taking the pipe, filling my lungs . . . with air!

I flushed with shame, recalling it, then groaned aloud, to drown out the scene, the two of them sitting there, grinning, as I told them how good it had been . . .

Terrific!

Swooning with embarrassment, I staggered out of the kitchen and into the other room, collapsing on the mattress.

Fool!

The word popped into my head. Not just *a* fool, but *the* Fool, the archetype for all fools. I bowed my head in profound disgrace, the world laughing at me.

Jumping up, I grabbed the dish holding the candle, hot wax spilling onto my hand as I lurched through the kitchen and into the back room, which I hadn't been in since painting the wooden floor a week before. I'd left the narrow window overlooking an air shaft open, to help it dry, but the room still smelled of wet paint, a persistent, lingering odor that summed up my predicament, though I couldn't say why—the mere fact that it occurred to me was enough to make it true—as I crawled over the bare floor, pushing the candle in front of me, my eyes inches from the black-painted wood as I looked for the hashish.

Why would it be in there? I wondered.

Because, I told myself, it was the only room I hadn't searched before.

I knew that didn't make sense, but more important than logic, I wanted to find the hashish to undo my humiliation . . .

Finally, reluctantly, I gave up, returned to the mattress and sat down.

I sighed with chagrin, and for a blessed moment my mind went blank . . .

And then I heard muttering. Indistinct voices.

I bolted into the kitchen and peered through the tiny hole at the hallway.

They weren't there. Of course. Why would they be? They'd already robbed me.

Returning to the mattress, I sat in silence a moment, then heard it again, the muttering. I looked around at the walls as it grew louder, though no more comprehensible. Voices, a conversation. I could nearly make out the words. There had to be a rational explanation, I told myself, and gazed at the wall where it seemed to come from, which separated my pad from the deserted apartment next door.

When I moved in, I'd been told that the old man was found when the stench became unbearable. He might have been dead for weeks. He had no family, no friends, no one at all. The door was open, and I decided to explore. Though a kitchen window was open, there was no breath of air inside, the apartment stagnant. The mildewed mattresses in the small bedroom were askew, half pulled off the box spring bed. The armoire next to it contained a well-worn suit jacket and pants, a few shirts and ties, a passel of wire hangers. The empty feel of the place spooked me.

A few days later I went back again, with Gloria, and we carried the mattresses and lugged the cast-iron stove next door. And then I went in again, without her, late in the day. A portrait of Saint Stanislaus was tacked to the wall over the kitchen sink, and the cupboards held dishes with a garland pattern on the rims, reminding me of my grandmother's china. It was twilight, the room a chalky gray, and it seemed I was an intruder, violating the dead man's life. In the bedroom, I thought I saw something move, at the edge of my vision, and turning quickly, saw a flicker, a specter, or the hint of it, hovering in the room. The presence of death.

That sense of imminence came back to me as I sat trembling amidst the susurrating voices, and I broke into a cold sweat, suddenly, absolutely sure that Death was speaking to me, telling me I'd sunk too low to merely die. That a deeper, darker death awaited me, one with no more lifetimes, no more chances, no rebirth.

I would not just die. I would perish.

My animating spirit extinguished.

I thrust the awful thought aside, clasping my hands against the tremors that roiled me. I told myself, lecturing, that I was not a teenager hanging out on the strip, believing that swirling flecks of light, moiré patterns, the rods and cones projected from my eyes, were ghosts. I didn't believe in ghosts. I was a rational being. Hallucinations, the supposed supernatural, could be explained. And there was a rational explanation for the voices that were not quite voices.

Against this onslaught of rationality, the muttering receded, and I grinned, at having chased them away, then chuckled.

"Heh-heh."

A made-up sound. The laughter of a comic book character in a cartoon bubble.

And in the wake of that artifice, the muttering returned, got louder, a confused chorus of voices building to a crescendo as I shook all over, the incomprehensible conversation surrounding me, coming now from above, below, and all sides; ceiling, floor, and walls. I pressed my hands to my ears to blot it out, heard my pulse pounding through my palms, the throbbing heartbeat announcing an incipient heart attack, to which the heart responded by beating faster, my hands quivering.

This is what it means to freak yourself out.

Relax! I told myself in response, and falling back on the mattress, linked my hands behind my head . . . which conjured the humiliating scene with Gazi and Roger. Abruptly I sat up, and into the cacophony.

I was hearing things.

It was apparent. There was no doubt about it.

I was hearing things.

And there was no one there.

I was insane!

It freaked me out.

INSANE! INSANE! IN-SANE! IN-SANE!

My hands jumped like a puppet's, out of my control, adrenaline coursing through me. I gasped for air.

IN-SANE! IN-SANE!

The repetitive meaninglessness of the word rendered it an even more powerful indictment.

CALM DOWN! I shrieked back, clutching myself. *Nothing is happening! You're driving yourself crazy over nothing!*

Surprisingly, I stopped quaking, and in the sudden calm, gazed at the room, noticed a photograph of a yellow flower snipped from a magazine, tacked to a wall. It looked silly. A dead thing. Why had I put it there? But its ordinariness was a confirmation.

It was true! Nothing was happening.

I tried to keep that in mind, discounted the soft muttering on the fringes, merely whispering now. Fearing its full-fledged return, I reached back for the sensibility I'd so recently attained, to silence the sounds—the discovery that nothing was happening. But the whispered muttering persisted, got louder. I looked at the walls, the ceiling, the floor . . .

I didn't have to stay! I could leave!

Yes, it was true!

With conscious deliberation, I got to my feet, crossed the room and methodically put on my coat, one sleeve at a time. Leaving the apartment, I closed the door softly, moving with careful restraint, controlling myself. One step at a time, I walked down the hallway to the stairs. My courage flickered at the first dark landing, and with an act of will I held myself in check, kept a steady pace, pushed panic away. Then I was on the ground floor, where I'd been robbed, and moving faster. And then on the stoop, where I'd been humbled by a dog and humiliated by my girlfriend and her lover. I sped up, to put that behind me, moved down toward the sidewalk, where I hesitated to take that last step and told myself it was okay. It was only a sidewalk. I walked on it all the time.

Approaching the spot where I'd asked the cop where to get a gun, I was moving fast. I couldn't help it. And beyond that, on the empty streets, the deserted late night tableau closed in on me and I broke into a run, toward wherever my feet were headed.

It was a well-lit building, which comforted me as I climbed the stairs, but unnerved me when I got to the top floor and knocked on a door. It was too bright now that I stood still, glancing over my shoulder at the stairway that led to the roof. It could have been the rooftop where they'd carved an X on the kid's belly; I assumed it was.

The door lock clicked, startling me, and I jumped, forgetting that I'd knocked or who I'd come to see. Then the door opened and I remembered. Gloria's friend Tanya stood there, groggy and disheveled. She wore a flannel nightgown that fell to her slippered feet.

"Peter!" she said. "It's so late. What're you doing here? Is something wrong?"

What could I say? That I'd been hearing things? Voices coming through the walls? That my apartment was haunted? How could I explain? It would sound unbelievable.

"What is it?" she asked, and I struggled for something to say, but nothing came to me.

"Did something happen between you and Gloria?"

"No, no," I said quickly, then blurted, "I can't stay in my pad! It's . . . I can't explain it. Can I stay here tonight?"

I sounded desperate, and she didn't hesitate, said, "Yes, "of course," and stepped back, inviting me in.

Inside, I looked around, wondering if I'd been there before. I must have, since I knew where it was, but I didn't recognize the large room that sprawled before me. It was dazzling, my pupils bouncing as I took in a couch, soft chairs, bookshelves, drapes across one wall, a rug on the floor . . .

Tanya finished locking up. "You have to be quiet," she said softly. "Danny's asleep."

"Danny?"

"In the bedroom," she said, gesturing across the enormous room, past the small kitchen, to a hallway and a door that was ajar.

I barely knew Tanya, but her concern as she gazed up at my face made my eyes water with affection, and out of that, her solicitude for someone else, asleep in another room, wounded me. "What's he doing here?" I asked, trying to keep the hurt out of my voice.

"Danny lives here," she replied.

It filled me with regret. Why hadn't I told her how I felt about her? Then it would have been me in that other room. I looked away, hiding my disappointment.

"Can I get you anything?" she asked, and reaching out, put a hand on my arm.

A lump lodged in my throat. Choked with grief, I looked down and shook my head.

"Something to drink? To eat?"

"No, no . . ."

"I can get you blankets and a pillow, if you want."

Everything she said, standing there in her flannel nightgown, her hair askew, made me love her more, and left me feeling worse. "No," I rasped. "Don't do that. I'll just stay here," and I pointed at the couch, then moved to it and sat down to demonstrate my meaning.

"Okay," she said doubtfully. "But if you change your mind, the blankets are in the closet down the hall, and if you get hungry, there's food in the refrigerator."

I didn't trust myself to speak, nodded, watched her pad away through the kitchen and to the bedroom door, where she turned back. "You sure you'll be all right?"

"I'm fine," I replied in a strangled voice, and after another moment's hesitation, she went inside, closing the door behind her.

Bereft, I took off my coat and sat on the edge of the couch, gazing at the ceiling, which gave meaning to my clasped hands; a prayerful posture.

What a fool I'd been not to marry her!

The thought astonished me.

Marriage? Why would I want that?

So I could own her.

The answer came unbidden, from that deep place that occasionally spoke to me. And in response, I frowned at my base instincts . . . and sighed, that I was so far gone, the exhalation becoming a sorrowful breath over the woman I'd lost because of my despicable, possessive attitude . . . and sighing again, became the wistful lament of an unrequited lover, pining away.

What was his name again?

Danny!

I looked at the bedroom door, as if I'd shouted the name, pictured the two of them there, in the dark, waking up at the thought-spoken sound, and quickly looked away, but it was too late. I'd caught myself watching them.

A Peeping Tom.

The lowest of the low.

I recoiled against myself.

I shouldn't have come! I couldn't stay!

I jumped up, my self-respect at stake, and crossed the room to the front door, where I paused, hand on the knob, and looked back at the brightly illuminated room, the couch, the soft chair, the rug, drapes, and bookcases.

Scene of my greatest happiness.

What happiness? What was I babbling about?

And then, recalling the turmoil in my apartment, it seemed I *had* been happy here, in this clean, well-lit place . . . So why was I leaving?

I went back to the couch and sat down again.

This is where I belong.

I looked at the bookshelves, and the spines were comforting.

If I'd only paid attention to Tanya, all this could have been mine!

Dramatically, I dug clenched fists into my eyes and rubbed, as if by rubbing hard enough I might blind myself to my misfortune . . . like Tiresias. Wasn't he the one who blinded himself? And with that, my selfishness flared again, rebuking me.

What a cad I was!

My moral self, which had pointed out that marriage was ownership.

A cad?

I stopped rubbing and looked up, blinked in the bright light. I was from Brooklyn, not society England. How could I be a cad?

But the word wasn't through with me yet, rendered Tanya an heiress, in that room with its drapes and bookshelves, and I recoiled from the implication: a marriage of convenience.

I was an opportunist! A conniver! A sneak! A rogue! A scoundrel!

The sight of what I'd coveted suddenly unbearable, I bolted across the room and flicked the light switch . . . and a moment later, standing in the dark, unable to see, flicked it back on, and dazzled by the sudden brilliance, flicked it off again, and then on. I was about to turn it off again when it struck me that anyone watching from outside, seeing the light flash on and off through the drapes, might think it was a plea for help, an SOS, and call the cops.

Alarmed, I moved to the couch, leaned over the backrest and surreptitiously parted the drapes just enough to peer out. In the nighttime darkness I saw the rooftop outline of buildings across the street. There were no lights on at all, anywhere. And I was on the sixth floor. Who would see me up there?

Someone sitting in their dark apartment across the way, I thought, watching.

Hastily, I closed the drapes, and they swung wildly from the brusque movement, revealing the light to unseen observers. I grabbed the swaying drapes, pulled them taut, and held them that way for several seconds, hoping no one had noticed.

When I turned back to the room, sinking onto the couch, I thought:

You are an asshole.

It was a stunningly profound statement.

I was an asshole!

It explained everything.

I yawned then, my mouth opening almost beyond its elastic limits. Though on edge, hyped up, I assumed it meant I was tired, and curled up on the couch, intending to fall asleep. I wasn't cold, but felt exposed. It would have been comforting to have something to pull over me. Why hadn't I accepted the blanket?

Because, I told myself with mock patience, you are an asshole.

In that fetal position, hands folded beneath my head in lieu of a pillow, my thumb was pressed into my cheek, inches from my mouth. I pulled it away, where it loomed before my eyes, asking to be sucked, and the frightened little boy I'd suddenly become brought on a fit of trembles. I tightened into my fetal ball to quell them, a posture that conveyed a greater fearfulness, the agitation spreading through my body, becoming quaking tremors. I gasped for air, and in an attempt to regain control, began breathing methodically, in and out, in and out, in and out . . .

Calm yourself and fall asleep, little boy. Everything will be all right if you just fall asleep!

The light!

Of course I couldn't sleep. The light was on!

I jumped up, lunged across the room, flicked it off, and returned to my protective curl, breathing in and out, in and out, heaving there in the dark, no closer to sleep than before, when it struck me that I wasn't sleepy, that it wasn't sleep I wanted.

What I wanted was to escape into unconsciousness.

It was a stunning realization, and yet, it didn't bother me. It was the truth, after all. I could see as much.

With the sudden poise of newfound maturity, I got up, crossed the room, and fumbled along the wall for the light switch. There! I thought when the room reappeared, its objects shimmering with an electric glow. I'd done the grown-up, mature thing.

I looked at the sofa where the boy had curled up, and pitied him, now that I was mature . . . and then that word, *mature,* turned on me, mocked me with its pretentiousness.

What a jerk!

. . . in a soda fountain drugstore where I worked behind the counter, in a small town somewhere in the Midwest. I lived in a back room and slept on a cot, an overage teenager, full-grown, and everyone laughed at me behind my back.

Oh what a jerk!

I hurried across the kitchen, past the closed bedroom door and down the hall to where the bathroom should have been, and felt momentary pride that it was there when I turned on the light and was rewarded with the gleam of a porcelain sink and the smooth surface of a mirror above it. Then my reflection caught my attention and I moved closer, over the sink, and stared into the mirror, becoming a teenager looking for pimples.

My face, I noticed, was gaunt, the flesh taut on cheekbones, eyes recessed in their sockets. It gave me a brooding look. Not bad, I thought. One might say handsome.

But as I continued to stare, the face in the mirror lost its definition, the lips, nose, and chin dissolving into a gelatin of flesh, the unrecognizable face an inhuman blob. Repelled, I turned, to flee, and in my haste smashed my knee against the toilet.

Whimpering, rubbing the knee, I stumbled in a half crouch down the short hallway and into the kitchen, a bumbling incompetent, a blithering idiot.

Blithering.

I was taken by the word; the way the syllables bumped into each other, so perfectly conveying its meaning. It marked a breakthrough—that I could see myself so unattractively and yet accept it. A sense of liberation washed though me.

The truth can make you free.

It seemed I'd coined the expression. No truer words had ever been said.

Meanwhile, not paying attention, I'd yanked open the refrigerator, and when the light popped on, out of old habit, took it as an invitation and peered inside.

It struck me as amusing, in a goofy way. The father in a television sitcom, tiptoeing downstairs and into the kitchen for a late night snack. As Ozzie Nelson, I surveyed an incomprehensible assortment of containers, jars, and dishes containing indiscriminate things, reached into one of the dishes and began shoving food into my mouth, though I had no idea what it was, chewing, rendering it into mush, a tasteless glop. Disgusted, I swallowed the cold lump, and as it cleared my throat and eked down my esophagus, I realized I wasn't hungry, had no reason to eat, and stepping away from the foolish mistake, watched the refrigerator door swing in . . .

Just before it shut, I lurched to catch it—too late! It closed with a thunk as I reflexively slapped a hand to my mouth to stifle the sound, catching myself in that pose—of someone with something to hide.

If anyone were to see me, they'd know everything.

The thought indicted me as I stood there, ghostly spots of light flitting before my eyes, the pointless flurry completing the portrait, summing up what I was: a compendium of irrelevancy.

Suddenly I felt heavy, worn-out.

I returned to the sofa and sat down, the weight of me sinking into the upholstery. I sat there without moving for a long while, drained, tired, wary of the identities that might form at any moment, in response to any thought.

Who was I?

What was at the core of me?

Was there anything real there?

I had no idea. My mind had gone blank.

I sat there a long while, not quite thinking, fragments flickering at the edges of my eyes as I stared into the room. I ignored them, refused to let them affect me.

At some point the light bothered me, and I squinted against its brilliance, looking at the switch on the opposite wall. But I no longer had the strength, or the desire, to get up and turn it off. There seemed no point to it.

Dark night of the soul.

The fully formed thought came to mind, perfectly describing my long ordeal. But it made me wary. Where would it lead? Who would I become behind it? Grimly I awaited the answer.

But nothing arose.

I'd gone blank again.

Gray Dawn

Eventually I parted the drapes and looked out. Above the rooftops, the sky was suffused with early morning light. I put on my coat, crossed the floor and absently flicked the switch. In the half-dark, I smiled without humor before closing the door softly behind me.

The overcast sky had brightened when I emerged on the street and walked up the block. The sun was somewhere, of course, but it didn't look like it would come out that day. Tenement buildings squatted beneath the gray ceiling, the parked cars lining the curbs a modern conceit of steel and chrome.

There was a light at the corner, but no cars or people. I stood there watching it change; red, then green, then red again. It was idiotic.

Ignoring it, I crossed and continued walking. There was no one about, the streets deserted, empty. In the gray dawn, it seemed a different city altogether, which I'd just stumbled upon from nowhere. Avenue A, Fifth, Sixth, Seventh, Eighth, Ninth . . . I followed my feet, turning into the park where the promenade ran through to the other side, treading heavily on the paving stones.

Up ahead I saw three figures, one leaning against a bench, the other two idling nearby. I recognized them; we'd met before. The boys shifted position as I approached, spread out and fell in step with me as I came abreast, the big one at my side, the other two behind.

"Give me your money," the big one said.

I didn't look at him, kept walking.

He kept pace alongside, pulled out his switchblade, clicked it open and pointed the tip at me. I looked at it, inches from my face, and kept walking.

It upset him. "I'll kill you, man!" he shouted.

"Then kill me," I said tonelessly.

He stopped walking, and the others did too. They stood there, bewildered, watching me continue down the promenade and out of the park.

The kitchen was somber, illuminated by overcast gray filtering in through windows in the other room. As I took off my coat, I spotted a scrap of brown paper on the table. It had a rough edge, had been torn from a grocery bag, and picking it up, I stared at it incredulously. A scrap of paper with nothing on it. It was a joke. It was hilarious! I'd never seen anything like it!

Absently, I turned it over, saw writing on the other side and brought the brown scrap close to my eyes. In large capital letters someone had scrawled:

I CAN'T STAND IT ANYMORE!! I'M GOING CRAZY!!!

What was this? I was flabbergasted, then recalling the voices that drove me out the night before, assumed I'd written it. I didn't remember doing that, and the writing didn't look like mine. But who else could it have been?

I saw the scrawled signature at the same moment I realized the dog was gone.

Gloria . . .

It came back to me then . . .

How one evening, in a delirious moment, we decided to get married. She told me her father, a salesman of some sort, would be in the city that night. She called him with the happy news, and we took the subway uptown and met him in a Hungarian restaurant. He was a dapper man, older than he tried to look, his hair dyed black, a ruby ring on his pinkie. In an ebullient mood, he ordered champagne and gestured a violinist to the table, who played as we ate, her father slipping him a tip afterward. When Gloria went to the bathroom, he slapped my shoulder, said he was delighted to meet me, confided that his daughter had been a handful since the divorce. I could see he was glad I would take her off his hands; the two of us buddies, conspirators discussing damaged goods. When she returned and called him "Daddy," I cringed.

A few nights later I took Gloria to meet my parents. They were embarrassed by her, hardly knew what to say as we ate dinner. When my father got up to clear the plates, I helped bring them to the sink, and in a confiding voice he told me he'd been a young man himself once, a marine in the Pacific, on leave. Lowering his voice, he said, "There's a difference between a piece of ass and a wife." Furious, I stormed out, dragging Gloria after me.

It was quiet as I sat at the kitchen table. The slow drip of the faucet entered the silence, and a while later the hiss of a radiator in the next room, and then, far away, a baby crying.

Who was this person about to go crazy? I wondered. What was she to me?

I let the brown scrap of paper fall to the floor.

I was still sitting there when the door opened and two girls walked in without seeing me and into the other room. I heard them flounce on the mattress. They talked awhile, a mumble from where I sat, and then it was quiet again and they fell asleep, breathing evenly. I got up, turned on the kitchen faucet and stuck my head under the flow. I turned it off, combed my wet hair back with a hand, and went into the other room.

Out one of the windows, I gazed at the rubble backyards, and across the way, at the horizon of tenement buildings against the gray sky. I stared at this scene, the brick structures with their lattice of fire escapes, erected long ago and surviving in this transition that was the present. And I thought: This is where I live.

Here, at this point in time.

I'd been born into it.

I'd always had a notion of history. Had always respected it, however much I'd disdained it for the momentary present. And now, standing there, looking out at the grim scene, I accepted it. For better or worse, it was mine.

I heard one of the girls in bed sit up behind me, and I turned toward them as the other sat up beside her. "What're you doing here?" I said, louder than I'd intended, and they shrank from my authoritative tone, clutching the blanket, pulling it up to their necks.

Instantly, I was disgusted with myself.

Who was I to question anyone? I was nothing. A nothing whose penis dripped a yellow stain. My mark. And this nothing who dripped pus had the gall to make demands!

"Gloria told us it was all right if we slept here," one of the girls said, apprehensive.

I was about to tell her it was all right, as a way of apologizing, but it seemed so much to say, and what did it mean anyway? So instead I merely replied, "I don't care," and left the room.

I put my coat on in the kitchen and walked out. At the far end of the hallway a thin middle-aged man, a Pole or Ukrainian, was occupied at his door.

I paused at the stairwell, said, "What're you doing?"

He looked up, pupils contracting to pinpoints. When he had me in his sights, he gestured at the framework of iron bars, half attached to the door frame. "This will keep the animals out," he said. And I could see it would.

I went downstairs to the entrance, noticed the hinges for the door that wasn't there, and continued down to the sidewalk. The air was cold on my damp hair. It felt good. Winter was coming.

I walked up the block, hands thrust into the deep peacoat pockets. The somber street was empty except for someone near the corner . . . a girl, I realized as I approached. She stood on the sidewalk amidst overturned garbage cans spilling empty containers, orange rinds, bottles, and coffee grounds on the pavement around her dirty bare feet. She was thin, had long, stringy brown hair that fell over her shoulders and down her back, wore a flimsy white dress that seemed to be made of gauze, and clutched her arms across her chest to ward off the cold.

When I got close, a few feet away, I hesitated, and she leaned in my direction.

"Peace," she said softly, her voice a plea.

I stopped and stared at her, tears filling my eyes, the outline of her fragile body wavering as I focused on her mouth, which was the beg of a smile . . .

And then something snapped in my chest and I bolted as if shot, moving quickly away.

Epilogue
Teenage Artie

While wandering the numbered streets and alphabet avenues during one of my annual pilgrimages to the old neighborhood, I was startled to see a familiar face. Or at least I thought so as I stood on a corner and he crossed the street, eyes on the pavement, ambling toward me. When he reached my side, he looked up and I saw what might have been a spark of recognition that flared out before it registered, his eyes flicking back to the pavement as he mounted the curb and walked past.

I moved on then too, resuming my periodic homage to the streets where the great revelations had occurred, then turned back to look again at what might have been Teenage Artie. If so, he was no longer thin and willowy, but chunky, having filled out. But he was the same height, his skin, from the glance we'd exchanged, was still tenement pale, and his splotchy beard brought to mind the wispy goatee that had been all Artie's glands could produce back then, when Patrick Malone, making one of his typically grand pronouncements, declared that Artie was wiser than any of us, despite, or perhaps because of, his age.

He'd made that declaration twenty-five years ago, in the wake of the living dead atmosphere at the communal apartment on Eighth Street. Crumpled cigarette packs, a half-eaten pizza long since grown cold, and burnt-out butts in jar lids littered the telephone spool table around which a half-dozen shattered people sat slumped and motionless on chairs and mattresses while a needle stuck in the groove of a record replayed the same scratch over and over again. No one had the energy or desire to get up and do something about it. Then Artie, who'd taken the same penultimate drug and gone for a walk, entered the pad, wondered aloud why everyone was so lethargic, and removing the needle from its groove, put an end to the static soundtrack.

Seven years later, I spotted Artie on a stoop on Bleecker Street during one of my nostalgic visits to the city, and that enervated scene at Eighth Street was the first thing I thought about. On Bleecker, Artie was as thin and smooth-skinned as he'd been as a teenager, but nervous, skittish, his pupils darting at movement on that busy nighttime street. I stopped and reintroduced myself, to remind him who I was, but he knew right away and was glad to see me, patting the step next to him, inviting me to sit. I asked him how he was and what he'd been doing, and he launched into a rambling response whose intensity took me by surprise, a tale of fugitive flight from a drug-related charge, from somewhere on Long Island to a farmhouse in Pennsylvania, where Leo was hiding, to New Mexico, and back to the city again . . . which was why, he remarked casually, he'd changed his name. He tossed this out as an aside amidst his jagged rap.

Changed his name?

Abruptly, I realized that he hadn't emerged from the psychic battering we'd all taken, though he'd clearly been changed by it, was a different person. The teenager I'd known had glided through life, seemingly without a care. And now as a young man he was ensnared in the side effects, the paranoia, the manic intensity. It had the feel of a bad trip.

Eyes still darting, he rambled on, interpreting our shared history with the certainty of my own younger days, pushing the thesis that everything that had gone wrong back then was the result of synthetic drugs, that had they been organic, things would have turned out differently. Laboratory drugs, he explained, could be diluted, altered, and outright falsified, and had been, which was why everything we were working toward had fallen apart.

That struck a nerve in me, for I'd also believed we were on the verge of something. It was a belief I'd never quite gotten over.

Which was why, he went on, his life was now dedicated to growing and distributing psilocybin mushrooms, to be ingested intact, in their natural state.

I recovered my senses then, hanging out on that ramshackle tourist street. It was no longer 1967, but the mid-seventies. The psychedelic bus had moved on, into memory. And no one I knew was clambering to get back on board.

Eventually I extricated myself and waved my way down the block, relieved to get away. I felt the same way about the retrospective television programs about the sixties, and when they interviewed hippies at Woodstock, it made me uncomfortable, I always turned it off before they were finished.

I assumed I'd never see Artie again, and now here he was again, in 1992, waddling up the block as I stood on a corner watching him. Suspended from one arm, Artie, or his aged resemblance, gripped a flimsy plastic bag, a grocery-store giveaway containing what might have been laundry detergent and a jumble of clothes, the bag swaying a few inches above the sidewalk as he ambled away.

Since seeing him on Bleecker Street, I'd lived in California, Manhattan again, the boroughs, and was now upstate. I'd shed friendships as I changed locales, and gradually, by fits and starts, adapted to a world that veered in unexpected directions and fell short of my expectations—its one constant. Along the way, disappointment had tempered my innate optimism, subdued the sociable exuberance that would once have compelled me to shout his name when I spotted him. Now, preferring anonymity, I merely watched Artie head up the block. But I was still a curious character, and furtively, like a protagonist in the novels of detection I read for pleasure and edited for a living, I discreetly followed him.

Crossing the street, I kept parked cars between us and avoided his line of sight, should he happen to turn around, tailed him up the block and around the corner, to Second Avenue, where he headed north. Crossing to the far side again, I dogged him obliquely, stopping as he paused at shop windows, which he perused with apparent indifference, and resumed my surveillance as he moved on. His manner, I noticed, was laid-back, incognito. But the bag he schlepped stirred my speculation. He'd already passed two Laundromats without a glance. If he wasn't transporting clothes and detergent, what was he carrying?

The answer came to mind immediately: drugs, hidden in dirty laundry, or perhaps in a tinfoil packet buried in a box of Tide. Drugs had been what motivated Artie, after all, as one of Leo's teenager couriers, and then years later on Bleecker Street, when he'd preached the benefits of homegrown mushrooms long after the psychedelic revolution was over.

But I was hardly a hard-boiled detective on that subject; the hippie past still had a powerful hold on me. Skimming past the flash and glitter of present-day drugs I'd only read and heard about, thinking instead within the mind-set of a bygone era, it wasn't cocaine he hauled in that too-innocuous plastic bag, but good old LSD. Still.

His demeanor, his casual modus operandi, buttressed the impression. I recalled Artie popping into my pad one afternoon while I was shaving to tell me about a shipment Leo was expecting later that week; the pills had been dubbed—ironically, in view of his present laundry bag—Blue Cheer. Having bought my doses one at a time to that point, I declined to buy what for me would have been bulk: twenty capsules. But Artie danced around me, pointing out spots I'd missed while pitching for the sixty dollars in my pocket. And when he left, I'd become a small-time dealer, one who never paid rent again, who would eventually live in febrile transience, peddling nickels and dimes for bigger businessmen than myself.

Several blocks farther north, as I crossed Eighth Street, and Artie, on the other side, meandered past the Ukrainian Hall, another explanation for the bag occurred to me. Simple soul that he'd always been, and simpler still, after taking drugs over the years, while clinging to the belief in a Utopia just a trip away, his brain was now scrambled beyond recovery, a logical extension of the fantasy he'd related on Bleecker Street. Whatever he might have imagined he'd attained, to a detached observer, he would have appeared one of the bag men who traipsed the streets with hoarded personal valuables; in Artie's case, old clothes and laundry detergent. Indeed, he continued to travel without particular purpose as he crossed the avenue to my side of the street, and looking neither right nor left, veered up Tenth, past St. Mark's Church.

This new interpretation plunged me into a funk.

By the early seventies, a crime-ridden period of junkie thievery, I'd left the old neighborhood with my first wife. And while not regretting it at the time, a decade later, divorced and remarried, disillusioned with my quixotic vocation as an unpublished writer, it seemed I should have stayed, that I'd fallen short of a personal ideal of acceptance: had I been capable of accepting *everything,* from deprivation to degradation, these streets where I now made my annual pilgrimage could have been a paradise, as they'd once briefly been. The notion of imagined others who remained when I'd fled (whoever they were) wormed away at me: an unseen community of former hippies, anonymous holy men and women who'd hewn to simplicity when I copped out . . . like this simple Artie, unashamedly toting his useless bag through the streets.

In truth, I knew of no one who stayed, except Tom Eckhart, and as Artie approached Fourth Avenue, it occurred to me that he might have been visiting Tom before I spotted him. He'd come from that direction, a pad on Third Street that was even smaller than Tom's old basement flat on Eleventh. Back then, though in his twenties like most of us, Tom had the look of an old man, with his creased, leathery skin and halting manner, and people gravitated to his pad and his reassuring stoic indifference.

Just the other day, while sorting through old memorabilia, I'd come across his name in a dog-eared pocket phone book and impulsively dialed his number at Third Street. I hadn't spoken to Tom in several years and had no idea if he would answer or what I'd say to him if he did. It rang four or five times, and

I was about to hang up when the receiver clicked and I heard the familiar, gruff voice: "Who is it?"

And I hung up, still not knowing what to say—I'd never known what to say to him back then either—but was oddly reassured that he was still there, lunatic or sannyasin, whatever he happened to be.

Distracted by these thoughts, I realized I was lagging farther behind Artie. Or perhaps, as with my call to Tom, suddenly unsure as to why I was following him, I'd become indecisive, lost my focus. He walked north toward Fourteenth Street and the blur of pedestrian color and movement thickening up ahead. I quickened my pace, but near the crowded subway entrance at Union Square, I lost him.

A month or so later, three thousand miles away, I spotted him again, in Eugene, Oregon. My family was on vacation, and we'd driven down from Corvallis, where we were renting a house for the month. It was a superb summer day, warm but dry, and a modest urban park in the downtown business district had been transformed into a Sunday marketplace of tent stalls selling fruits and vegetables, fabric and pottery, T-shirts and cassettes and stuff they used to sell in head shops, when that was a thing. The incense wafted me back to the old days, and because it was the West Coast, to Haight-Ashbury, where I'd begged on street corners and slept in crash pads, while holding onto the giddy dream that I was part of something monumental, a profound transformation of society into something I could embrace as mine.

In the ad hoc marketplace setting in Eugene, a second or third generation of flower children occupied patches of grass between walkways and aisles, and their presence, the incense, and the sun-splashed day brought Golden Gate Park to mind. But I also viewed the scene with another eye, noticed the obliviousness of these young hippies to the world around them, heard the old slang, often my old words exactly, spoken as fervently, and bemused by my dual perspective, felt excluded from their alternative society.

My wife, whose own experience of the sixties had been gentler and less drug-oriented, was off somewhere, circulating among the booths. My daughter, seven years old, sat on a stone balustrade a few feet from me, holding patiently still while a butterfly was painted on her cheek.

Then Artie appeared.

I don't say reappeared, because this was a different Artie than the suspect I'd tailed to Union Square. For one thing, he was thinner than his recent look-alike, and his pasty face as he walked along a row of booths in the bright sunlight was pinched; with some discomforting preoccupation, it seemed. For another, he was dressed in clothes that weren't baggy. They fit him well. He wore a beige short-sleeve shirt with a collar, corduroy pants, leather shoes. Since our last actual encounter, on Bleecker, when he told me he'd changed his name, his life had taken a more complicated turn. Though still restless, he appeared to know, or might have been on the verge of discovering, that whatever contradictions plagued him were not in his circumstance, but in himself.

Like his chronological peer on the lower east side, this Artie was in no hurry, and yet his posture and bearing bespoke self-consciousness. Was he ill at ease in his neat, more formal getup? Unnerved by the wide-open setting with its expansive sky, so different from the claustrophobic tunnel world of tenement Manhattan? Or, like me, was it the past itself, juxtaposed to this present, that bothered him, octaves of regret intoned by the hippie scene and its disturbingly familiar vibes?

I observed him.

He made no attempt to enter the hippie enclave beneath the trees. Hewing to the concrete path, he dallied at the booths; not with serious intent to buy, but like a conflicted tourist among the serious shoppers poking and fingering the tie-dyes. Gradually, he gravitated toward a pair of musicians strumming guitars and singing old songs, classics of the Hendrix era. And there he lingered awhile, trying to relax, which only made him more edgy, his posture that of audience to performer. It made me nervous just to look at him.

I imagined that this Artie, uneasy within his skin, was wrestling with limitation. His parallel other, whom I'd tailed, had been closer in his languid ease to the teenager I somewhat knew. Which was better off? Or more evolved? To me, it meant the same thing, and being who I am, I took sides, seeing less in the Artie who still roamed the tenement streets than in the one who'd gone west and wound up here, squinting against the sunshine, not quite sure who he was.

When he wandered off, or rather, willed himself to move on, I had no urge to follow. I was with my daughter, after all; a father, not a sleuth. But I might not have followed anyway, for this Artie touched me in a way the other hadn't, reminding me of myself at a time when I was confused and vulnerable and wanted nothing more than to be left alone.

Two years later I saw him again. By then I'd also spotted Michael, in the lobby of an office building, checking the directory. My old pal, who had become a burden, was still the Hasidic Jew he'd chosen to define himself as twenty years before, when he recoiled at my suggestion that he see a psychiatrist and tried to push a menorah on me. I broke off relations then, and hadn't seen him until I walked into the lobby. He wore a suit and an overcoat, though it was summertime. A Moses beard covered most of his face, and he tugged at it with the same old distracted self-hatred. I ducked out of the building before he noticed me.

I also spotted Rose, leaving the Museum of Modern Art. I'd heard she was a performance artist, and seeing her, regretted not knowing her well enough to reintroduce myself. I hadn't gotten to know any of the women back then, except as an observer. I was too much in thrall to a drowning version of desire, and too intimidated by the other sex to be comfortable with companionship. Rose looked self-confident, oblivious to the crowd, but aware, I suspected, of the lay of the land, the details, which was her saving grace and kept her from turning cynical.

I saw Gazi too, on the upper west side, prowling the fringes of a blanket on which he'd spread old magazines and books for sale on the street. I'd crouched down, feigning interest in something while observing him, and he moved closer, as if I had it in mind to steal the dog-eared book in my hands. When I put it down and straightened and looked directly at him, he stepped back, still eyeing me with hooded suspicion. He had no idea who I was.

Nor did Roger, when I paused at a subway entrance where he was deriding someone for not giving him money. He was a scary wretch, shouting, waving a fist, personifying a philosophy of entitlement that was the sorry stereotype of the homeless in that era.

And I ran into Arnie Glick, in a bar. He was pleased to see me, bought me a drink, for old times' sake. An agent in the gentrification game, he was married, with three kids, and living in a building he owned. Yet he knew a lot about the old gang. He told me about Rose, and that Emery worked on Wall Street, and had heard that Leo moved to the coast, where he was dealing cards in a town with legalized gambling. Emily had married an artist, and Lila lived a few blocks from him with her daughter, Tom's child, and taught art in a public school. She was the only one he'd actually seen recently; he ran into her in the supermarket occasionally. Then I began telling him about the book I was working on, and he interrupted to declare that he never thought about what happened back then, that it was a waste of time.

"The way I see it," he said, in his high, thin, abrasive voice, "we were all crazy. None of what we thought was important made any sense at all. None of it was real."

There wasn't much to say after that, and I took his number, as if I might call and we'd get together again, and split.

And then I saw Artie again, or his facsimile, in Beaufort, South Carolina.

He had a neatly trimmed fu manchu mustache and was engrossed in conversation with a companion who also wore sandals and shorts. This Artie stood out on the conservative small-town street, in his yellow knit sport shirt with a maroon racing stripe across the chest.

At once it was apparent he was too far removed from the ambling character on the lower east side and the uptight Artie in Oregon to be the descendant of either one; certainly not in two years' time. No, this Artie was a completely different extension of the teenager who'd watched me shave, and of the skittish young man I'd last spoken to on Bleecker Street.

The sun was high, and puffy, picturesque cotton clouds idled in a blue sky; heaven up there, but down on the restored and renovated main street of the southern town, heavy, humid, clammy. It was August, and the three of us were on vacation again, car-tripping through the South, on our way to bringing my daughter to Disney World. She was nine now. We'd stopped for lunch, and afterward my wife and daughter went into a bookstore while I looked for a post office.

Taking in this Artie's manner and demeanor at a glance, and seeing in it neither self-absorption nor self-consciousness, I thought of him as a peer. In truth, I hadn't with his other likenesses. And unlike my reaction to each of them, no psychological analyses came to me. I wondered, merely, what he was doing there, in South Carolina, of all places. Seeing him with his somewhat older companion, their heads bobbing close, intimately, as they conversed, and taking in their apparent ease with each other, it struck me that Artie was gay.

Back then, it never occurred to me that he might be. In fact, I'd never thought about that now commonplace subject. But in ruminating on the book I was reworking for the third or fourth time, and thinking about Carl and Gary, I'd begun to wonder whether Patrick Malone had been gay as well. All the hints were there: the partnership he suggested, his monastic experience, his discomfort with women. Now, in Beaufort, it seemed possible that Patrick might have been attracted to Artie when he declared that Artie was wiser than any of us. Had Artie reciprocated this affection, or only acknowledged his inclinations later, between Bleecker Street and Beaufort?

Not that it made a difference. The way he carried himself now, as a person, was more significant. It left me feeling good about him, and I moved up the street without a backward glance, glad to see him happy, if in fact it was him.

41204506R00150

Made in the USA
Lexington, KY
03 May 2015